CW00409548

CURRENT ISSUES IN
DEVELOPMENT ECONOMICS

CURRENT ISSUES IN ECONOMICS

General Editor: David Greenaway, University of Nottingham

Current Issues in Microeconomics
Edited by John D. Hey

Current Issues in Macroeconomics
Edited by David Greenaway

Current Issues in Labour Economics
Edited by David Sapsford and Zafiris Tzannatos

Current Issues in International Monetary Economics
Edited by David T. Llewellyn and Chris Milner

Current Issues in Development Economics
Edited by V. N. Balasubramanyam and Sanjaya Lall

Forthcoming

Current Issues in Public Sector Economics
Edited by Peter Jackson

Current Issues in Industrial Economics
Edited by John Cable

Current Issues in Monetary Analysis and Policy
Edited by K. Dowd and Mervyn K. Lewis

Current issues in Welfare Economics
Edited by Nicholas Barr and David Whynes

Current Issues in Agricultural Economics
Edited by A. J. Rayner and David R. Colman

Series Standing Order

If you would like to receive future titles in this series as they are
published, you can make use of our standing order facility. To place a
standing order please contact your bookseller or, in case of difficulty,
write to us at the address below with your name and address and the
name of the series. Please state with which title you wish to begin your
standing order. (If you live outside the United Kingdom we may not
have the rights for your area, in which case we will forward your order
to the publisher concerned.)

Customer Services Department, Macmillan Distribution Ltd
Houndmills, Basingstoke, Hampshire, RG21 2XS, England.

Current Issues in Development Economics

Edited by

V. N. Balasubramanyam

Professor of Development Economics
Management School, Lancaster University

and

Sanjaya Lall

Lecturer in Development Economics
Oxford University Institute of
Economics and Statistics

MACMILLAN

First published 1991
Published by
MACMILLAN EDUCATION LTD
Houndmills, Basingstoke, Hampshire RG21 2XS
and London
Companies and representatives
throughout the world

Typeset by TecSet Ltd
Wallington, Surrey

ISBN 0–333–51323–1 hardcover
ISBN 0–333–51324–X paperback

A catalogue record for this book
is available from the British Library.

Printed in Hong Kong

Contents

List of Tables

List of Figures

Series Editor's Preface

The *Current Issues* Series has slightly unusual origins. *Current Issues in International Trade*, which Macmillan published in 1987 and which turned out to be the pilot for the series was in fact 'conceived' in the Horton Hospital, Banbury and 'delivered' (in the sense of completed) in the Hilton International in Nicosia! The reader may be struck by the thought that a more worthwhile and enjoyable production process would start and finish the other way round. I agree! Be that as it may, that was how the series started.

As I said in the Preface to *Current Issues in International Trade*, the reason for its creation was the difficulty of finding suitable references on 'frontier' subjects for undergraduate students. Many of the issues which excite professional economists and which dominate the journal literature take quite a time to percolate down into texts; hence the need for a volume of *Current Issues*. The reception which *Current Issues in International Trade* received persuaded me to do something similar for the other subject areas we teach. Macmillan agreed with my judgement, hence the series. Thus each volume in this series is intended to take readers to the 'frontier' of the particular subject area. Each volume contains ten essays, nine of which deal with specific current issues, with an overview setting the relevant current issues in the context of other recent developments.

As series editor the main challenge I faced was to find suitable editors for each of the volumes – the best people are generally the busiest. I believe, however, that I have been fortunate in having such an impressive and experienced team of editors with necessary skills and reputation to persuade first-class authors to participate. I would like to thank all of them for their cooperation and assistance in the development of the series. Like me all of them will, I am sure, hope that this series provides a useful service to undergraduate and postgraduate students as well as faculty.

With regard to the present volume, development economics is an area of great interest to economists – both theoretical and applied. It is a sub-discipline which is far harder to delineate than other areas, such as industrial economics or public sector economics. After all, the 'development economist' may be interested in issues and problems which cut across these and other sub-disciplines. Moreover, development economics has also been an area of great controversy for most of the post-war period. The editors of this particular volume therefore faced a demanding task in identifying appropriate topics for inclusion. In my judgement they have done an admirable job. Issues in agriculture, industry, trade, macroeconomic stabilisation, debt and structural adjustment are all covered. In addition there is still space to include papers on the evolution of the subject and new issues like services. The resulting blend is comprehensive, fresh and stimulating. As well as informing readers of current issues in this field, the papers should also testify to the vibrancy and policy relevance of recent developments. I am grateful to the editors and to the contributors for producing a worthwhile addition to the *Current Issues in Economics* series.

DAVID GREENAWAY

University of Nottingham

Notes on the Contributors

V. N. Balasubramanyam is Professor of Development Economics, Management School, Lancaster University.

Timothy Besley is Assistant Professor at Princeton University and Fellow of All Souls College, Oxford.

David Bevan is Fellow of St John's College, Oxford and a member of the Unit for the Study of African Economies, Oxford University Institute of Economics and Statistics.

Paul Collier is Reader in Economics at Oxford University, a fellow of St Antony's College, Oxford, and a member of the Unit for the Study of African Economies.

David Greenaway is Professor of Economics, and Director of the Centre for Research in Economic Development and International Trade (CREDIT), University of Nottingham.

Jan Willem Gunning is Professor of Economics and Director of the Economic and Social Institute at the Free University, Amsterdam, and a member of the Unit for the Study of African Economies.

Brian Hindley is Senior Lecturer in Economics, London School of Economics.

Ravi Kanbur is Professor of Economics at the University of Warwick and currently with the World Bank as Editor of *The World Bank Research Observer* and *The World Bank Research Review*.

J. B. Knight is Senior Research Officer at the Oxford University Institute of Economics and Statistics and a Fellow of St Edmund Hall, Oxford.

Sanjaya Lall is Lecturer in Development Economics at Oxford University Institute of Economics and Statistics and a Fellow of Green College, Oxford.

K. A. Ingersent is Senior Research Fellow in CREDIT, University of Nottingham.

Alisdair I. MacBean is Emeritus Professor of Economics, Lancaster University.

Paul Mosley is Professor of Development Economics and Director, Institute for Development Policy and Management, University of Manchester.

A. J. Rayner is Professor of Agricultural Economics and Assistant Director of CREDIT, University of Nottingham.

P. N. Snowden is Senior Lecturer in Economics, Management School, Lancaster University.

1 Current Issues In Development Economics: Introduction and Overview

**V.N. BALASUBRAMANYAM
and SANJAYA LALL**

Since the decade of the 1980s both the march of events in the Third World and the novelty of analytical tools employed by the development economist to analyse them have outpaced the textbook writer and surveyor of development issues. Teachers and students of development economics have been hard put to find suitable literature on rapidly unfolding issues such as the macroeconomic effects of commodity booms on LDCs, novel solutions to the debt problem, the structural adjustment and stabilisation policies of the Fund and the Bank, and implications of the recent industrial organisation-based theories of international trade for trade policy of the LDCs.

This volume brings together ten essays written by specialists on these and other issues. They are designed for final year undergraduate and graduate students and provide a succinct survey of theoretical developments and analysis of policy prescriptions. Each of the contributions speaks for itself, and there is little need here to belabour their subject matter. We merely highlight the main themes of the essays, the novelty of their analysis and alert the reader to opposing points of view.

The days when we worried about the status of development economics as a sub-discipline of economics are long gone. The volume, variety, and the distinctive quality of the literature on development issues during the decades of the 1960s and 1970s served to establish development economics as a specialist discipline on par with, say, labour economics or monetary economics. We now appear to have swung to the other end of the spectrum with the question: is there a need for a separate sub-discipline with the title 'development economics'? It is often argued that development economists are but mainstream economists who apply the tools of their trade to analysis of problems of developing countries. Much more disconcerting to the development economist is the view that the sub-discipline has not succeeded in slaying the dragon of backwardness, that it is dead as a discipline, and that its demise should be welcomed as it may have done more harm than good for the interests of developing countries.

John Knight provides an analysis of these issues in Chapter 2 on 'The Evolution of Development Economics'. His essay would serve to assure the student of development economics that the subject is not only alive, but kicking. Indeed, Knight's 'shopping list' of topics awaiting research and analysis is an invitation to students and specialists in other sub-disciplines to join the quest for solutions to development problems. His view that 'to a surprising extent, technology, institutions and the state are amenable to the sort of formal modelling that is the hallmark of the economics profession today', should reassure the mainsteam economist concerned about the intellectual rigour of the discipline. His enunciation of the compatibility of neoclassical and structuralist approaches, depending on the validity of their underlying assumptions, deserves careful study: if all development economists spelled out their premises and checked their empirical value, a great deal of fruitless debate would be avoided.

Poverty, hunger, inequalities, and the role of the state in the development process are some of the issues in Knight's list of topics awaiting further research. The next three essays in the volume address these issues. The first of these essays by Tony Rayner and Ken Ingersent (Chapter 3) discusses institutional and technological change in agriculture. They subject received wisdom on issues such as the allocative efficiency of traditional agriculture, the relationship between size of farms and productivity, the impact of the 'green revolution' on productivity and economic welfare of farmers, and the reasons for the failure of the green revolution in sub-Saharan Africa (SSA) to intense scrutiny, and find it deficient in many respects. They argue, for instance, that, contrary to received wisdom, the green revolution which involves the use of complementary capital inputs with built-in indivisibilities may have placed small farms at a disadvantage relative to large farms. They question Shultz's celebrated thesis that farmers in traditional agriculture are poor but efficient, in terms both of the neoclassical assumptions underlaying the thesis and the policy conclusions that flow from them. They examine the thesis that the green revolution, with its impact on output and profits, is an harbinger of institutional change, and suggest that institutional change may be a prerequisite for the green revolution to result in growth with equity. Indeed, they argue that the failure of the green revolution in SSA may be a consequence of inefficiencies of public institutions in providing the required research inputs. They are dubious about the 'getting prices right' prescription for improving agricultural supply and productivity. Citing the Chinese experience, they argue that an institutional system which links rewards to individual responsibility may be a better bet than the policy of merely getting prices right. While the defenders of the neoclassical faith may not quarrel with this thesis, they may argue that it is narrow in conception, applicable only to specific locations and culture. Nonetheless, the thesis does cast the 'getting prices right' prescription in a new light. The reader will also find in this essay an analysis of the world beyond the green revolution, poised to take shape with the biotechnology revolution, a topic yet to figure in the mainstream literature on agriculture.

Alisdair MacBean is also sanguine about the prospects of increased food supplies in the world as a result of technological change (Chapter 4). His concern is the problem of hunger amidst ever-growing supplies of food. Why are so many Third World countries hungry despite the fact that production of food has outstripped the growth of world's population? Answers to this question are to be sought not only in economics but also in ethics and politics, a clear case where economists cannot avoid crossing the boundaries of other disciplines. Macbean's essay on 'Achieving Food Security' does so, drawing upon Amartya Sen's well-known theme that food deprivation arises out of lack of command over resources to buy food, and not because of declining availability of food. The policy prescription that follows from Sen's thesis is that raising the real incomes of the poor is the most powerful and systematic method of preventing food insecurity. MacBean discusses these and other issues, including the costs of food insecurity and measures of dealing with transient as opposed to chronic food insecurity.

The essay on targeting by Tim Besley and Ravi Kanbur (Chapter 5) focuses on a subject of great current significance, the design of efficient policies for poverty alleviation. The ideal policy of targeting would, they suggest, be one where all transfers went only to the poor. Such an ideal policy faces three sets of problems in the real world: the administrative and informational costs of implementation; individual responses and incentive effects; and political economy. These inherent problems lead Besley and Kanbur to be sceptical of the applicability of ideal targeting policies. However, they suggest two kinds of targeting that, while not theoretically ideal, may be useful in certain circumstances: *statistical targeting* and *self-targeting*. They go on to conclude that real progress in devising poverty alleviation schemes can be made only by conducting detailed empirical analyses of particular countries, echoing the conclusions reached in John Knight's survey.

David Bevan, Paul Collier and Jan Gunning introduce the reader to the 'new macroeconomics' of open developing economies subject to external shocks (Chapter 6). The 1980s have witnessed a growing concern with the effects of serious macroeconomic shocks in several parts of the developing world. Received theory has, however, been unable to analyse these shocks satisfactorily. Bevan, Collier and Gunning use the theory of the 'Dutch Disease' as a starting point, but develop and refine it to take account of short-run dynamic effects, distinguishing between capital and consumer goods in the tradable and non-tradable sectors. They consider the impact of shocks with and without government regulation (in the form of exchange control on holding foreign assets), and argue that such regulation usually amplifies the impact of the shock. They analyse the design of appropriate fiscal policies to deal with shocks, and find that the usual control regimes in developing countries lead private economic responses to be socially sub-optimal. They conclude that the problems of finding an appropriate policy response under these conditions are often insuperable. As with the Besley and Kanbur essay, Chapter 6 ends on a pessimistic note concerning the feasibility of designing or implementing ideal government policies.

Sanjaya Lall's essay on 'Explaining Industrial Success in the Developing World', (Chapter 7), takes a rather more positive view of the role of government intervention in the industrialisation process. He takes the trade strategy debate as the starting point for an analysis of the determinants of the success of the newly-industrialising countries (NICs). It is evident that export orientation has turned out to be a superior strategy to import substitution, but export oriented strategies do not provide a sufficient explanation of industrial success. Neither do they support the case for non-intervention. Lall is sceptical of both the strong version of the outward-oriented approach to development (which eschews intervention of any sort) and the weak versions (which accept functional but not selective interventions). Drawing on the experience of the East Asian NICs, he presents the case for selective intervention within the broad framework of outward-orientated policies, based on market failure in product, factor, and technology markets. In essence, his case for economically selective intervention, including protection where necessary, rests on what may be termed as the 'infant-industry' argument in the age of technology. He distinguishes such interventions sharply from the non-selective, non-economic interventions practised by most import-substituting regimes in the past. Lall's detailed analysis of the intricate and complex process of technology acquisition and development of indigenous capabilities leads him to the conclusion that selective intervention may be essential for the development of entrepreneurial talent and technical abilities in more complex industries in developing countries. Another related theme of importance discussed in the essay is the role of human capital in the development process. Despite a general consensus that skills and technological effort are critical to industrial success, the development literature on industrialisation has largely ignored these factors when drawing lessons from the dynamic performance of the NICs. The bulk of the most dynamic manufactured exports of developing countries today comes from industries that underwent a 'learning' process behind protective barriers, and this poses important questions on the standard policy prescriptions that have emerged from the trade strategy debate.

International aspects of development economics are invariably headline news. Recent developments, including the issue of liberalisation of trade in services, the birth of new theoretical explanations of trade grounded in industrial organisation theory which also appear to provide novel arguments for protection, and imaginative solutions to the debt problem have all been the subject of intense debate. The next four essays in the volume address these issues.

David Greenaway's essay on 'New Trade Theories and Developing Countries' (Chapter 8), surveys the new theories of trade and analyses their applicability to the trade policies of developing countries. The twin pillars on which the new theories rest are economies of scale and product differentiation. It is also these two characteristics of modern industry that underlie the observed growth in intra-industry as opposed to inter-industry trade. Drawing upon the extant econometric evidence Greenaway demonstrates that much of the existing intra-industry trade is confined to trade between developed countries and to a lesser extent to the trade of the NICs. This provides indirect but strong evidence in favour of the proposition that the twin characteristics of economies of scale and product differentiation on which the new theories rest are scarcely to be found in developing countries. Hence Greenaway's conclusion that the new trade theories may be of little relevance to an analysis of the trade problems of developing countries. Greenaway concedes, however, that they may be of some relevance to the NICs and may assume significance for other developing countries as their incomes grow. Subject to these caveats he is willing to concur with the positive aspects of the new theories, but he is reluctant to embrace the normative policy implications. The new theories are often invoked to justify protection on grounds of externalities and as a method of preserving rents in oligopolistic or duopolistic industries (where such industries are confined to domestic markets), or for transferring rents from one country to another in cases where the relevant market is international. Greenaway finds these arguments for protection unconvincing as few developing countries harbour industries of the sort that generate substantial rents. One would be hard put to find examples of such industries except for the much publicised case of the aerospace industry. He finds little that is new in the argument for protection based on externalities and argues that in cases where externalities do exist they are best captured by subsidies rather than through intervention in free trade.

Nick Snowden's essay on 'Managing the Debt Legacy: Approaches to Resolution' (Chapter 9), provides an overview of the origins of the debt problem and analyses many of the suggested solutions. Especially noteworthy in this context is his analysis of debt–equity swaps and voluntary debt relief or debt forgiveness. He does not find much merit in debt–equity swaps as a method of reducing the financial burden on the debtor countries, for debt–equity swaps merely alter the pattern of external claims on the debtor country with little impact on the total value of such claims. Indeed, debt–equity swaps may serve to benefit mainly the creditors. Snowden's argument in support of this claim is that a reduction in the debt burden of the debtor as a result of the swap may improve the debt profile of the country and serve to increase the value of the remaining portion of the debt. While this benefits the creditors it does little for the borrowing countries, especially so if full repayment of the debt is not on the cards in any case. Snowden, however, concedes that the swap arrangements may confer real benefits on debtor countries to the extent that they generate additional foreign investment flows.

In his analysis of the intricacies of voluntary debt reduction, Snowden finds several benefits to both creditors and debtors. Such debt reduction arrangements not only enhance the investment capacity of debtor countries, but may also provide them with an incentive to invest A reduction in the debt burden releases resources for investment. Debtor countries will have an incentive to invest as a result of debt relief if it allows them to enjoy a minimum level of consumption. In the absence of debt relief, however, the country is likely to indulge in above-average consumption in the knowledge that additional investment is likely to enhance their ability to service debt and favour the creditors. For these reasons debt relief is likely to favour both debtors and creditors. There is though a snag in all this: while creditors as a whole may gain from debt relief, individual creditors may be inclined to let others grant the debt relief while holding on to their original claims. This is the so-called 'free rider' problem to which Snowden offers several solutions.

In recent years the debate on the liberalisation of international transactions in services has attracted increasing attention. At the heart of the debate is the reluctance of most developing countries to lower the variety of non-tariff barriers to trade in services they have erected. In large part, their reluctance to do so arises from their traditional distrust of multinational enterprises, the major producers and purveyors of services. Brian Hindley's essay on 'Economic Development and Services' (Chapter 10) analyses the case of developing countries for the regulation of trade in services and finds it deficient in many respects. Hindley's critical examination of the case for regulation is grounded in an analysis of the concept of services, the distinction between goods and services, and the received theories of regulation. Especially relevant to a discussion of services is the 'capture theory of regulation', which posits that members of a regulated industry will often succeed in capturing the powers of regulators and using them for their own purposes. Because of the unique features of most service industries providers of services may be well placed to capture the powers of regulators for their own use; in these cases, Hindley argues that service users may be better off with no regulation at all rather than having a framework of regulations devised and implemented by captured regulators. The reader will also find in this essay a provocative critique of the 'infant industry' argument for protection often invoked in the context of services. Hindley's critique of the argument stands in strong contrast to Lall's defence of intervention in Chapter 7, and readers may also examine the differing assumptions made about the costs of the 'learning' process involved and the realism of these assumptions. Such controversy is the stuff of development economics, but its ramifications stretch well beyond academic debate.

No less controversial and intricate than the debate on services is the issue of structural adjustment identified with the package of policies for developing countries advocated by the World Bank. Like services, 'structural adjustment' is a nebulous concept which seems to mean all things to all men. As Paul Mosley remarks in his essay on 'Structural Adjustment: A General Overview, 1980–9' (Chapter 11), 'in the 1980s the phrase [structural adjustment] was used by many as a synonym for appropriate development policy and treated, like motherhood, as a good and necessary thing in itself'. Mosley, however, provides a precise definition of the term: it is that part of development policy which is devoted to achieving a boost to the supply side of an economy by the removal of market imperfections. Thus defined, structural adjustment is distinct from stabilisation, which seeks to control the demand side. The emphasis of the Bank's structural adjustment policies is on the

removal of 'distortions' through the reduction of state intervention. Mosley analyses the nature of structural adjustment policies
and proceeds to evaluate their effectiveness. He treats the reader
to a blend of economic theory, historical perspectives, and statistical evidence in arguing his case that the policy has not been
universally successful, and what may be an appropriate structural
adjustment for a NIC may be entirely inappropriate for a resource-
poor economy with a shattered infrastructure. Structural adjustment policies have to be tailored to suit the stage of development
countries have reached; a headlong rush into outward-looking
policies, for instance, on the part of countries which are stagnant,
poor in human resources and infrastructure, and compelled for
political reasons to propitiate rent-seekers may be a recipe for
disaster. Much of this supports the case presented by Lall in
Chapter 7 that the success of export-orientation depends on many
other factors than 'getting prices right'. Mosley's wry comment
that structural adjustment may be a middle-income country item of
consumption is worth pondering over.

These ten essays do not aim at providing a comprehensive
review of development economics. So broad and diverse is this
subject today that any such attempt would end up being either too
long, or too superficial, or both. The present selection focuses on
some issues that are emerging, or recognised, as significant in the
area of analysis and practice. Each of the essays offers useful and
original insights, which students of development problems may
fruitfully use as guides to existing knowledge or as pointers to
further research.

2 The Evolution of Development Economics

J. B. KNIGHT

2.1 EVOLVING FASHIONS

Development Economics (DE) rose to prominence as a separate sub-discipline in economics in the 1950s. Some would say that it had its heyday in the 1960s and early 1970s, and that from the mid 1970s it was on the wane. In certain senses, this is true. For instance, fewer First World students showed an interest in the Third World, and this affected the popularity of development courses. There has also been a blurring of the demarcation lines between development economics and other sub-disciplines of economics. Thirdly, DE initially achieved considerable lustre and excitement because people thought that it could slay the dragon of backwardness. By the 1970s, greater realism was setting in. As Sen (1983, p. 745) put it: 'the would-be dragon slayer seems to have stumbled on his sword'. Yet this is all rather misleading. The important fact is that both the quantity and quality of research on less developed economies has continued to increase.

What ought to constitute DE has been quite a lively issue in recent years. Perhaps its most aggressive critic has been Lal, who concluded his polemical monograph (1983, p. 109) as follows: 'The demise of development economics is likely to be conducive to the health of both the economics and the economies of developing countries'. A sensible definition of DE would be what people studying less developed economies do. But Lal obviously does not mean that. What he is really attacking is what he calls 'dirigiste dogma', the particular diagnosis of, and prescription for, the economic problems of developing countries offered by certain influential development economists writing particularly in the 1960s. He characterises the dirigiste dogma as anti-price mechanism, pro-planning, pro-government controls and intervention and pro-trade protection.

It is true that in the period up to the mid-1970s, the prevailing attitude among development economists was more anti-price mechanism, pro-planning, pro-intervention and anti-trade, than it is today. In part this was the general attitude towards government at the time – government was getting bigger and becoming more active everywhere. In part it reflected the fact that developing countries, especially those that had been under colonial rule, had failed to make progress under laissez-faire economic systems, and governments – especially the newly independent ones – seemed the obvious instruments for accelerating the pace of development. It was commonly felt that capitalism could not 'deliver the goods' in developing countries, and that, at the least, a mixed economy was required. In some countries political independence was achieved without significant economic independence – governments wanted to secure the latter as well by becoming more active in the economy. For all these reasons, and no doubt for some others, development economists faithfully reflected the prevailing fashions, perceptions and ideologies, when in their positive analyses they stressed the deficiencies of markets and in their normative analyses were generally pro-intervention.

In place of the dirigiste dogma Lal argued for general reliance on the free market, both in the domestic economy and in trade, and for a limited government role and limited intervention. Where market imperfections existed and where government did intervene, it should do so by harnessing the price mechanism (e.g., through taxes and subsidies, or by using shadow prices in public sector decisions), rather than by means of direct controls – price controls, quotas, rationing, government allocation, and the like. In support of this stance he cited the failures of some countries (e.g., India), which had pursued dirigiste polices, and the success of others (e.g., South Korea, Taiwan and and Singapore), which appeared to rely on private enterprise, market forces and free trade.

The direction that Lal prescribes is of course the direction in which DE has moved since about 1975. The prevailing paradigm has changed. This has occurred not only among development economists studying Third World economies, but also in the First World and in the Second World, such as Eastern Europe and China. It is a universal fashion. But it is not just fashion – it seems to reflect also an underlying change in circumstances since the 1960s. Then, many governments were too small, and it was natural that much economic advice would involve additional government activities. Now, many governments are too big and the consequences of their actions can be better evaluated, and it is to be expected that much advice will involve curbing government.

There is also another change in development economists' perceptions of government. They used, perhaps naively, to view government as a powerful, well-informed overlord, determined to promote the interests of society, defined in terms of some defensible social welfare function. Perhaps as a result of the experience of the last quarter-century, development economists are now more sceptical, even cynical, about government, its competence and its motivation. Sometimes it is seen as an actor in the economy, promoting its own interests (i.e., those of the politicians or the bureaucrats) or the interests of small but powerful groups, and using government interventions to do that. Government is sometimes seen as part of the problem, not part of the solution.

Keynes (1926, p. 12) explained the rise of the doctrine of laissez-faire in the nineteenth century in the following terms: 'The ineptitude of public administrators strongly prejudiced the practical man in favour of *laissez-faire* . . . Almost everything which the state did in the eighteenth century in excess of its minimum functions was, or seemed, injurious or unsuccessful'. In the same way – and, of course, to a more limited extent (because what is now regarded as the minimum function of government is far greater than it used to be) – the same reaction is apparent today among development economists, especially those working for such influential bodies as the IMF and the World Bank.

One ought to be aware of the trends in the thinking of development economists. I should rather say 'cycles' instead of 'trends' because I doubt whether the trend I have described can be projected far into the future. These attitudes and ideological frameworks not only affect normative economics (i.e., policy recommendations), but they also infiltrate into positive economics (e.g., in the choice of topic to be researched, in the relationships and variables within the analysis that are stressed, and so on). There does seem to be a correlation between the political alignment of development economists and the positive economic analyses that they produce or accept. For instance, development economists of the 'left' tend to be structuralist in their approach to macroeconomics and those of the 'right' tend to be monetarist. Mind you, one has to be careful with the terms 'left-' and 'right-' wing economic policies because the distinction can correspond more closely to the motive for than the extent of government intervention.

2.2 DIFFERENT APPROACHES: SUBSTITUTES OR COMPLEMENTS?

'A study of the history of opinion is a necessary preliminary to the emancipation of the mind' (Keynes, 1926, p.116). Feeling emancipated, I turn now to current approaches. One of the important questions which frequently gets asked and which ought to be addressed is: should there be a separate sub-discipline of DE, or can it all be subsumed under general economic analysis? The answer depends in part on whether less developed economies are inherently or systematically different from developed economies in their structure and operation. The distinction can best be made by means of examples – concerning the extent of market failure, the degree of responsiveness to change, and the role of institutions in obstructing or promoting development.

Although the emphasis given by development economists to the role of government in development and to government intervention in the economy has been subject to changing circumstances, ideology and fashion, even today a wide variety of approaches to these issues can be found. This reflects the fact that the evidence is by no means conclusively in favour of one paradigm rather than another. Take, for instance, the success of the newly industrialising countries like South Korea and Taiwan. Their success has been taken by some economists as evidence in favour of laissez-faire and free trade. It is true that their governments may be less interventionist that some other governments of developing countries. Yet Sen (1982), Wade (1988) and others have argued that their success is in no small part due to the active role of powerful governments – providing protection, steering resources, correcting market failures, and planning long term – and that reliance on market forces is not enough.

The terms 'structuralist' and 'neo-classical' are sometimes used to contrast the competing paradigms. The term 'structuralism' originally arose out of Latin American writing on inflation, which argued that one had to understand the structures of these economies to understand their high inflations. It can be more widely understood to mean that the economies of poor countries are inflexible: change is inhibited by obstacles, institutions, bottlenecks and constraints; the supply of most goods and factors is inelastic; product and factor markets are often very imperfect. These structural problems impede the development process. The structuralist approach tends to provide a rationale for not relying on market forces and for managing change by administrative action. By contrast, neoclassical economics begins from the assumption that the economies of poor countries are flexible. Such economies are characterised by rational economic behaviour, with economic agents maximising risk- and time- discounted profits or utility. Factors are mobile, supply curves are elastic, institutional influences are limited, and this ensures that product and factor markets are characterised by a good deal of competition. Neoclassical economics is thus a paradigm that investigates markets and prices and expects them often to work well (Little, 1982, pp.25–6) and, where they do not, looks for market and pricing ways of correcting them (e.g., taxes and subsidies).

Much polemical heat can be generated in contrasting and trying to defend one of these paradigms and attacking the other. The standard smear technique is to take a non-extreme version of one's own paradigm and compare it favourably with an extreme caricature of the other. The paradigms can be thought of as two ends of a spectrum: it is easy to criticise either of them by taking it to its extreme. In practice, what we need is a blend of the two – how much of each depends on the particular economy being studied, and the particular problem being studied within that economy; there is not really a conflict between them. Neoclassical forces tend to be at work wherever there are markets, and they have to be qualified and supplemented as an explanation wherever markets are not fully competitive. The danger of the neoclassical approach lies in the superficial or mechanical application of orthodox economics without thorough knowledge of the economy and its economic institutions: it is the skill of applying general economic principles to the intricacies of particular developing countries contexts that development economists exercise. The standard neoclassical analysis is normally relevant, but it cannot be applied automatically without good knowledge of the economy or the market in question, its actors and its institutions.

As an example of the difference between the opposing paradigms, consider the role of institutions in developing countries. A view that development economists commonly took in the past was that institutions were relevant to development but were exogenous and tended to be a brake on progress because they were slow to adapt and even dysfunctional. A contrary view which has recently gained currency among development economists is that institutions should not be taken as given: they are endogenous, they perform a useful economic function, and they respond rapidly to changing circumstances. Stiglitz (1986) and others, for instance, have argued that the institution of sharecropping in developing countries is readily understandable as an economically efficient response to the problems posed by the risk-aversion of peasants and the supervision costs of landlords. For any actual institution, it is likely that both views will be relevant. It is quite possible that an institution does have an economic rationale, that it does evolve in response to an economic need, but it is also possible that it will fail to adapt rapidly enough to changed circumstances and will outlive its usefulness.

The difference in approaches outlined above does not correspond to the structuralist – neoclassical dichotomy. At the time when structuralists thought of institutions as exogenous obstacles, neoclassical economists assumed them away. What I am describing, therefore, is the advance of DE in that the right questions are now being posed. Provided that development economists combine the application of economic analysis to institutions with a thorough knowledge of those institutions, then the improvement in the questions asked will be accompanied by an improvement in knowledge gained.

Another way in which development economies has improved in recent years is through the greater availability of good data; the use of specially designed surveys for research purposes in developing countries has increased rapidly. Partly, this reflects the greater opportunities for analysis provided by computers. Partly, it stems from greater recognition that the information needed to answer important questions has got to be collected. And, thirdly, it is due to the better research training of development economists. This trend is likely to continue. The extension of the frontiers of many topics will require the design, conduct and analysis of microeconomic surveys in developing countries, in which the researchers themselves will often have to take the initiative. Although such research is time-consuming and expensive, a cost–benefit analysis might well favour it over more intensive analysis of the existing official statistics.

As a result of these data improvements, DE is now more quantitative and – reflecting the much greater research output – is more concerned with 'nitty-gritty' issues. The days of grand generalisations about the process of development with limited facts are receding. Development economists have mostly descended from the rarified atmosphere of the high sierra and they are now grappling with the undergrowth on the plains. Nevertheless, by comparison with other, more prestigious, tribes occupying territories further away from poverty and deprivation, the Devecon generally manage to keep sight of the big questions and, in their choice of small questions, show a sense of economic reality and policy relevance. Stern (1989, p.599) has argued that DE derives its distinctive flavour and richness from its blending of big questions, small questions and problem-solving techniques – for instance, the development of broad ideas about how poor economies function, or misfunction, by means of hypothesis-testing in microeconomic case studies.

A promising methodological development of recent years has been the rigorous use of comparative analysis to examine particular issues. There is a tradeoff here between breadth and depth. For some purposes it is appropriate to examine large samples of countries in order to discover international patterns (for instance, Chenery, Robinson and Syrquin, 1986). The alternative approach is to compare only a few well-chosen countries, the advantage being that there is then more opportunity to select countries that are similar in all the relevant respects except the one of interest to the researcher, and to gather precise and appropriate data. An example might clarify the method. Kenya and Tanzania, the two East African countries, are very similar in many relevant respects but differ sharply in the quantity of secondary education; this has generated very different stocks of educated labour in their urban sectors. By means of specially devised and rigorously comparable sample surveys in the two countries, the effects of this difference could be analysed and the alternative policy regimes evaluated (Knight and Sabot, 1990). Development economists should increasingly exploit the existence of 'natural experiments' of this sort of wide range of issues.

Because of these various changes there is now a school of thought that suggests that DE as a separate subject is on the way out. Now – they say – we ought to be labour economists, or industrial, or monetary, or trade, or agricultural economists – people who include developing countries among their countries of study, but not exclusively so. According to this view, our task as professional economists would be to apply advances on the fronties of (say) labour economics – both methodological and substantive – to labour markets in poor countries. If we are not good labour economists – if we regard ourselves as development economists who dabble in labour issues – the research will be shoddy.

There is some truth in this view, but it is not the whole truth (Lewis, 1984). There is a danger involved in picking up a data set on some little understood economy and proceeding to analayse it, or in flying in to some poor country, equipped only with sophisticated economic techniques, and thinking one can do something useful. There are many specific research questions which will not even be thought of without a good knowledge of the economy in question. Those questions can be much better answered, and quantitative results better interpreted, if one has a general understanding of that economy, of its institutions and of its political scenario. That is an important reason for being a development economist with a good knowledge of a particular geographic area or of particular countries. We thus have an onerous life – we need to be both development economists and subject specialists.

It is arguable that the best research is problem-orientated, not technique-orientated. One ought to choose a problem and then apply all the relevant available techniques to try to understand it and to solve it; it is necessary but not sufficient only to theorise.

Theorising on its own can easily become sterile because it is difficult to evaluate one's theories except in terms of their logical and aesthetic appeal, unless other approaches are adopted as well. Nor is it sufficient to go in for number-crunching and econometric analysis. The 'bottom line' of that analysis must be interpretation. The quality of interpretation depends on the ability to theorise, and also on a thorough knowledge of the phenomenon being studied. This may well require a willingness to cross the conventional boundaries of economics and examine history, politics and institutions. It also requires perceptiveness, acute observation and common sense – which are the qualities that often distinguish good economists from economists who are merely well educated.

It is likely that all three of the approaches outlined above will shed some light on the chosen problem. Yet surely there are advantages of specialisation and economies of scale in research which might be lost. There is often a good case – particularly in large research projects – for the researchers to assemble a balanced team, with different strengths complementary to each other. I suspect that is the direction in which economic research on developing countries will move.

2.3   UNDERDEVELOPED TOPICS

Much of the discussion so far has been about methodology and about alternative general approaches. Very little has been said about the substantive issues which have been opening up, and will do so in the future. There are certain issues which development economists tended to neglect in the past, and which deserved more attention in the future. The issues listed below are necessarily subjective but deliberately thematic. The common theme is that economic analysis should be extended into areas unfamiliar or suspect to market-orientated economists – broader welfare objectives, technology, institutions and the state.

1. First, Sen (1983, 1989) has argued that development economists can be criticised for concentrating too much on economic growth and too little on the ultimate objectives of development – alleviating poverty, raising life expectancy, promoting participation, enhancing freedoms, improving health and

avoiding famine – what Sen refers to as the expansion of peoples' 'capabilities' – their capabilities to be and to do things. His complaint, therefore, is that development economists have been too narrow in their approach and that they have a useful role to play in broadening the approach to development. The underlying value judgement is an appealing one. It has led Griffin and Knight (1989) to argue the case for a 'capabilities-orientated' rather than a 'goods-orientated' social welfare function – even though it involves reflective rather than mechanical evaluation – and for a corresponding redirection of policy emphasis in the 1990s.

2. A second issue concerns technology, emphasised by Toye (1985). Development economists have tended to neglect technology, partly because they lack technological knowledge and partly because the conventional tools of analysis, concentrating on prices, tend to push it out of view. Yet economic agents in less developed countries find it difficult to learn: much learning is by doing, and the ability to learn is itself partly learned. There are important externalities in the learning process which cannot easily be internalised, and the outcome can be a low technology equilibrium (Stiglitz, 1989). Moreover, technology has important economic and social implications: it raises fascinating analytical issues concerning externalities, market failure and imperfect information; and it offers scope for cross-disciplinary work with technologists.

3. A third issue, to which I have already referred, is that of institutions. The analysis of institutions is now more common than it used to be, but there is a lot of interesting work to be done in analysing the extent to which particular institutions are functional or dysfunctional. Endogenous theories of institutions have been produced by both the transaction cost school and the imperfect information school: institutions can be seen as ways of dealing with high transaction costs and information problems. Having plenty of both, less developed economies are hospitable territories for institutional analysis (Bardhan, 1989). The term 'institution' is used here in a general sense, to mean a set of rights and obligations affecting economic agents – including property rights, conventions, types of contract, and authority (Matthews, 1986). Markets are a potentially important set of institutions in the organisa-

tion of all economies. However, even in developed countries much production is mediated not through markets but through large firms, so internalising externalities, improving information and reducing risks. Market failures are still more pervasive in developing countries, and the non-market institutions that ameliorate the consequences of market failure are not always effective, or may fail to develop without government support. There is accordingly a need for the microeconomic explanation and evaluation of rural and industrial organisation is less developed economies (Stiglitz, 1989). It may often be the effectiveness of the relevant institutions that determines how well the economy responds to price signals.

4. The fourth issue has also been touched on already. Development economists in the past tended to be naive in their implicit theory of the state, often displaying a touching faith in the intention and ability of government to correct market imperfections and market failures and efficiently to promote development. By contrast, the literature is now awash with accounts of interventionist failures. It is less concerned, however, with explaining the reasons for these apparent failures. There is a need to endogenise policy-making (Ranis and Fei, 1988). This is true of both normative and positive analysis.

Much policy discussion is conducted without an adequate understanding of government behaviour. Development economists should recognise that national policies are often the outcome of conflicts among sectional interests; in offering policy advice, they should analyse interest groups and examine the causes of conflict. It may then be possible to suggest ways in which conflicts can be moved towards successful outcomes.

A satisfactory theory of the state in developing countries is likely to encompass a variety of approaches. These might include the Marxist view of the state as representing dominant class interests; the neoclassical view of the state as an arena for competition among interest groups; the view that government, or its bureaucracy, pursues its own interests – for instance, using economic policies to purchase the support and secure the leverage necessary for retaining power; and the notion that urban bias in development policies is due to the disproportionate political power of urban dwellers.

The theory of the state should also be influenced by the growing literature on rent-seeking in developing countries. The underlying notion is that, when rents are created by natural monopolies or government intervention, economic agents in the pursuit of rents will, via 'directly unproductive activities', divert resources to unproductive uses. The rent-seeking literature is in danger of becoming too much concerned with reversing conventional trade theory results (which itself rapidly becomes a DUP activity!). However, another strand of the literature has attempted to link rent-seeking with government policy (for instance, Srinivasan, 1985). Although this 'new political economy' has been rather dominated by right-wing economists only too willing to conclude that the deficiencies of government interventions must outweigh any deficiencies of the market, the rent-seeking approach is potentially instructive. It provides a theoretical framework for understanding why a variety of government policies are what they are, why apparently irrational policies may in fact represent the rational pursuit of government objectives, themselves influenced by rent-seeking pressures, or why some liberalisation policies are not adopted, or fail.

Progress in understanding government motivation and behaviour is likely to come not from grand theorising *ab initio* but from generalisation based on many studies of diverse cases. It is possible, for instance, to explain the inefficiency of irrigation projects in terms of the incentives for canal officials and their masters to secure the rents flowing from subsidised water (Wade, 1982); or to model a 'government response function' arising from pressures for the creation of labour market rents and so explain the phenomenon of surplus labour in the public sector of developing countries (Gelb, Knight and Sabot, 1988).

A further important question has not yet been fully answered in the literature: why is it that some states pursue effective development policies and some do not (Bardhan, 1988)? It would not be surprising if the answer were found in the ability of the state to insulate economic management from the pressures of short term rent-seeking by powerful interest groups. In other words, in the more successful economies the state has more relative autonomy than in other developing countries; it has the ability to make policy changes when they are required because it can afford to upset entrenched interests. However, that answer would in turn raise deeper questions, in which orthodox economics might well be out of its depth.

To a surprising extent, technology, institutions and the state are amenable to the sort of formal modelling that is the hallmark of the economics profession today. However, it is unlikely that the important questions to which these topics gave rise can be answered solely by means of formal economic analysis. Development economists should not be afraid to cross the conventional boundaries of economics, or at least to seek advice across the boundaries. A contrary view is that economists should do the things they are trained to be good at, and not dabble in the things at which they are amateurs. Moreover, if DE is to be taken seriously as an academic sub-discipline, it should be as intellectually challenging and rigorous as other areas of economics, and not contaminated by 'softer' subjects. On the other hand, if we are ultimately concerned about things like poverty, hunger, inequality, 'peoples' capabilities to be and to do things', and so on, and with policies to make improvements, then we must recognise that economics is interdependent and cannot be isolated. In our approach to development economics, as in so many economic situations, there are awkward tradeoffs to be made.

3 Institutional and Technical Change in Agriculture

A.J. RAYNER
and K.A. INGERSENT

3.1 INTRODUCTION

This essay is based on the premise that expanding the output of domestic agriculture and the size of the agricultural surplus is a major objective of government policy in most Less Developed Countries (LDCs). Our primary emphasis is on the role of technological and institutional innovation in increasing food production and raising output–input ratios of the primary inputs employed in agriculture. Technological advance releases the constraints on production imposed by natural resources and human labour and is typified by a shift from a 'resource-based sector to a science-based' industry (Ruttan, 1982, p. 3). Institutional innovation facilitates the development and adoption of appropriate technology. Examples of institutional innovation are the setting up of a publicly financed agricultural research system directed toward biological research and changes in property rights concerning rules of access to land that provide incentives to efficient resource utilisation.

It is argued here that a successful transformation to a dynamically efficient food production system is fundamentally dependent upon appropriate technological advance and the complementary adaptive response of institutions. Market and non-market links between agriculture and the rest of the economy are relevant to this success. For example, a modernising agriculture purchases inputs and services from other sectors, requires a transportation and marketing infrastructure to deliver output, relies on a continuous stream of innovations supplied by public research institutions and private firms, and is aided by general education and the provision of information to farmers on available innovations in farm systems. Hayami and Ruttan (1985) have hypothesised that these linkages provide a mechanism whereby technological and institutional innovations are, in part, endogenous to the economic development of agriculture.

These innovations occur as a response to disequilibrium or imbalance in the food production system. For example, in a land scarce developing country, the expansion of public sector biological research and technical advances in high yielding crop (HYV) varieties responsive to fertiliser might be induced by the rising demand for food coupled with land prices increasing relative to wage rates. However, technological change is also, in part, autonomous. Similarly, whilst institutional changes may be induced by demand forces, they also exhibit an element of conscious design. More generally, the supply of institutional innovations depends upon the creativity of politicians, administrators, lawyers, economists, etc. in framing new institutions, and the ability of the innovators to mobilise political resources to bring about change.

The neoclassical analysis of agricultural development highlights the transformation of traditional agriculture by the removal of the productivity constraints imposed by those factors of production in most inelastic supply and institutional restraints most inimical to the generation of new income streams: government has a positive role to play only in the provision of public goods such as research institutions and physical infrastructure. However, critics have proposed a more interventionist role for government. Specifically they have argued that peasants are not only resource poor but also that their resource allocation is bound by village tradition, hindered by imperfect knowledge and targeted to avoid risk. Consequently, the 'interventionists' state a *prima facie* case for interventionist measures to improve the efficiency of peasant farming.

3.2 EFFICIENCY OF PEASANT AGRICULTURE

The 'poor and efficient' hypothesis postulates that the poverty of small producers is the consequence *not* of inefficient resource utilisation but of restrictions in the kinds and quantities of resources they command. The results of a celebrated case study of peasant farming in India were advanced in support of this hypothesis (Hopper, 1965; Schultz, 1964). It was claimed from the empirical results that the case study farmers were apparently behaving as neoclassical profit maximisers and were *allocating their resources with optimum efficiency*. The results of another larger-scale study of Indian agriculture conducted in the 1970s appeared to point to the same conclusion. (Yotopoulos and Nugent, 1976). Since these results appeared to validate the 'poor and efficient' hypothesis, its proponents proceeded to infer that because peasant farmers were allocatively efficient, they could raise their output (and, by implication, their income) *only* through technical innovation. This pointed to the conclusion that agricultural policy in LDCs should concentrate upon accelerating technical innovation rather than improving the utilisation of existing agricultural resources.

However, there have been two main criticisms of the 'poor and efficient' model: (1) the choice of the neoclassical model to represent the behaviour of peasant farmers, and (2) the distinction between allocative and economic efficiency. The essence of the first criticism is that peasant farmers are typically confronted by major uncertainties as well as numerous institutional and cultural restraints. Moreover, because they are poor they tend to be *risk-averse*. Consequently, the implicit assumption of Hopper that the farmer maximises expected profit is incorrect: rather, the peasant is willing to sacrifice some long-run profit in order to avoid possible major short-term losses (Lipton, 1968). Other more recent studies suggest that peasants trade off profit against risk reduction via the application of 'safety margins' in committing resources to production at the intensive margin and the giving of priority to less risky production enterprises over more risky and potentially more profitable ones (Wolgin, 1975; Schluter and Mount, 1974; Roumasset, 1976). The general findings from studies of village economies tend to support the conclusions that farmers are risk-averse and that local customs, although flexible, influence

economic activity (Stern, 1989). Nevertheless whilst village economies do not always fit the simple model of perfect competition
under certainty, input markets are important in allocating resources and agents and institutions can respond quickly and flexibly
to changing economic opportunities. In the context of *transforming* traditional agriculture, these studies would appear to indicate
the importance of incentives in order to bring about change in the
face of the risk-aversion of peasants and the information costs
which tend to preserve existing institutions and customs.

The second criticism is concerned with the theoretical distinction between *allocative* efficiency and *economic* efficiency. Economic efficiency combines *technical* efficiency with allocative effi-
ciency (Farrell, 1957). Thus whereas economic efficiency is conditional upon allocative *and* technical efficiency, allocative efficiency
is not conditional upon technical efficiency, or vice versa. The
pioneering study by Hopper did not explicitly consider technical
efficiency. However, the results of other studies of peasant
agriculture, which were explicitly concerned with technical efficiency, suggest that most producers operate inside the outer bound
production frontier due to lack of knowledge or other reasons
(World Bank, 1978). This evidence points to the conclusion that
scope exists for improving the technical efficiency of peasant
farmers via agricultural extension and farmer education.

A further important aspect of the efficiency of peasant agriculture is the relationship between efficiency and holding size. *A
priori*, traditional agriculture utilising land and labour as principal
inputs, might be expected to yield constant returns to increasing
farm size, subject to the important proviso that factor prices are
common to all farmers regardless of farm size. But there are sound
a priori reasons for expecting labour to be relatively cheap and
land relatively dear to the operators of *small* farms. An obvious
implication of this line of reasoning is that the reverse situation of
dear labour and cheap land applies to *large* farm operators. The
rationale of the wage differential is labour market dualism.
Whereas large farmers hire workers in the labour market at the
going wage rate, small farmers are self-employed and make little
use of the labour market. Moreover, due to a dearth of alternative
employment opportunities, the opportunity cost of the peasant
farmer's own labour, and that of his family, is typically very low.
The expected differential in land prices (and rents) is also a

consequence of inequality within the agricultural sector. By behaving monopsonistically, large-scale farmers tend to have preferential access to the land market where they buy or rent land relatively cheaply. But because of their weaker bargaining position in the market, smaller-scale farmers are obliged to pay more for land or a higher rent.

If, in fact, the price of land declines with increasing holding size, whereas the price of labour increases, the land:labour ratio will tend to vary directly with holding size and, *ceteris paribus*, labour will be used most intensively on the smallest farms and least intensively on the largest holdings. Moreover, under a relatively labour-intensive system of agriculture, where output per unit of land area is directly related to the corresponding labour input, the *productivity* of land is largely a reflection of labour intensity. Given the expected inverse relationship between labour intensity and farm size, it follows that the productivity of land (as reflected by crop yields, for example) will also tend to be inversely related to farm size. Furthermore, if land is scarcer than labour, as it often is in LDCs, this argument carries the important policy implication that smaller farms may utilise resources more efficiently than larger farms. Moreover, there may be a direct link between a country's farm size structure and its aggregate level of agricultural production. More specifically, a large farm structure may not be consistent either with efficient resource allocation or with reaching the optimum level of aggregate production.

The results of empirical analysis, based on data pertaining both to India and a wider cross-section of LDCs in several continents, support the hypothesis that, in traditional agriculture, output per unit of constant quality land is inversely correlated with farm holding size (Yotopoulos and Nugent, 1976; Berry and Cline, 1979). However, the validity of the inverse relationship between land productivity and farm size has been questioned, with supporting evidence from India, on the ground that the relevant empirical studies have failed to allow for land quality differentials (Bhalla and Roy, 1988). Moreover, even in LDCs, the apparent superior efficiency of the small farm is limited by two considerations. First, because it derives from labour market dualism, the superior efficiency of small farms is destined to disappear as labour becomes scarcer and its opportunity cost rises. Second, and even more importantly, the superior efficiency of small farms under the conditions of *traditional agriculture* is vulnerable to the impact of agricultural technical change in LDCs. Virtually all the evidence on the superior efficiency of small farms predates the 'green revolution' which, since the mid-1960s, has had a substantial impact on methods of agricultural production at least in some less developed regions.

It is often argued that being readily divisible, certain modern farm inputs, such as chemical fertilisers and seeds of high-yielding varieties (HYVs), are 'scale neutral'. But the adoption of green revolution technology involves the use of other complementary inputs which are less readily divisible, such as irrigation equipment and even field machinery such as tractors and mechanical harvesters. Due to the indivisibility of fixed capital inputs which are an integral part of the new technology, unit costs must tend to be lower, and profits higher, on the *larger* farms. To the extent that a higher profit per unit of output reflects superior efficiency, large farms may thus well become more efficient than small as a consequence of the modernisation of traditional agriculture. Due to a dearth of empirical evidence on the relative efficiency of large and small farms in LDCs where green revolution technology has been widely adopted, the proposition that small farms are losing their traditional advantage in terms of efficiency, where the scarcest resource is land, is based on *a priori* argument. Empirical evidence to confirm (or reject) the argument is badly needed, particularly for the guidance of policy-makers.

3.3   CONCEPTS OF TECHNOLOGICAL AND INSTITUTIONAL INNOVATION

Origins of new agricultural technology

Technological progress 'raises' the production function. Regardless of whether it is seen as being 'embodied' in specific production inputs, or as a 'disembodied' shift variable, technical progress is thus a prime source of resource productivity gain.

In recent years two main theories have been advanced to explain the origins of technical change: the 'supply-push' and 'demand-pull' theories (Thirtle and Ruttan, 1987; Jarrett, 1985). The supply-push theory postulates that scientific progress is an autonomous process owing little to economic forces. Scientists pursue knowledge for its own sake, but some scientific discoveries prove to be 'useful' and lead on to applied R & D and, later still, to commercial production, sales and profits. A related theory is that firms pursue their own internal R & D to develop 'new products' with a good market potential. New discoveries can also be made by trial and error or 'learning by doing'. Prior to the present century, this was the main source of agricultural innovations, such as the adoption of crop rotations and advances in animal breeding made by enterprising farmers in the now developed countries. Whilst scope still remains for agricultural advances to be made on this basis, particularly in LDCs, professionally conducted R & D is generally considered to be cheaper, in social terms than learning by trial and error.

Compared with supply-push theory, the demand-pull theory of technical change and innovation ascribes a larger role to economic forces (Hayami and Ruttan, 1971; Ruttan and Thirtle, 1989). The crux of the theory of induced technical change is that the research and investment, which necessarily precedes the new discoveries leading to technical progress, responds to market forces. In agriculture, changes in the relative scarcities of resources, as expressed by input price ratios, induce a derived demand for technical innovations to facilitate the substitution of relatively plentiful and cheap factors for scarcer and dearer ones. So, in a labour scarce economy, capital in the form of labour-saving machinery tends to be substituted for human labour. But in a land scarce economy, yield increasing and land saving inputs such as fertilisers, irrigation and HYVs are substituted for land. More formally, the theory of induced technical change is equally well adapted to explaining both *biological* innovations which save land, and *mechanical* innovations which save labour.

Although induced innovation theory emphasises the role of producer *demand* in determining the pace and character of technical change, it does not preclude supply-side forces from playing a contributory role. By lowering the cost of technical innovations, general scientific progress may influence the rate of technical change independently of changes in factor proportions and demand (Thirtle and Ruttan, 1987, p.10.). Thus, by allowing both demand-side and supply-side forces to influence technical change within the economic system, induced innovation theory is better 'balanced' than pure supply-side theories.[1]

Induced technical innovation theory is based on all the usual neoclassical assumpions. It is thus assumed that markets 'work' and that market prices reflect both private and social opportunity costs. Equally important is the fact that it is also assumed that R & D already exists as an institution, either in the public or the private sector (or both), and that it is responsive to market signals which producers are capable of giving. Critics of the relevance of induced innovation theory in LDCs have queried the validity of all these assumptions. If induced technical innovation fails to work in LDCs, what is the policy implication? A possible prescription is government intervention on the supply side to promote and finance R & D. But a more orthodox approach is to argue that *institutional* innovation is needed to complement technical innovation.

Hayami and Ruttan recognise that in LDCs induced technical change tends to be impeded by institutional barriers. In agriculture, there is a general lack of adequate research institutions to foster the discovery and application of new scientific and technical knowledge. Institutional innovation is therefore needed to break this bottleneck. Moreover, the main onus of responsibility for organising and financing agricultural research falls mainly on the government for two reasons. First, the prospective pay-off from agricultural research in LDCs may be too small or uncertain to attract private investors. Second, because it is generally easier for firms to protect or internalise the gains from a *mechanical* innovation (e.g., by taking out patent rights on the design) than those from a *biological* innovation, such as an HYV, any agricultural research conducted in the private sector of an LDC is likely to be biased in favour of the former. But mechanical innovations, which are generally labour-saving, are not well suited to the needs of peasant farmers for whom capital is scarce and dear, whilst labour is plentiful and cheap. Rather their need is for labour-intensive biological innovations, such as HYVs. For these two reasons, and to ensure that an LDC's agricultural research programme is compatible with national objectives of agricultural policy, it will thus normally be advantageous for the government to oversee the programme as well as providing many of the resources needed for its implementation (Ruttan, 1974).

Factor-biased technical change and its distributional consequences

A technical change is said to be 'factor-biased' if its adoption results in a change in factor proportions. Although, in theory, technical change is not *necessarily* factor-biased, in practice it usually is. Moreover, the change in factor proportions resulting from technical change must imply some change in the total levels of factor employment. Although the adoption of new technology with a labour-saving bias does not necessarily displace labour, it may do so depending upon the relative strengths of the 'changed factor proportions' and 'output adjustment' effects (Donaldson and McInerney, 1973).[2]

In most LDCs the creation of new employment, including new jobs in agriculture, is a major policy goal. Encouraging producers to adopt labour-using technologies, rather than labour-saving ones, might appear to be an appropriate short-run method of achieving the goal. Specifically in the context of agriculture, a distinction has been made between *land-augmenting* and *labour-displacing* technical change (Yudelman *et al.*, 1971., Ch.II). A land-augmenting technical change (LATC) induces an increase in total output either through enlargements of the cultivated area or through higher crop yields. *Ceteris paribus*, LATC expands the demand for labour since the higher output will tend to increase labour requirements. A labour-displacing technical change (LDTC) saves labour but does not directly affect output. Its economic rationale is to substitute other inputs for labour in order to reduce unit costs. But whether labour is actually reduced in practice is an empirical question.

The most obvious examples of LATC are biological and chemical innovations which increase crop yields. But mechanical innovations may also be output-increasing, either through a crop area or a crop yield effect. Indeed, upon closer examination the distinction between LATC and LDTC proves to be ambiguous, particularly regarding their different effects on output and employment. This ambiguity, and the near impossibility of identifying, technologies which are *invariably* labour-displacing casts doubt upon the policy relevance of the distinction between LATC and LDTC, particularly with respect to the adoption of 'selective mechanisation' as an objective of agricultural policy in LDCs.

Selective mechanisation means 'restricting mechanisation to where it contributes to increasing employment or is necessary to break a seasonal bottleneck' (FAO, 1973). The effective implementation of such a policy would involve restricting the use of agricultural machinery to situations in which it was land-augmenting and not labour-displacing. But, for a mixture of technical, economic and administrative reasons, it is highly doubtful whether the necessary government controls would be feasible, even if they were economically desirable.[3]

Agricultural technical change and employment in LDCs

Technical change in agriculture affects employment, not only in agriculture itself, but also in all the industries linked with agriculture through the inter-industry input–output matrix.[4] The effect of technical change on employment in agriculture itself can be termed the *direct* employment effect, whereas the effect on employment in other sectors is the *indirect* effect. The relative magnitudes of these effects cannot be determined *a priori*, but only by the results of empirical investigation.

Most empirical studies of the *direct* employment effects of farm technical change in LDCs have concerned mechanisation with tractors. The evidence on whether tractors displace labour is mixed, with the results of different studies pointing to diverse conclusions (Roy and Blase, 1978; ODM, 1976; Yudelman *et al.*, 1971; Clayton, 1972). This is not surprising because the substitution of machine power for human labour is not the sole motive for adopting tractors or other machinery. The motive may be to increase output (through LATC) rather than displace labour. Moreover, mechanisation is a gradual and piecemeal process taking a long time to complete. At any particular time the process is likely to be more advanced in some places – be they individual farms, regions or whole countries – than in others. The evidence provided by contemporaneous but geographically separate studies may thus cover many different stages of the mechanisation process.

A more broadly-based study of the direct employment effects of agricultural technical change in the state of Punjab in India distinguished between 'crop-mix', 'cropping intensity' and 'pure technology' effects (Krishna, 1975). The principal crops were wheat and rice and the empirical findings showed that despite positive crop mix and intensity effects, technical change over a five year period resulted in an overall net loss in total employment on both crops due to a large negative technology effect. This was apparently due to a bias inherent in the new technology adopted by farmers.

Fewer studies have been made of the indirect employment effects of technological innovation in agriculture in LDCs. However, the results of a projection study based on the Indian agricultural sector, using a comparative static input–output model, showed conditions in which technical change in the farm sector would induce a higher level of aggregate employment despite labour displacement from agriculture itself. In other words, the extra employment created by farm technical change in the non-farm sector outweighed the loss of farm jobs (Krishna, 1975). Although this result derived only from a projection based on a particular set of assumptions, it is very effective in drawing attention to the difference between viewing the consequences of farm technical change in the farm sector alone, and in the economy as a whole.[5]

3.4 BIOLOGICAL TECHNOLOGICAL CHANGE: THE GREEN REVOLUTION

Development, spread and production impact[6]

The development and diffusion of high yielding cereal varieties (HYVs) has been the major technological change in agriculture in the LDCs, particularly in Asia, in the years 1970–90. In comparison with traditional varieties (TVs), the seeds of the HYVs embody greater genetic potential for response to fertiliser in a favourable environment and HYVs are described as short, stiff-strawed, fertiliser-responsive plants.[7] Typically the HYVs have a shorter growing period than TVs. The HYVs have had an important impact on production in those countries where there has been significant adoption. Specifically, higher yields have been obtained by using larger quantities of fertilisers, controlling weeds, pests and diseases more effectively and managing the use of water. The shorter growing season has also permitted an extension of multiple cropping. The new seed–fertiliser technology has been termed the 'green revolution' (GR). The HYVs spread quickly and widely following their introduction; by the mid-1980s they accounted for just over half the wheat and rice area in the LDCs. However, the GR has been confined mainly to wheat and rice areas with a plentiful supply of water (largely supplied by irrigation). Some regions, especially, in Africa, have not benefited from the GR.

The varietal improvement of food crops through systematic breeding in agricultural research institutes is a relatively new phenomenon in the developing countries. Agricultural development strategies in the 1950s and 1960s emphasised the screening of internationally available technology for effectiveness, and transfer of this technology through extension services. However, agricultural technology, particularly with regard to crops, was found not to be readily transferable, and this strategy was largely unsuccessful. Rather, biological agricultural technology exhibits an overriding element of location specificity: that is, there is a strong interaction of improved agricultural technology with soil and climatic factors which impedes the diffusion of technology across broad regions.

The failure of direct technology transfer to raise substantially agricultural output led to increased emphasis by national policy-makers and aid institutions on expanding agricultural research capacity in the developing countries. The development assistance agencies also established international agricultural research centres (IARCs) both to provide a lead in designing new varieties of food crops for use in the Third World and to train agricultural scientists from the developing countries.[8] Substantial investment of international bilateral and multilateral aid in IARCs and in the national research programmes reflected a belief that this would produce low cost agricultural growth, a corollary of the poor but efficient hypothesis discussed in section 3.2 above. Essentially, the system of national and international research would permit the indirect transfer of technology: research findings could be adapted to specific local agroclimatic conditions.

The international research system (IRS) represents a major social invention which has enabled high returns to be realised directly from agricultural research and indirectly by facilitating research coordination and indirect technology transfer. As a generalisation, the IRS produces R & D technologies which improve the capacity of national agricultural research systems (NARSs) to develop new production technologies. An IARC might thus produce new seeds which are screened and adapted by an NARS or germ plasm which is incorporated into the breeding programme of NARSs.[9] Whilst the IRS has significance as a 'leading edge', it now represents a small if strategic element in agricultural research in the developing world. In the mid-1980s, the budgets of NARS represented about 95 per cent of agricultural research expenditures in developing countries with 5 per cent being provided by the IRS. There was a large expansion of NARSs between the 1960s and the 1980s and comparable increases in extension activities (Judd *et al.*, 1986).

The impact on cereal production has been impressive in the regions able to use HYVs, following low growth rates in output in the 1950s and early 1960s. For example, the annual average percentage growth rate in cereal production between 1961 and 1985 was 3.7 per cent in Asia (3.1 per cent excluding China), 3.4 per cent in Latin America, 2.2 per cent in the Near East/N. Africa but only 1.7 per cent in Sub-Saharan Africa (SSA) (Alexandratos, 1988, p. 86). Herdt and Capule (1983) in a study of eight major rice producing countries[10] estimated that an increase in rice production of 120 million tons between 1965 and 1986 could be attributed almost equally to improved varieties, increased fertiliser, an increase in the irrigated area and a residual (changes in land area, labour and complementarity amongst factors).[11] The HYVs have also indirectly increased production because most varieties have a shorter growing season than TVs. This characteristic facilitates a more intensive multiple cropping system whereby an additional crop of the HYV or some other plant may be produced during the year. 'Wheat, for example, has become an important winter crop, between rice crops in Bangladesh' (Dalrymple, 1985, p. 107).[12]

The impact of HYVs of rice and wheat has, however, been largely confined to areas with irrigation or relatively favourable rainfall. These two crops have also taken a substantial proportion of research resources, and varietal improvement in other crops (except export crops) has not been so rapid. Nevertheless by 1984 over 6 million hectares of maize in the LDCs was planted to varieties derived from the work of the IARCs. New varieties of other crops such as cassava, millet, cowpeas, field beans and potatoes derived from research at the IARCs (and that show an improvement in trials over TVs of these crops) have been released in recent years.

Adoption and distributional issues

The introduction of a new technology at the farm level results in a period of disequilibrium whilst the farmer learns about and experiments with the innovation. Costs of information acquisition, transactions, set-up and evaluation are involved in the adoption process. Constraints on adoption can be imposed by risk-aversion, lack of access to or high cost of credit, inadequate incentives associated with farm tenure arrangements, insufficient human capital and inappropriate transport structures (inadequate market linkages). The fixed costs and constraints imposed on adoption by institutional deficiencies can affect the pace of adoption and the distribution of gains from the employment of new technology.

HYV technology is essentially divisible and hence technically scale neutral but the implications of its adoption for income distribution has generated considerable controversy, particularly during the initial years of the GR. In particular, critics argued that gains in production were offset by increasing income inequality. However, more recent evidence,[13] suggests the following generalisations concerning the adoption process and income distribution impacts of the GR:

1. The HYVs were adopted at rapid rates in those areas where they were technically and economically superior to local varieties.
2. There has been a wide diffusion of the HYVs among farmers over time, irrespective of farm size and tenure status. Whilst smaller farmers tend to lag behind larger farmers, the lags disappear after a few years. Small-scale farmers are laggards either because they can avoid risk and lower fixed costs by observing the experimentation of the larger farmer or because they cannot purchase scarce inputs. Larger farmers capture innovator rents through differential adoption. Owner operators do not adopt more readily than tenants unless tenants are credit constrained.

3. Small-scale farmers and tenants ultimately adopt and utilise HYV technology as intensively as large farmer and owner operators. Indeed yields may be larger on smaller farms because they apply more labour per hectare (see section 3 above).
4. HYVs raise labour demand per hectare, especially at harvest time. But the large, mobile and growing rural labour force prevents real wage rates rising significantly. Nevertheless, landless labourers have gained in absolute terms.
5. HYVs raise the demand for land but because land supply is inelastic, rent and land values rise. Landowners gain more than tenants and labourers from the adoption process.
6. The adoption of HYVs widens wage and income differentials between regions. The location-specific nature of agricultural technology limits the applicability of HYVs. Differential adoption across regions is also influenced by variations in physical and institutional infrastructure: the differences in availability and cost of water and irrigation, credit and fertiliser and the extent to which regions are connected to market centres by transportation networks.
7. Consumers have gained from the increases in output, moderating increases in the price of food and from a smoother supply of food throughout the year stemming from increased multiple cropping. For semi-subsidence producers, a portion of the consumers' gain remains with producers.
8. The HYV technology has helped to lower the threshold of viability of small farms. For example, in the Indian context a two acre farm – the medium size – might be viable with the new technology. HYV technology provides the opportunity for investment in the small farm sector to be productive.

Conclusions and issues

The GR is an example of technological and institutional innovation that has been appropriate to relative resource scarcities or factor constraints in many developing countries. Specifically the GR has released constraints in economies which were land scarce with population pressure pushing against an inelastic supply of land and agricultural science poor with high training costs for scientists and high costs of developing and operating research programmes. In such countries the shadow prices for land and research science were high, these being the effective constraints on increasing agricultural output. Fertiliser was a potentially cheap substitute for land and the adaptation of foreign technology and its dissemination via extension was a potentially cheap alternative to domestic agricultural research. However, such substitutes could not be used effectively without necessary investments in interacting technological and institutional innovation. The application of fertiliser is thus a low cost source of growth only if compatible biological technology is available; such technology is available only if investment is made in location specific biological research. Adaptive research depends on the ability to purchase research resources at a low price – that is, the basic research underlying new biological technology is developed at 'foreign' institutions and disseminated at low cost. Extension workers are cheap but their effectiveness in diffusing technology depends on complementary institutional investments in farmers' education and training, physical infrastructure including roads and irrigation, electricity to power irrigation systems, and the elimination of inefficiencies in resource allocation associated with credit and land tenure systems.

Whilst the GR is in itself an example of a technological innovation, it is the product of a major institutional innovation – that of the IRS. Whilst prototype HYVs were being developed in some LDCs in the early 1960s, the IARCs speeded up the development of the new varieties and the enlargement of national research capacities. The facilitating and coordinating role of the IRS in research represented a discrete shift in the supply of institutional shift to the right. This institutional change thus reduced the cost of overall research compared to the parallel development of separate national research systems. In part, it would appear that the inauguration of the IRS was a response to growing evidence that agricultural growth and rises in productivity were not being achieved in the 1950s and early 1960s by simple technology transfer and the perception of aid agencies that direct food aid tended to have a depressing effect on domestic production incentives in recipient countries. At the same time there was a shift to the right in the non-market demand for biological research arising out of the perceived 'food crisis' in the developing world in the early 1960s (population growth tending to outrun the rise in food production and the emergence of large food deficits). Consequently, both the nature and production of the GR give some support to the theory of induced innovation expounded at length by Hayami and Ruttan (1985).

Whilst the GR has been, in general, a story of success of agrarian technological innovation, it has given rise to several issues.

1. There was considerable academic controversy during the early stages of the adoption of the GR regarding the equity implications. There was concern over institutional rather than technological bias in the distribution of returns. Experience with the GR suggests that it can meet both productivity and equity criteria if the complementary institutional structures are in place. Whilst Hayami and Ruttan have argued that the availability of HYV technology can induce appropriate institutional change because of demands resulting from increased output and profit, the supply of such institutional innovation may not be forthcoming. It is thus a debatable question as to whether or not prior institutional reform affecting the supply of inputs is a precondition to growth with equity from the GR, or whether the initiation of the GR induces institutional responses to provide growth with equity.

2. Why has the GR in sub-Saharan Africa (SSA) apparently failed? This region stands out as a major exception in a world context. In the 1980s, SSA faced major food deficit problems despite significant increases in agricultural research and extension expenditure between 1959 and 1980 (Judd *et al.*, 1986). Moreover the size of NARSs relative to agricultural output is apparently large in SSA compared to other developing regions (Lipton, 1988). The implication is that public sector agricultural research in SSA has yielded low returns whilst it has shown high internal rates of return in other LDCs.[14] Why has the agricultural research in SSA apparently not been cost effective? Many studies have suggested that the main reasons for the poor performance of agriculture in SSA have been constraints imposed by inappropriate fiscal and pricing policies (disincentives to agriculture), inadequate extension, marketing and physical infrastructures, trade policies not based on comparative advantage and political mismanagement (see World Bank, *Development Reports*, 1985; 1986; 1987).

Perhaps as important has, however, been the inappropriateness of available technological innovations in the African context and inefficiencies in research organisation. Binswanger and Pingali (1988) have argued that the GR has been inappropriate to the land-abundant, thinly populated rural areas lacking infrastructure covering much of SSA. The development of plant varieties embodying stress resistance to drought and disease rather than a yield response to fertiliser would constitute a more appropriate technological strategy. Lipton (1988) has identified inefficiencies in research organisation and imbalance in research portfolios for the poor performance of public sector biological research investments. The small size of most countries has not allowed NARSs to reap economies of size and regional research cooperation is difficult because of an assurance problem – the fear of 'free riding'. In organisational terms, the NARSs have suffered from a dispersion of research at many institutions and high turnover of scientists. Finally, there has been insufficient research on mass consumption crops (cassava, sweet potatoes and maize) which can yield large domestic benefits, with excessive research on export crops where the benefits flow to foreign consumers if the export demand schedule is price inelastic. In short, the low productivity of research effort may be the major constraint on improving the performance of agriculture in SSA and this constraint would seem to be imposed by inefficient public institutions.

3. Is the GR sustainable? There is concern over the potential loss of genetic diversity as a wide range of TVs are displaced by HYVs based on a narrow range of genetic materials coupled with worries over the intensive use of chemicals to control pests, diseases and weeds such that the natural resistance and competitive ability of crops is reduced. In part, this issue focuses attention on the importance of maintenance research in agricultural crop science. A related issue is that of spillover effects or environmental costs associated with the GR. The increased use of fertilisers, chemicals and irrigation has led to a rise in chemical pollution costs, an increase in salinity and in water borne diseases and costs associated with soil erosion. Institutional change to regulate environmental costs may be more difficult to achieve than that to increase output, since

such changes are not induced by private profits derived from technological change.

3.5 AGRICULTURAL SUPPLY: CONSTRAINTS AND INCENTIVES

In the 1960s and 1970s the 'technological fix' approach to agricultural development was fashionable. More specifically the World Bank, and other development agencies sought to promote agricultural development primarily through micro-level *development projects*. Most such projects involved the introduction of new technology 'packages', such as the seeds of HYVs combined with fertiliser and irrigation, which farmers in the project area were encouraged to adopt.

More recently the development agencies became somewhat disillusioned with this approach to agricultural development. Too many projects failed once the technical and financial support of the aid donors was withdrawn. In seeking the reasons for the limited success with the project approach to agricultural development, the development agencies reached the conclusion that a large part of the failure was due to misconceived macroeconomic and agricultural policies in the host countries. An influential World Bank report on SSA (1981) was especially critical of the damaging effects of government policies on domestic agriculture in that continent. This was later developed into a more general criticism of the agricultural price policies in LDCs (World Bank, 1986; Timmer, 1986). The crux of the argument was that in LDCs government policies keep domestic producer prices below 'border' prices; 'low' producer prices depress domestic production and encourage food imports; income is transferred from agricultural producers to consumer and taxpayers.

The 'negative' price policy which is said to be typical in LDCs is thought to be partially deliberate and partially accidental. The deliberate or direct element is said to reflect the urban bias of LDC governments which give way to pressure from urban consumers and industrial employers to keep food prices low (Bates, 1983, Ch. V). The accidental or indirect elements of negative agricultural price policy are a consequence of industrial protection and exchange rate over-valuation, both of which are very common in LDCs (Krueger *et al.*, 1988). The reasons for exchange rate inflexibility are partly political – that is, because exchange over-valuation benefits consumers of imported goods and producers of non-tradables, these groups have a vested interest in opposing devaluation, and exert political pressure to that end. Like producers of other traded goods, farmers lose from exchange rate over-valuation in both the domestic and overseas markets. Domestic market prices are depressed by the entry of 'cheap' imports, whereas export prices have to be cut, in terms of *domestic* currency, to match world prices denominated in stronger currencies.

The neoclassical economist's reaction to negative agricultural price policies in LDCs is to prescribe agricultural price reform to equate domestic producer prices to 'border' prices – that is, ignoring marketing costs and product quality differentials, domestic producers should receive the equivalent of the landed price of imports. On this view, the lack of an adequate producer price incentive is the main constraint on agricultural development. Once this constraint has been removed by 'getting prices right', domestic agricultural production and farm incomes will increase, and food imports will decline, to the benefit of the balance of trade.

Although there is substance in the case for allowing agricultural prices to rise in order to encourage farmers to produce more for the market, as well as improving their own welfare, placing such a price policy at the centre of agricultural policy reform in LDCs is clearly open to several criticisms. In the context of the major subject matter of this essay, over-emphasis on the importance of producer price incentives neglects the importance of the impact of technical innovation on agricultural productivity and aggregate production. But additional criticisms include neglect of the impact of higher food prices on the welfare of poor consumers, and of the possible benefits of relative price stability to both producers and consumers. Before proceeding to discuss the first criticism at greater length, we shall first deal briefly with the other two.

Just as the pursuance of a negative agricultural price policy transfers income from producers to consumers, the 'correction' of such a policy implicitly transfers income back from consumers to producers. Whilst virtually all policy adjustments affect income distribution, and the welfare implications of redistribution are sometimes difficult to evaluate, the welfare losses which higher food prices in LDCs might impose on low income households, including landless rural households, are difficult to ignore. The case for raising agricultural prices to improve the welfare of farmers and related benefits is matched by the case for keeping food prices low in order to avoid damaging the welfare of the very poor. Resolving the conflicting interests and welfare needs of agricultural producers and poor consumers in LDCs has been termed the 'food price dilemma' and various policy prescriptions have been suggested for dealing with it, including targeted food subsidies (Timmer, Falcon and Pearson, 1983).

The world market prices of many agricultural commodities are notoriously unstable. Commodity price instability is partially the consequence of unstable supply due to natural causes, such as weather variations, interacting with inelastic demand. But a further cause of unstable prices is the behaviour of developed countries in subsidising the disposal of commodity surpluses on export markets. The variability of agricultural prices imparts major uncertainty to price formation which can inhibit investment and curtail production by risk-averse farmers. Stabilising prices by public buffer stocks might then seem an attractive policy option to aid producers. However, Newbery and Stiglitz (1981, p. 444), suggest that 'the optimal buffer stock is very small', and point to the dangers that significant buffer stock intervention may simply transfer storage from private agents to public agencies. Newbery and Stiglitz point to the potential of futures and credit markets as being more effective ways of reducing the costs of risk to producers. Specifically, they advocate policy to make future markets more accessible to small producers. However, they are less sanguine about the practicality of improving the workings of credit markets in LDCs.

The instability of food prices also affects consumers. Indeed, because food grains constitute a large fraction of expenditure by low income consumers in LDCs, an increase in cereal prices relative to income can literally be a matter of survival. Possible instruments that can be used to protect consumers from 'excessive' food price variability are (a) public storage and (b) ration shops coupled with food entitlements. Newbery (1988, p. 20) has argued that the latter is more effective than the former provided that 'the coverage of the scheme is reasonably high and the level of intervention is modest'.

Few, if any, governments of LDCs, in fact follow the precepts of the border price paradigm model. Most *do* intervene in order to regulate agricultural and food prices in some way, often to the apparent detriment of domestic producers. Although successful lobbying of the government for cheap food by urban interests may help to explain price intervention in some countries, the evidence suggests that price stabilisation, rather than deliberately keeping domestic prices below border prices, is an explicit policy in some LDCs (Timmer, 1989; Rao, 1989). In practice the effects of price stabilisation may be difficult to distinguish from those of following a negative price policy, especially in the short term.

We return now to the point that over-emphasis on 'getting prices right' as an agricultural policy prescription for LDCs neglects the importance of technical innovation to enhance agricultural productivity and aggregate production. In many LDCs agricultural commodity supply elasticities are fairly small, implying a high ratio of fixed to variable costs of production: this, in turn, suggests the existence of major supply constraints other than an adequate price incentive (Smith, 1989). So, for example, supplies of purchased farm inputs may be constrained either by bottlenecks in domestic manufacturing capacity, or by a shortage of imports, or simply by infrastructural defects affecting distribution to farmers. But a major reason for slow agricultural growth in an LDC may above all be inadequate investment in agricultural R & D to equip farmers with improved technology to enhance their productivity.

Furthermore, production responses to price and research policies are influenced by the rewards system operating in agriculture. Whilst liberalising prices offers incentives for increased input usage and the development of biological innovations offers the potentiality for shifting the production function outwards, lack of incentives to labour effort in farming may lead to a shirking of labour, a stifling of initiative and an under-realisation of productivity gains. An institutional system which links rewards to individual responsibility provides strong incentives in agricultural production because of the importance of the personal attention to detail required in good farming practice and the consequent high costs of supervision of a collective labour force.

The results of the reform of agricultural institutional arrangements in China after 1978 provide strong supporting evidence for the importance of incentive effects on farm production. From the late 1950s to the end of 1978, Chinese agriculture was organised via a communal system of decision-making and rewards. The commune (equivalent to a local government unit or township) was the top decision-making unit but the production team comprising some 20 to 40 families (equivalent to a village) was the basic unit for organising farm labour. The 'reform' process started in 1979 introduced a 'personal responsibility system.'[15] Individual household farming with land leased from the state had virtually replaced the collective system of 1983 (Nolan, 1984): the individual peasant rather than the production team was the basic unit for decision-making. Other policy changes occurred after 1979 in particular, a policy of regional self-sufficiency in grain was abandoned and state procurement prices for farm products were substantially increased. Sharp increases in agricultural output and productivity occurred between 1978 and 1984 with a slow-down in 1985–6 (see Johnson, 1988; Perkins, 1988; Riskin, 1986; Wong, 1983). A study by McMillan, Whalley and Zhu (1989) suggests that some three-quarters of the total factor productivity increase between 1978 and 1984 could be attributed to the introduction of the household responsibility system and the strengthened individual incentives that it generated.[16] Rising total factor productivity after 1978 was also a contrast to stagnant or declining productivity between the late 1950s and early 1960s and 1978 (Rawski, 1982; Tang, 1980; and Wong, 1987). Yet the collective period embodied positive policies towards biological technological change and investment in inputs (Wiens, 1982). The rapidity with which output increased during 1978–84 reforms suggests, first, that the investments made during the collective period shifted the agricultural production possibility frontier substantially to the right but, second, that the increased technical capability was realised only by major improvements in allocative and X-efficiency induced by the reform policies regarding individual and price incentives.

3.6 AFTER THE GREEN REVOLUTION: THE BIOREVOLUTION?[17]

The cluster of emerging agricultural technologies generally known as biotechnology[18] will affect global agriculture via (1) plant genetic manipulation and breeding, (2) industrial tissue culture,

(3) animal applications of embryology and genetically engineered products and (4) the use of genetically manipulated microorganisms to produce or displace agricultural products (Buttel *et al.*, 1985, p.34). The coming 'biorevolution' is likely to have both greater and different impacts on third world agriculture than the GR even though 'the actual impact on levels and costs of production is unlikely to be appreciable until after the year 2000' (FAO, 1988, p.242).

The biorevolution promises to raise productivity on a wider scale than the GR. Whilst the GR has utilised traditional plant breeding techniques to improve yields of a limited range of crops in favourable agroclimatic settings, the biorevolution is likely to be applicable to both crops and animals across a broad spectrum and in diverse agro-ecosystems. In this sense, the biorevolution can build on and extend the GR. However, the biorevolution differs sharply from the GR in several important characteristics. First it is being produced by investments made largely in the private rather than in the public sector. Second, biotechnology is high cost hi-tech – that is, it is relatively expensive compared to traditional agricultural science. Third, industrial tissue culture introduces the possibility of producing naturally occurring drugs, flavours, dyes, etc. through industrial processes rather than via the cultivation of plants. Fourth, biotechnology will develop products that will displace agricultural commodities; for example, fructose corn sweetener has already eroded the market for sugar whilst there is substantial work on genetically engineering microorganisms to convert methanol into single cell protein, a process which if successful will displace traditional protein-rich animal feeds. Fifth, biotechnology systems will be knowledge-intensive as well as capital-intensive, so that adoption may be 'biased' towards the well informed and capitalised progressive farmer rather than the smallholding peasant farmer. Sixth, the broad front of biotechnology research portends rapid but disjointed (because of different lead times) changes from many directions: impacts will be more pervasive, more complex and occur at a more rapid rate than has been experienced in the past, creating difficulties in the design and implementation of agricultural development strategies.

Private sector dominance in biotechnology agricultural research stems from several sources. First, crucial scientific breakthroughs (e.g., genetic engineering) have increased the potential productivity of agricultural research. Second, technical advances with regard to hybridising crops,[19] such as wheat and rice and legal changes in the developed countries such as plant variety protection acts and the patenting of genetically modified life forms have increased the extent to which returns from biological research can be appropriated. Third, funding of public sector national agricultural research and the IARCs is under pressure whilst biotechnology industries receive subsidies by developed country governments.[20] Fourth, large chemical and pharmaceutical corporations with established research bases have been actively acquiring seed companies.

The heavy involvement of the private sector in biotechnology research in the developed world raises several issues with regard to Third World agriculture.

1. The extent to which private firms will engage in technology transfer to and development in the LDCs. According to Buttel *et al.*, (1985) seed companies and their transnational parents already have sales outlets in most and research facilities in a number of LDCs. Potentially, the Third World offers a large market.
2. The form of technology transfer: joint ventures between biotechnology firms in the industrialised world and agro-industrial firms in the LDCs are one possible route. The essentially private character of biotechnology suggests that the transfer, unlike the GR, may well not happen via NARs.
3. The influence of proprietary rights on technology transfer. This was not a consideration in adaptive transfer under the GR since new seed varieties were released via public agencies. The extension of plant variety protection to the LDCs would facilitate private sector transfer to the Third World by creating the conditions for enhanced profits. However, variety protection and the upholding of patents on genetically engineered organisms will increase the cost of adoption and impede the free flow of scientific information. The requirement of the private sector to acquire proprietary returns is also likely to influence research priorities in a different manner to those followed under the GR research.
4. The implications of the growing private sector for the future role of the IARCs and NARSs, since these are competitors to

the private seed firms. Biotechnology research is comparatively more expensive than traditional plant breeding in terms of fixed costs and the public sector institutions may not be able to acquire sufficient funds to develop new technology directed at third world agriculture.[21] In addition, the IARCs and NARSs may face proprietary restrictions or have to pay royalties for the acquisition of information and genetic material from the private sector. Further, there are doubts concerning the ability of NARSs in the LDCs to carry out biotechnology research: 'the more technically advanced LDCs have begun to establish national biotechnology programs at the same time that other LDCs lack the capacity to do the most routine plant breeding' (Buttel and Barker, 1985, p. 1173).

5. The extent to which industrial tissue culture will erode the market for primary products exported from the LDCs. It is possible that the plant species providing the genetic material from which a particular compound is produced will originate from LDCs but that the tissue culture industry itself will be located in the developed world.

6. The implications for the Third World of the biorevolution in animals. Unlike the GR, the biorevolution will raise the productivity of animals through advances in hormones, vaccines and reproductive technologies. Successful commercialisation of these technologies would lower costs of livestock production and increase the availability of livestock products, enhance the capacity of developing countries to produce livestock and raise the productivity of breeding animals. The consequences of these are likely to be lower cost protein foods and increased exports, and dislocations such as the displacement of food crops grown by small farmers and forests by livestock production.

7. The effect of the biorevolution on distribution: it is possible that the adoption of the new technologies will bypass peasant smallholders and the rural poor because of the requirement for innovators to secure commercial returns and the likelihood that adoption will depend on a high level of management skill and information knowhow.

In summary, the coming biorevolution has a greater span of applications than the GR and as a consequence, has the potential to raise the productivity of Third World agriculture on a broader front. However, the dominance of private sector involvement, the high investment costs, and the high degree of proprietary protection raise unresolved issues concerning the impacts of technology transfer to the LDCs in the context of an ongoing reorganisation of agricultural research. In a manner analogous to the GR, technological and institutional innovations are combining to generate a forthcoming biorevolution. This biorevolution will probably exceed the GR in its consequences, but at this stage in its development assessment is largely conjecture.

3.7 CONCLUSIONS

Continued population and income growth in the LDCs indicates a rising demand for food well into the next century (FAO, 1988). Expanding agricultural output and productivity is likely to remain a policy goal in most of those countries. Our review in this essay has highlighted the past success in many regions of Asia and the past failure in Africa. The lessons from this record point to the complementarity of appropriate technological advance and institutional innovation. Vital elements appear to be the strengthening of the capacity to promote technical advance (the research system) and the provision of incentives to farmers. However, the emerging issues in agricultural development strategy concern the opportunity and challenge provided by the forthcoming biorevolution. Policy-makers in the LDCs and international aid agencies will need not only to absorb the lessons from the past, but also to face up to the implications of the changing milieu of agricultural research if they are to promote agricultural development in the future.

4 Achieving Food Security

ALASDAIR I. MACBEAN

4.1 INTRODUCTION

In a world of plenty hunger continues to grow. That is the terrible paradox of hunger today. Food production has continually outstripped the growth of the world's population; yet the numbers who go hungry continue to rise. Nor has the world been able to avoid the terrible crises of famines. Many countries and hundreds of millions of people have felt the ravages of hunger, and many more the insidious effects of chronic under-nourishment from inadequate diets. They suffer from lack of food security.

But are not these problems basically questions of technology and ethics? What, if anything, does economics have to offer by way of analysis and prescription in this area? It could well be argued that for many poor countries the solutions lie in improvements in the technology of food production: new seeds, irrigation, fertiliser, biotechnological revolutions in developing new and improved varieties and in plant protection methods. By such means these countries could become self-sufficient in food. But would that be a necessary and sufficient condition for the achievement of food security? Technology could also serve to improve information, communications, transport, weather and pest-attack prediction, storage systems and so on. All of these could contribute to solutions, but still the problems could remain. All of these approaches require resources which have competing demands placed upon them. Resources, finance, knowhow and human skills are limited. This scarcity immediately creates the classic economic problem of choosing how to allocate scarce resources among a myriad of claims for them.

Ethics and politics clearly play a role. Hunger is almost always a problem of the poor, and especially of the poor in poor countries. Decisions on whether to provide famine relief from food surplus countries to food deficit ones are clearly a matter of ethics and political judgement. The same is true within countries, both in times of famine, and over the long run. But again economics has a key role to play in analysing the basic reasons for hunger and in calculating the benefits and costs of alternative policies for achieving both short- and long-term solutions. In the last fifteen years economic analysis, particularly the work of the distinguished economist A. K. Sen (1982 and earlier works cited there), has refocussed discussion in this field and profoundly affected policy prescriptions for creating food security.

Food security exists when people have access to enough food on a regular basis to meet their needs for energy, growth and maintenance of health while leading a normal active life. A nation enjoys food security when it has access at all times to enough food through domestic production, stocks, or international trade to satisfy these needs for virtually all of its population.

Transitory food insecurity occurs when people are temporarily unable to obtain enough food. Common causes are natural disasters such as drought, flood or pests; wars and civil strife; instability in food prices; loss of employment, fall in wages, or other sources of income (loss of entitlements to food in Sen's terminology (1982, Ch. 1)). Famine is the extreme form of transitory food insecurity. Chronic food insecurity is the deep-rooted and more widespread problem which occurs when households suffer from a persistent failure to gain enough food.

This essay reports the incidence of food insecurity in less developed countries (LDCs), analyses its causes, and examines various proposed remedies. Section 4.2 concentrates on the incidence and the social costs of food insecurity. Section 4.3 discusses various diagnoses of the problem, including Amartya Sen's 'entitlement' analysis. Section 4.4 considers some of the more important policy suggestions while section 4.5 presents a summary and some conclusions.

4.2   INCIDENCE AND COSTS OF FOOD INSECURITY

That undernutrition is widespread can be seen from Table 4.1 (which shows its incidence in the major developing regions).

Different definitions of an adequate nutritional standard produce widely varying estimates of undernourishment. The estimates in Table 4.1 are relatively conservative. Measuring food insecurity is complex and uncertain (see Appendix). An alternative estimate in a 1986 World Bank Study put the figure of under-nourished in 1980 as high as 730 million people (excluding mainland China because of lack of data). As Table 4.1 shows, the percentage of the population suffering chronic food insecurity is highest for Africa South of the Sahara. In general the problem seems to be related to the level and distribution of income, but largely independent of a country's degree of self-sufficiency in food (World Bank, 1986a, p. 55). It affects surplus countries like Malawi, self-sufficient countries like Kenya, and deficit countries, like Ethiopia (Commission of the European Communities, 1988).

Table 4.1 shows that the absolute numbers suffering undernourishment have risen over the last 25 years because of population growth. In regions with rapid economic growth such as East Asia and the Middle East both the share and the numbers of under-nourished in the population have fallen. In South Asia and Sub-Saharan Africa (SSA), where growth was slow or negative, the share of the population with deficient diets increased slightly (World Bank, 1986b, pp.1–3).

Transitory food insecurity in the form of famines has dominated the headlines of the media on many occasions since the food crises in the Sahele in the early 1970s. But households in many countries suffer less dramatic, yet severe food insecurity as a result of fluctuations in harvests, prices or family incomes. Lack of data makes it impossible to assess how frequent and severe such incidents are.

Chronic food insecurity increases vulnerability to illness and parasitic infections. These reduce strength, energy, alertness and vigour. As a result work and schooling suffer. Absenteeism from work increases and performance suffers. There is also a vicious circle of poor nutrition leading to infections which in turn lower the ability to benefit from food. These effects lower workers'

TABLE 4.1 Undernourished population in developing countries

	number (m)		
	1969–71	1979–81	1983–5
Sub-Saharan Africa	63	78	105
Near East/North Africa	28	16	15
Asia	190	191	191
Latin America	35	35	37
Total	316	320	348
	% of population		
Sub-Saharan Africa	23.5	21.9	26.0
Near East/North Africa	15.7	6.7	5.6
Asia	19.5	15.6	14.3
Latin America	12.7	9.8	9.5
Total	18.6	14.7	14.6

Note: Figures are for 89 countries, some small countries are not included; estimated population with energy intake below what is needed for a normal life (diminished physical activity, slowdown of growth, vulnerability to infection, increased mortality risk).

Source: FAO, *Agriculture Toward 2000* (Rome: FAO, 1987).

productivity, dampen economic growth and handicap families' and nations' efforts to escape from poverty.

At its worst, transitory food insecurity causes deaths from hunger and hunger-associated illness and disease. Famines in Bengal, China, Ethiopia, the Sahel, and Kampuchea have cost many millions of lives in the last 50 years. The stability of governments has been threatened and riots have occurred when food insecurity has struck or threatened vulnerable groups in societies.

4.3   CAUSES OF FOOD INSECURITY

Food availability decline (FAD)

A fall in the quantity of food relative to the size of population is an obvious likely cause of hunger. Such food availability decline (FAD) has been the focus of attention in many studies of famines. Analysis of statistics on changes in food availability has been a common approach to the prediction of famine situations. Fear that population growth would outstrip food production either globally or within individual countries has motivated much research and many publications (Erlich and Erlich, 1972; Meadows *et al.* 1972). So far, such fears have proved groundless.

At the global level history shows that food supply has generally grown faster than demand. In real terms, the trend in world cereal prices has been downward from the 1960s to the 1980s. Table 4.2 shows these trends for the main cereals (wheat, rice and maize) from 1960 to 1984. An index of annual average prices in constant US dollars for cereals, taking the average price for 1979–81 = 100 shows 1976 as 115. 1986 as 55 and 1987 as 47. The indexes for 1988 and 1989 are higher, at 59, due mainly to drought in the United States (World Bank, 1989). But such fluctuations are common. There seem to be no fundamental reasons why the general trend in cereal prices in real terms should not continue downward into the foreseeable future. World Bank and FAO projections show production continuing to outstrip population to the end of the century (World Bank, 1989a; FAO, 1987).

TABLE 4.2   Trends in world prices of wheat, rice and maize, 1960–84, 1980 constant dollars

Grain	% per year
Wheat	-0.4
Rice	-1.0
Maize	-0.6

Source: World Bank (1986a) Figure 2.1, p. 15.

Biogenetic research, research on the timing and placement of fertilisers, investment in more efficient devices for water control, pest control, and better transport, marketing and support services for agriculture, together with policies which improve farmer incentives hold out excellent prospects for continued expansion of food production without the need for new land. Barring some environmental disaster world food supply should keep ahead of the demand produced by rising population and incomes (World Bank, 1986a, p. 15). As productivity is likely to continue to rise in distribution, information, transport, selling, stock control, etc. average world food prices seem likely to continue to decline in real terms.

On a regional basis also, the production of food has so far kept ahead of the growth of population save in SSA (see Table 4.3). Bangladesh and Nepal in South Asia, and most of the African Sahelian countries have very low supplies of food per head. These countries could be regarded as food deficit areas where, given problems of communication, weak institutions, and poor distribution systems both chronic and transitory food insecurity are likely to be common. But even in SSA agricultural production has improved greatly since 1985 (see Figure 4.1). Harvests in 1989 are reportedly at record levels (*International Agricultural Develop-*

TABLE 4.3 Average index of food production per head (1979–81 = 100)

	1984–6 (average)
Developing economies	110
Oil exporters	105
Exporters of manufactures	116
Highly indebted countries	101
Sub-Saharan Africa	97
Industrial market economies	103

Source: World Bank (1988d) Table 7.

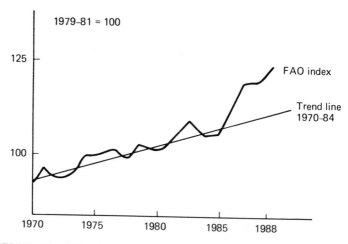

FIGURE 4.1   SSA agricultural production

ment, March–April 1989, p. 4). Some of this improvement can be attributed to better rainfall and other natural causes, but some can justly be claimed to be due to better incentives for farmers and more efforts by governments to boost agriculture as part of structural adjustment policies (World Bank, 1989a). Such increases in food availability, however, would not end food insecurity. Higher prices for farmers can hurt the urban poor, or any whose money incomes have not risen along with food prices.

Food availability is seldom the fundamental cause of hunger. Most of the world's hungry live in countries where there is ample food to provide an adequate basic diet for all if the food were more evenly distributed. The trouble is that the hungry are also the chronically poor and the politically weak. Such people suffer whether the distribution system is driven by market forces or administered by bureaucrats. That is the major conclusion of a seminal study of *Poverty and Famines* by Amartya Sen (1982). His diagnosis has been largely accepted by the World Bank, in its analysis of food insecurity (World Bank, 1986a and 1988a) and has influenced the attitudes and policies of most donor agencies.

Entitlement and deprivation

Sen's thesis is that food deprivation arises because the victims lack command over resources to produce enough food or to buy food.

The loss of real income, for example, provides a better explanation of why famines occur than does a decline in the availability of food. Typically, the victims are small-scale farmers or tenants whose crops have failed and who can find no other employment, or landless labourers who cannot find work when production falls, or who face high food prices when their incomes are stagnant, or falling, pastoralists who lose animals or cannot sell them at a reasonable price, and so on. In a market system entitlement to food depends mainly on the ability of families to pay for food or to grow it for themselves. Ability to pay in turn depends upon whether people can sell crops, other goods and services or their labour for cash. The ability to grow food depends on entitlement to land and other resources. A decline in food availability in a country may or may not be associated with famine, but it is seldom the fundamental cause of that famine. There can be starvation when food availability has declined little, or even risen, as in Bangladesh in 1974 (Sen, 1982, pp. 138–47). Indeed, Sen's studies of four severe famines: the Great Bengal Famine of 1943, Ethiopia in 1972–4, the Sahel in 1973, and Bangladesh in 1974 show that a decline in food availability was rarely the cause of famine.

But is Sen's approach as general as some writers have claimed? People may suffer undernutrition, and even death from hunger or related causes, for more reasons than lack of legal entitlement to foods, as Sen is well aware. He deliberately excludes some of these other possibilities from his analysis – for example, ignorance, religious or social convention may lead people to starve themselves or their children. He also excludes theft and, by implication, acts of war or civil strife which physically prevent the distribution of food. His main aim is to explain why, in a society where property rights are defined and legally protected, people can starve even when there is enough food available for the society to feed everyone. He is certainly right to attack the food availability decline approach at world or national level. But does the entitlement approach succeed better when simplified to the possession of the means to produce or purchase food for one's family?

Most recent famines have occurred in conditions of war or civil war: Ethiopia, Somalia, Sudan, Kampuchea, and several of the Sub-Saharan countries like Chad and Uganda. Even countries at peace such as Malawi and Zambia have been affected by wars in neighbouring countries through influxes of refugees and disturbance to transport. In Sen's analysis of the Bengal famine of 1943 he seems to have underplayed the effect of government procurement on the availability of grains outside of Calcutta and the damage to transport caused by the destruction of boats, the main transport system. The problems arose at least in part as a result of the policies of denying boats for use in a Japanese invasion which seemed imminent, and diverting food to essential war workers in Calcutta's factories. The real availability of grains did go down in many parts of Bengal (see Alamgir, 1980; Basu, 1986; Kula, 1988). Political factors certainly do play a role in starvation. Some groups in some societies are deliberately disadvantaged through discrimination. Even in socialist, centrally-planned economies such as China, as we now know, many millions of deaths can occur due to catastrophic famines. Sen, writing in 1981, did not have access to this information.

None of these comments detract from the importance of Sen's work. They do not touch upon the essential validity of his critique of the 'food availability decline' diagnosis of hunger. Nor do they invalidate the findings that in most countries chronic food insecurity is a problem of poverty, and that in most famines people starve because of lack of entitlement to food. Nor do these criticisms undermine the policy implications that raising the real incomes of the poor is the most powerful and systematic way to prevent both chronic and transitory food insecurity in many, perhaps most, countries and most institutions.

4.4 POLICIES TO COMBAT FOOD INSECURITY

What then are the most promising approaches to the alleviation of hunger?

1. Should nations aim at self-sufficiency or self-reliance, where 'self-sufficiency' means producing enough food to meet the nation's needs, while 'self-reliance' means being able to afford enough food?
2. Should fluctuations in domestic production be met by the accumulation and decumulation of domestically held stocks, or by exporting surpluses and importing to meet deficits?

3. Does the world community need to invest in public international stocks of basic foodstuffs, or is an increasingly
   integrated, well-informed world market and its privately held
   stocks (plus the public stocks of USA, Canada, Australia and
   the EC) adequate to meet all foreseeable emergencies?
4. Given the widely dispersed rural communities and poor
   transport links typical of much of Africa, do regions within
   countries have to be self-sufficient in production and hold
   their own emergency stocks, or would it be more efficient for
   them to maximise incomes, improve transport and rely on
   trade to meet both normal and emergency food needs?
5. Can countries which take the self-reliant route depend upon
   the international financial system including the IMF's Compensatory Financing Facility and its Food Financing Facility,
   to provide adequate credit for food emergencies?
6. Within each country can farmers and their workers who
   specialise in export crops rely upon credit to buy food when
   either their revenues drop or food prices shoot up unexpec-
   tedly?

These issues have been considered in many reports by officials
of the World Bank, the UN Food and Agriculture Organisation
(FAO) in conference papers and in academic writings. As the way
in which the questions have been posed hints, there is a broad
division between those who believe that the main solutions require
direct government participation in the production, stockpiling and
distribution of food, and those who believe that government
policies have been, and often still are, the main cause of the
problem. The latter group tend to favour the privatisation of
government farms and parastatal marketing organisations, and the
restoration of incentives to farmers to produce those crops which
are most profitable. They also argue that farmers and their
countries should specialise along the lines of (dynamic) comparative advantage – i.e., farmers and nations should do the things that
will earn them the highest (social) rate of return on the resources
at their disposal. This does not mean simply looking at current
costs, but involves looking to the future, allowing for risk and
uncertainty, making intelligent guesses about future trends in
demands and costs and keeping an eye on the competition. For
some countries, it will mean putting more resources into food

production, whether to replace imports or to develop exports. For others the most efficient use of resources may be to grow export crops, develop or expand mineral exports, shift resources into processing, or increase manufactured exports and by these means obtain more food indirectly through trade than they could by producing it directly for themselves.

The market approach

The role of government, as seen by this school, would be to make sure that its citizens and managers were faced with the right market signals or social accounting prices so that their decisions would be made on the basis of full information about the costs and benefits of the strategies they adopt. Generally this would mean that prices as set in international markets should be the guide to domestic prices. If a good or service can be obtained more cheaply from abroad, then very special reasons would be required to justify producing it at home (e.g. overriding defence priorities, distribution of income objectives or positive externalities, such as a pronounced complementarity with some other socially profitable domestic production). Governments would also have a role in seeing that the poor were protected from hunger by distributional or employment policies.

Until quite recently, most developing countries neglected agriculture with much less resources invested than in other sectors. Research, particularly in subsistence crops, was neglected. Marketing boards and other state organisations paid prices to farmers which were well below international prices. They did this on food crops in order to keep down food prices for urban workers and on major cash crops to raise government revenues. At the same time, manufactured goods prices were kept high by severe restrictions on imports because of the desire to protect domestic industries and to ration the use of scarce foreign exchange. Over-valued exchange rates further lowered the incentives to export and distorted the prices of imported inputs (Bates, 1981, part I; World Bank, 1986a, Ch.4). The effects of such domestic distortions were to lower national output and slow growth with no apparent improvement in income distribution (World Bank, 1986a, Chs.4, 5 and 8).

Just how damaging government policies can be to a major export is illustrated by the case of the Ghana Cocoa Marketing Board. The Ghanaian government's share of cocoa sales revenues rose from 3 per cent in 1947–8 to 60 per cent in 1978–9. In addition, the Marketing Board took as much as 20 per cent to cover operating costs. As a result the cocoa farmers' prices by 1979 averaged about half their 1963 level, even after allowing for subsidies on seeds and other inputs. Farm prices also remained highly unstable. Cocoa production fell from 540,000 tons in 1965 to 250,000 tons in 1979. The volume of exports fell by 80 per cent and an estimated 45,000 tons of cocoa a year were smuggled to neighbouring territories where prices were higher. From being the dominant exporter in the world Ghana dropped below both Brazil and the Ivory Coast. The foreign exchange loss to Ghana was about 15 per cent of average export earnings (World Bank, 1983, p. 77).

In terms of direct production of food Ghana's failures are equally dramatic. Taking 1974–6 as 100, food production *per capita* in Ghana in 1982–3 was 73 while Ivory Coast and Sri Lanka, two countries which have moved towards policies of efficient pricing and management, have achieved 108 and 127 respectively (World Bank, 1986a, Table 6).

Such observation, combined with the *a priori* reasoning of neoclassical economics, leads many economists to the view that long-term food security and long-term economic development can be achieved by the same policies. Countries which get their macroeconomic policies right – e.g., equilibrium exchange rates, no excessive government borrowing, non-inflationary monetary policies – on the one hand, and adopt pricing systems which reflect marginal social opportunity costs, on the other, should on average become self-reliant. They would argue that on the whole such policies would not have adverse distributional effects because most of the poor live in rural areas and have been discriminated against by past economic policies. International prices would give them better prices for their crops and would stimulate more labour-intensive production. Better prices and more jobs would raise rural incomes. Higher prices would, of course, hurt the urban poor, but they would have more job opportunities and if necessary they could be assisted by job creation, income transfers or their food consumption could be subsidised through food stamp programmes, ration shops or subsidising the prices of their staple foods.

Criticisms of the market strategy approach to food security

Critics of the approach outlined above would stress its risks to both nations and individuals. For nations, food insecurity can stem from fluctuations in domestic production of food, in world prices for food and from prices for exports. A policy of self-reliance may expose the nation to greater risks than one of self-sufficiency. Self-reliance requires that the country should always be able to obtain adequate supplies of food through trade. But if its need to import more food coincides with a year when world supplies to the international market have declined or demands from other nations have surged such as 1973–4, the food deficit nation can be exposed to very high import prices or it may have to accept political, economic or commercial strings to get food. In the worst possible case, its own export earnings could have declined in the same year. If it cannot pay for adequate food imports from current earnings and use of reserves it would have to borrow commercially, use IMF or other official concessionary borrowing facilities or seek food aid. Resort to such external sources could prove costly in terms of treasure or political independence, high interest costs or political strings attached to aid. These considerations may lead many developing countries to consider self-sufficiency the preferable policy.

It is also a worry of some governments and observers that the policy of devaluing exchange rates, reducing levels of protection and reducing taxes on exports may cause serious problems for countries which rely mainly on a few primary commodity exports. If many LDCs simultaneously adopt such policies the volume of their raw material exports could rise fairly quickly. But these products generally face demands which are both slow growing and price inelastic. Their world prices would then drop sharply and their export earnings would fall. As a result of the adverse shift in their terms of trade they could suffer 'immiserising growth' (Bhagwati, 1958). Given the high overhead costs of tree crops and mining this situation would not be remedied quickly by automatic responses of supply to the falling prices. These same conditions, plus the random shocks to supply and demand characteristic of such products, also make their prices and earnings relatively unstable. The result of uncoordinated actions of producers responding to increased farmgate and minehead prices could increase both long- and short-term uncertainty and place their national food security in jeopardy.

Such considerations lead many governments of LDCs to aim to be nationally self-sufficient in food through increased domestic production and stocks held nationally, or by regional or UN organisations in which they have a substantial, if not controlling, voice.

Rather similar arguments can apply to small farmers. Even if, on the average, the incomes earned from more specialised production of cash crops promised to be higher than from growing their own food, many farmers – and particularly the poorer ones – might find the risks too great. They are the ones who find it the hardest to obtain credit when their crop is poor or food prices exceed their current income. They cannot afford to place themselves in this double jeopardy.

Practical policies

In food security, as in all other areas of development economics it is essential to recognise the diversity of developing countries and of the families that live there. Each is faced by different opportunities and constraints. Such considerations argue the need for a very pragmatic approach to their problems.

Raising the rate of economic growth and reducing income inequality can reduce, and probably eliminate, chronic food insecurity. But in the present world climate where world growth has slowed and debt problems seem endemic, growth cannot go fast enough for many LDCs to alleviate chronic food insecurity for some groups in the near future. Other policies to speed the attainment of food security are necessary. What are the most cost-effective ways of doing this?

Experts from the World Bank suggest that possible types of intervention are: (1) to increase food supplies, (2) to subsidise consumer prices, (3) to create jobs for the poor, or transfer income to them.

Changing food supplies can be achieved by increasing production of non-traded foods, by increasing imports or by reducing exports. But food security will be improved only by increasing supply if it increases the real incomes of the groups who go hungry. This requires either that the policy lowers the prices of food for which they are net consumers, or raises their income from producing food either as farmers or as rural labourers. Increasing production of traded food may do nothing to lower food prices; it may simply replace imports or increase exports. It will thus necessarily improve food security only if it provides income and employment for the poor. Policies which lower food prices will help the urban poor, but may harm the rural poor if they are net sellers of these foods; they may reduce effort, or switch to alternative crops.

Policies of national self-sufficiency need not reduce food insecurity; it depends on their effects on the real income of the poor. National self-sufficiency policies may not even increase food availability if the increased production of food merely replaces imports.

Subsidising food prices without lowering producer prices can help alleviate chronic food insecurity. But such policies have to be very carefully designed if they are to avoid an excessive drain upon the budget. If they simply lower food prices, all consumers – rich, as well as poor – benefit. The costs of the subsidies can become exorbitant, but a large body of opposition to reducing the subsidies is created. The alternative is to target the subsidised food on defined groups who are poor. But there are problems with such schemes. These include the difficulty of controlling access to the targeted group, the costs of administration, the incentives to fraud and corruption, the risk that food sold at low prices and intended for human consumption may be used to feed livestock or make alcohol. Food subsidy schemes work best if foods can be identified on which the poor are dependent; if the scheme can be confined to a geographically restricted area; and if the food is of a processed type such as flour, bread or tortillas, and where a few centrally located firms do the processing.

Transferring income to the poor by giving them cash, food or ration cards can be cost-effective means of improving food security. Usually such schemes aid only the urban poor through such methods as rationing food to a target group. Food can be sold at low prices through special shops or given free at health centres. This is more difficult with scattered rural populations, but subsidising farm inputs which are bought infrequently can effect income transfers to poor farmers. As with subsidised food prices, it is difficult to avoid leakages to non-targeted groups. There is usually a tradeoff between reducing leakage and administrative costs.

Public employment programmes such as the rural public works schemes used in Pakistan and India can raise rural incomes by providing jobs when the seasonal demand for agricultural labour is low; they can construct feeder roads, irrigation ditches, flood protection, schools and village dispensaries. Potentially such schemes can be excellent; the main difficulty is the choice of projects and administration. Often funds are misappropriated, projects of interest to the local landlords, rather than to the poor, are constructed and the quality of the work is often very poor so that roads are washed away in the next flood. Sometimes schemes to provide employment prove extremely costly in relation to the benefits; one, in Malaysian small-scale dairy farming, was costing over $3 for every $1 actually reaching the participating farmers.

Clearly the choice of approach depends on the characteristics of the groups who suffer food insecurity and on the administrative capacity of the country. Most countries will have a variety of target groups and therefore need a combination of measures. In SSA, most of the afflicted are farmers who produce and sell food, but there are also some urban poor and some landless workers. An appropriate approach is likely to be to raise producer prices, especially as they are usually below international prices, and complement this with food subsidy or ration programmes for the rural poor and job creation for the landless. But if, as in most of Latin America, the food insecure live mainly in the cities and shanty towns, policy should aim mainly at lowering food prices, preferably through schemes targeted on the urban poor. If the numbers are large and the administrative costs of operating tightly controlled schemes are excessive, a feasible approach could be to lower import prices of those foods which tend to be consumed mainly by the poor.

Dealing with food emergencies

Crises arise which lead to famine situations as a result of sudden changes which reduce food supplies, raise food prices beyond the capacity of the poor to pay, or reduce the incomes of the poor. In most of the recent famines war and civil war have also played a role in damaging production and disrupting transport and communications.

National buffer stocks are a frequently recommended policy for stabilising supplies and prices. But in developing countries they are a high cost method. Storage facilities have to be built to a capacity which can hold the maximum required stock; but as buffer stocks rise and fall most of that capacity is unused most of the time. In tropical countries, storage losses are high from pests, fungus attacks and deterioration of quality; the opportunity costs of capital tied up in stocks are also high. Most countries would find it much cheaper to use exports and imports to balance food surpluses and deficits, relying on commercial credit or loans from the IMF's Compensatory Financing Facility to pay for excess requirements of food imports. Even if they have to pay higher than normal prices for cereals when they need imports, over the long run this will normally prove cheaper than carrying domestic stocks. Commercial, government and international stocks of grains and other foods are more plentiful and more widely dispersed than in the past. It is extremely unlikely that a developing country which has accessible ports and its own, or borrowed, foreign exchange could not now obtain supplies of food without paying an exorbitant cash or political price. The events of 1980–1 proved the reliability of the trading system in the face of a fall in world supplies of food.

Even for landlocked countries domestic buffer stocks should be a last resort. Measures to stabilise domestic production through irrigation and plant protection, together with improvements in information and distribution systems are generally more cost-effective. Regional cooperation in trade in food can help. Improvements in early warning systems which can enable swift identification of the early development of a crisis, and the nature of its causes and likely effects, are crucial. They should enable early placing of orders for shipments and arrangements for emergency transport systems when these are necessary. If such warning systems cannot be relied upon, then emergency stocks at convenient locations at district level within countries may have to be held.

But even if supplies of food on average are adequate and prices stabilised, groups such as landless labourers, whose employment or wages are depressed by drought conditions, or farmers whose crops have failed or prices fallen, or the urban poor whose jobs have disappeared, need special help. They need income support with payments in cash or kind and, if effective work programmes can be mounted, temporary public employment.

4.5 CONCLUSIONS

At the global level the world has succeeded in maintaining a faster growth of food production than population. The trend prices of the main internationally traded grains have been falling for years. The progress of technology, particularly the new developments in genetic engineering and plant breeding, seem likely to raise the capacity of the world's agricultural land to continue to grow food fast enough to avoid world hunger. The progress in adopting economic policies in developing countries which stimulate farmers to produce more means that capacity is likely to be realised much more fully than in the past. Despite these gains, the absolute number of people suffering malnutrition and undernutrition continues to rise; transitory food insecurity, famine, continues to haunt many in Africa and Asia.

More often, enough food is available within the stricken countries to meet both chronic and transitory problems; or is physically available either commercially or through aid from the rest of the world. The key problems of avoiding hunger within countries tend to be social and economic. People starve because they lack the means to grow food for themselves, or to buy it. Overcoming poverty will automatically alleviate chronic food insecurity, but not fast enough. Special measures to assist disadvantaged groups will usually be necessary for a long time to come, in some cases indefinitely. The best approach in most situations in most developing countries is to target income support or subsidised food on the groups most in need. Sometimes this can be done through clinics aimed at mothers and small children. But more ambitious targeting on larger groups of urban or rural poor can be very expensive in terms of administrative costs. There are times when general subsidies to foods most used by the poor may be the only practicable way of giving help. But then the budgetary costs must be watched carefully.

Appendix: Measuring Food Insecurity

Estimates were based on two energy standards corresponding to 90 per cent or 80 per cent of FAO/WHO requirements calculated for individual countries. These are based on the intake of calories required to meet energy outputs and childhood growth. For particular populations requirements were established for a reference man or woman who was assumed to be moderately active and whose weight and age were representative of groups whose energy use and food consumption had been studied. Then demographic data for each country were used to calculate its diet requirements.

This information was combined with information on income distribution so as to estimate the share of the population who were likely to be inadequately nourished because of insufficient income to buy enough food energy. Income distribution data were available for 35 countries (with about 70 per cent of LDC populations). For these, an energy consumption function was estimated by allocating the total energy in the nation's food consumption among the different income groups (for a more detailed description of the methods, see S. Reutlinger and M. Selowsky, 'Malnutrition and Poverty: Magnitude and Policy Options'. *World Bank Staff Occasional Paper*, 23, or World Bank, 1986c).

5 The Principles of Targeting[1]

TIMOTHY BESLEY
and RAVI KANBUR

5.1 INTRODUCTION

The question of how to design policies to effectively alleviate
poverty is one of great practical significance. In nineteenth century
England, J. S. Mill succinctly characterised the problem as one of
giving the greatest amount of needful help with the smallest
amount of undue reliance upon it. This characterisation fits well
with the dilemma faced by modern day policy-makers. It is
important to use available resources efficiently: this means direct-
ing them as much as possible towards those who need them most.
This is the basic idea which motivates discussion about targeting.

Hence, it is often argued that the 'best' solution to the problem
of poverty alleviation is one which identifies who is poor and then
directs benefits towards that group. The debate on targeting is an
old one, and moreover it has been as much a topic of controversy
in developed as in developing countries.[2] Many commentators
have emphasised the costliness of identifying the poor and the
effects on incentives which may attend income tested programmes.[3] The counterpoint is to recommend universalistic programmes which provide benefits which are paid independently of
income. However, it is in the wake of macroeconomic and
structural adjustment that targeting seems to have attained a
special significance in developing countries, as more and more
governments have come under pressure to reduce expenditure.
Indeed, targeting has become a panacea in the area of poverty

alleviation, whence it is suggested that policy-makers can have their cake and eat it too – improved targeting means that more poverty alleviation can be achieved with less expenditure! Alas, the real world is not quite so straightforward. There are good reasons why this best of all possible worlds is not available to policy-makers in developing countries, and hard decisions will have to be made that weigh up the costs and the benefits of targeting.

The object of this essay is to provide a framework for considering the principles of targeting to alleviate poverty. Since the focus is on the *principles*, much of the discussion will be at a general and abstract level. However, these principles are intended to be applicable in particular Less Developed Countries (LDCs) whereupon the flesh of institutional knowledge must be added. Section 5.2 begins by stating the basic problem in a very simple framework, and here we present the ideal solution: a case of 'perfect targeting'. Sections 5.3–5.5 take up three central problems with this solution – administrative costs, high marginal tax rates and political economy considerations. Each of these militates against fine targeting and suggests the advantages of more universalistic schemes. In Section 5.7, we consider self-targeting schemes; section 5.8 concludes the discussion.

5.2 THE BASIC PROBLEM AND THE IDEAL SOLUTION

Any discussion on targeting for poverty alleviation presupposes agreement on what is meant by 'poverty' – i.e., agreement on (1) a measure of the 'standard of living', (2) a 'poverty line' which distinguishes the poor from the non-poor, and (3) a 'poverty index' which aggregates together information on the standard of living of the poor. Each of these is an important and controversial topic and would demand a separate study on its own.[4] For our purposes, we shall assume that these problems have been 'solved', in order to focus attention directly on targeting.

Let us suppose, initially, that we have a household income distribution which measures 'income' correctly, and adjusts for households facing different prices, household size and composition.

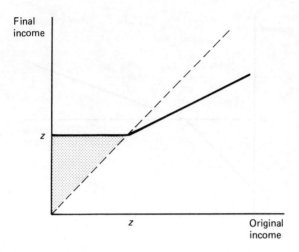

FIGURE 5.1

Suppose, furthermore, that the poverty line is given by z, so that all those with incomes less than z are in poverty. The object of policy is to reduce poverty to zero. The 'ideal solution' would be one where income can be observed accurately and costlessly, and where no incentive effects prevent the state from plugging the gap between the poverty line and income. The ideal solution is depicted in Figure 5.1, which plots final income (i.e., post-transfer) against original income. Along the dotted 45° line there is no difference between original and final income.[5] A point above this line indicates a subsidy or transfer, while a point below indicates a withdrawal or tax. The ideal solution is given by the solid line. For anybody with original income y less than z, the government transfers exactly the amount $z-y$ so as to bring final income up to z. This completely eliminates poverty. The financial cost of this strategy is given by the sum of these transfers $z-y$. If the distribution of income was uniform then this cost would simply be depicted by the triangular areas between the horizontal solid line and the 45° line.

The structure of the scheme for those with income above z depends on the nature of the budget constraint. If the transfer–poverty alleviation scheme is to be self-financing, then those with incomes above z have to be taxed. This is shown in Figure 5.1 by

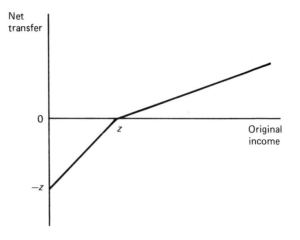

FIGURE 5.2

the solid line beyond z lying below the 45° line. The larger the tax revenue to be raised, the shallower this line will have to be in order to balance the budget. Figure 5.2 makes explicit the transfers to and from the government as a function of original income. Below z, the transfers are from the government and are therefore shown as negative, whilst above z they are to the government. The slope of the solid line in Figure 5.2 is the *marginal* tax rate. Figure 5.2 shows that the 'ideal solution' imposes a higher marginal tax rate on the poor than on the non-poor. We return to this point in section 5.4 below, where the disincentive effects of high marginal tax rates are discussed.

If the government is perfectly informed, the ideal solution is clearly the least cost method of alleviating poverty. If external resources were at stake, or if internal resources had to be raised to finance the poverty alleviation program, the ideal solution would be preferred. But is it feasible? It relies on being able to transfer exactly the right amount to each indivdual below the poverty line without affecting their incentives to earn. The administrative costs of this in a developing country context are taken up in section 5.3. Here we will present the opposite extreme to the ideal solution, by way of contrast. This is a completely universalistic scheme which gives *everybody* a transfer of z (i.e. regardless of income). This is depicted in Figures 5.3 and 5.4. This scheme also eliminates poverty, but at a far greater budgetary cost. It is easy to see why this is so. Now everybody, even someone with original income exceeding z, receives the transfer of z from the government (as shown in Figure 5.4). The budgetary cost of this is simply z times the population size. If this is to be recouped through taxation, then the marginal tax rates on the non-poor will need to be higher than in the ideal solution, although the marginal tax rates on the poor are now lower. Figures 5.5 and 5.6 depict such a scheme, which is discussed further in section 5.4 below.

These two extremes (ideal means testing and universalistic benefits) serve to anchor our discussion of the principles of targeting. As will become clear by the end of this essay, neither extreme is particularly appealing. The benefits of the ideal solution are clear. Sections 5.3–5.6 will discuss some of its costs.

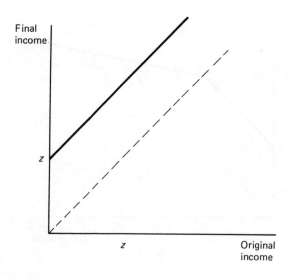

FIGURE 5.3

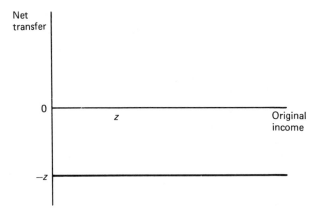

FIGURE 5.4

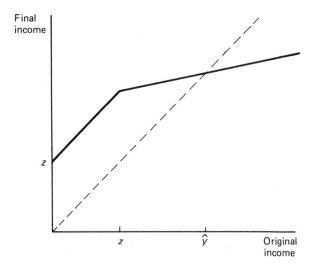

FIGURE 5.5

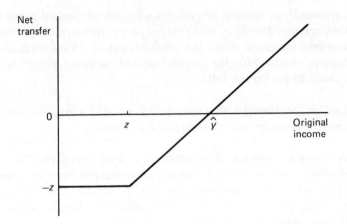

FIGURE 5.6

5.3 ADMINISTRATIVE COSTS

Although section 5.2 developed its argument using the language of income transfers, it is also relevant to other institutional settings – e.g., the analysis of various food subsidy programmes. Prior to the reforms of 1977, ration shops in Sri Lanka provided rice rations to all Sri Lankans below market prices. As Besley and Kanbur (1988) have shown, this is equivalent to an income transfer equal to the ration times the effective subsidy if any unwanted rice can be resold. Hence it is like a universalistic programme. After 1977, this system was gradually replaced by a food stamp programme which restricted benefits to those households whose incomes were below a critical value (the details are given in Anand and Kanbur, 1987). This involves a move towards the ideal solution in section 5.2.

However, a World Bank study (1986a) points out some difficulties with this attempt to effect the 'ideal solution':

One problem is inflexibility in the way of a program determines who is eligible, as exemplified by Sri Lanka's food stamp program. The target was identified by household size and earnings, but, because households were never checked to see if they remained eligible, many stayed on the rolls even after their earnings increased above the eligibility cutoff. Households that became eligible after the program started, however, never had a chance to get on the rolls.

Lest it be thought that this is an isolated case, the same document provides other examples, e.g. Brazil:

A coupon program that distributed food every two weeks through government-run supermarkets used income to determine who could participate in Recife, Brazil. The program revealed several problems . . . It is difficult to target income if income reporting is arbitrary . . . A coupon program requires extensive book keeping and administrative cost . . . Building on lessons from the evaluators, the Brazilian program was modified, with apparent success, to reach very low income neighborhoods without coupons or downpayments. Common basic foods are now subsidized for all customers of many small neighborhood stores in selected poverty areas. Any leakage of benefits to people not in need is much less expensive than administering the cumbersome coupon program.

One of the main lessons of the above is the difficulty of assessing and verifying low incomes. This is not even easy in developed countries, with their systems of regular employment and with a literate population accustomed to filling in tax returns (see, for example, Kay and King, 1978). In developing countries, where much employment (especially that of the poor) is irregular, where there is production of agricultural output for home consumption and where the definition of a 'household' is problematic, one would suspect *a priori* that the administrative costs involved in the ideal solution would be high. The frequency of testing is also necessary, as the Sri Lankan case illustrates, to ensure that those genuinely in need are in the scheme and to weed out those who are not. The administrative capacity to do this simply does not exist in many (perhaps most) developing countries. Macedo (1987) identifies cases in Brazil where the authorities relied on local committees to identify the needy, and he points to the difficulties to which this gave rise.

The quantification of administrative costs by programme will not be an easy task, particularly if costs are shared by several programmes. However, some allocation formulae might be feasible. The revenue required R, of a programme can be divided into three categories:

$$R = A + NP + P$$

where A are administrative costs, NP are transfers (leakages) to the non-poor or more generally to those not in the target group while P is the effective transfer to the poor.

A measure of the fineness of targeting is then given by

$$F = \frac{P}{P + NP}$$

i.e., the fraction of the total non-administrative outlay that reaches the target group.

The administrative costs as a proportion of the revenues are:

$$C = \frac{A}{A + P + NP}$$

It is hypothesised that C rises with F and at an increasing rate. This is illustrated in Figure 5.7. Figure 5.7 also assumes that there is a minimum level of administration costs needed to get any programme going, and that a basic minimum level of targeting can always be achieved. For example, if the total non-administrative budget is divided equally among the population, with no attempt at targeting, the fraction of the outlay that goes to the pre-transfer poor is given by the fraction of poor people in the population – i.e., the incidence of poverty. This much targeting is always possible, even with the opposite extreme of the ideal solution. It is the shape of the curve between F and 1 upon which we require more information, yet it is the one about which we are most ignorant at present.[6]

Quantifying administrative costs of poverty alleviation programmes is clearly an important issue for future research since the efficacy of means tested programmes depend upon it in an important way.

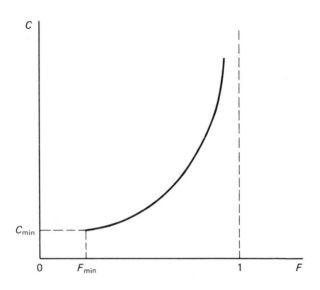

FIGURE 5.7

5.4   INDIVIDUAL RESPONSES AND INCENTIVE EFFECTS

The incentive effects of the 'ideal solution' must also be weighed up in assessing its applicability; Besley (1988) examines one aspect of this – that certain individuals might not participate in finely targeted programmes because of the costs involved in subjecting themselves to very detailed assessment, filling out of forms, attending interviews, etc. Alternatively they might just be the psychic costs of the social stigma that attaches to participation in programmes specifically meant for the poor.[7]

Besley (1988) hypothesises that if an individual's costs of participating in a finely targeted poverty alleviation programme are c, then those with income greater than $z-c$ will not take part in them. This means that those with incomes between z and $z-c$ will remain below the poverty line. The alternative is to have a universal scheme which gives everybody an amount m, such that the total budgetary outlay is equal to that of the targeted programme. These two alternatives are illustrated in Figure 5.8. As can be

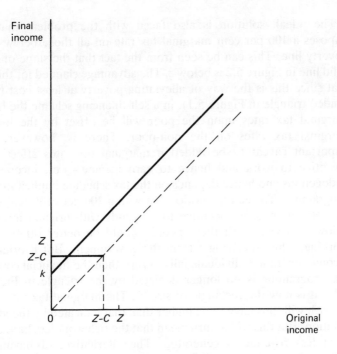

FIGURE 5.8

seen, the finely targeted programme tends to exclude those just below the poverty line, while the universalistic programme with the same budget does not do as much for the poorest of the poor. Besley (1988) provides some quantification of these tradeoffs for assumed income distributions. His numerical simulations indicate that the introduction of take-up costs does not turn the tables against income testing.

Incentive problems are in significant measure related to problems of imperfect information. If the government found individuals transparent (i.e., knew their tastes and abilities) then taxes and benefits could be made to depend directly upon immutable characteristics. In fact, only income is observable (and perhaps not even that) and by altering their behaviour to alter their income agents can alter the amount of tax–benefit which they pay–receive. This is the root of the incentive problem.[8]

The 'ideal' solution is also faced with the problem that it imposes a 100 per cent marginal tax rate on all those below the poverty line. This can be seen from the fact that the slope of the solid line in Figure 5.2 is below z. The advantage claimed for this is that since this is the way of alleviating poverty at least cost (the shaded triangle in Figure 5.1), in a self-financing scheme the high marginal tax rates upon the poor will be offset by the lower marginal tax rates on the non-poor. There is, however, an important caveat to be added if marginal tax rates affect the incentive to work and hence to earn income – i.e., income is endogenous and hence depends on the tax schedule implicit in the programme. To see this, notice that with a 100 per cent marginal tax rate there is no incentive for anybody with original income below z to work. All these people would be better off by not working, while receiving z from the government. But if original income for these individuals falls to zero then the financial cost of the programme is no longer depicted by the triangle in Figure 5.1 – it is now the rectangle of size z[9]. The marginal tax rates on the rich will thus have to be higher than that indicated by the ideal solution. But this will in turn mean that the rich work less hard and even less revenue is generated. The alternative, of having a universalistic scheme, will have medium level marginal tax rates on everybody. The choice is between having a distribution of high marginal tax rate skewed in the direction of the poor, and a more even spread of marginal tax rates.

Clearly, the final decision rests with the specifics of the case.[10] Kanbur and Keen (1987) provide a general theoretical analysis of the issues. However, what is needed is detailed country-specific analyses for developing countries. In the past such analysis may have been thought to be problematic given the lack of adequate micro-data. But recent advances in micro-level data collection makes this excuse less plausible. Policy analyses and research programmes utilizing this data, and addressing the issue of targeted versus universalistic schemes, are now pressing.

5.5 THE POLITICAL ECONOMY OF TARGETING

A purely 'technocratic' approach to the problem of poverty alleviation asks only how the informational, administrative and other costs can be taken into account. Whilst useful, it neglects the issues of distributional and political conflict which lie at the heart of the problem. It is interesting to consider the political support that various types of poverty alleviation programmes might enjoy. The 'ideal solution' of Figure 5.1 will rationally be supported only by those with incomes below the poverty line. But this group is unlikely to have sufficient political power to predominate against those above the poverty line who have to pay. The universalistic scheme of Figure 5.5 has the advantage that it brings into the net of beneficiaries some people with incomes above the poverty line. It pits the 'middle classes' between z and y in Figure 5.5 against those with the highest incomes. This contrasts with the 'ideal solution'.

Tullock (1982) espouses the view that universalistic schemes are a way of minimising net transfers to the poor:

When we consider the political forces which may lead to the expansion [universalisation] of a programme it is, in general, clear that if people who are interested in expanding the programme are trying merely to help the poor, they have chosen an inept way of doing it. Only if they feel that they can trick members of the middle and upper class into voting for a programme to help the poor by that indirect method which is more generous than they are willing to give in a direct and open way, is it sensible.

Tullock's views are however controversial (see Downs, 1982). Nevertheless the considerations that he raises are relevant to the recent debate in developing countries on moving away from universalistic schemes (such as general food subsidies) towards targeted schemes such as food stamps based on income criteria. If a constant budget is maintained this entails a net loss to the middle and upper income classes.[11] The tolerance of the political system then becomes an issue. Bienen and Gersovitz (1985) have analysed recent attempts to remove food subsidies (in the context of a larger stabilisation and adjustment programme). Their work demonstrates the importance of particular countries' circumstances – i.e., the existing configurations of power and the possibilities for power realignment:

IMF programes may also incorporate cutbacks in subsidies for goods, especially those disproportionately purchased by the urban poor, such as food. Many of these so-called basic needs programs, it should be noted, benefit urban middle classes. Mexico's middle classes, for example, frequently shop in subsidized retail outlets . . . But elites are reluctant to make precipitous policy changes that threaten their support . . . Exceptions include regimes in Sri Lanka (1977), Turkey (1984) and Zimbabwe (1984) that did successfully cut consumer food subsidies.

However, if a universal programme is in fact removed and targeted programme is substituted, this means that the poor are isolated in terms of political alliances. The history of Sri Lanka since 1977 in relation to food subsidies (see Anand and Kanbur, 1987) is particularly instructive. After the introduction of targeting with food stamps, the real value of food stamps was allowed to fall during an ensuing period of inflation, with severe consequences of poverty and undernutrition. With the new institutional arrangements, the interests of the middle classes lay elsewhere (the maintenance of public sector wages, for example) and the poor were to some extent abandoned to their own political devices. With generalised subsidies the middle classes would have been linked to the poor in a significant way.

In his fascinating account of the targeting of social programmes in Brazil, Macedo (1987) has also highlighted political aspects of poverty alleviation strategies. He concludes that 'if policy changes were introduced at the highest levels of decision-making in Brazil, then many changes would follow at the level of programmes, both in their design and management'.

The political equilibrium is a significant determinant of what types of poverty alleviation programmes may be sustained. Proper consideration of it might lead one away from programmes which give benefits only to those with income below z towards those which are more universal and a source of political cohesion.

5.6 TARGETING USING INDICATORS

In view of the informational and administrative difficulties encountered in implementing the ideal solution, it may be worthwhile enacting poverty alleviation programmes through targeting key indicators (e.g., a household's region or the age distribution of its members). In LDCs where income is very difficult to measure this solution may be particularly pertinent. However, such targeting may be more widely relevant (see Deaton and Stern, 1986 and Akerlof, 1978). World Bank (1986a) discusses the use of geographical area for targeting. Under such a scheme, all individuals *within* an area are treated identically – as with the universalistic scheme depicted in Figures 5.3 and 5.4 – but only certain areas are chosen to receive benefit. These are the low income neighbourhoods which are easier to identify than individual incomes. The aim, in general is to find an indicator which is less costly to identify but is sufficiently correlated with income to be useful for poverty alleviation. Whilst there is bound to be some leakage, no indicator being perfectly correlated with income, it is hoped that any leakage of benefits to those who are not in poverty will be much less expensive than administering the cumbersome ideal solution.

Continuing the regional metaphor, household income and expenditure surveys[12] can be used to evaluate the poverty characteristics of individual regions as finely as sample size will allow. How can this information be used to develop a priority ranking of regions? This problem has been analysed in Kanbur (1986). The answer depends upon the precise objectives of the government, and how the expenditure devoted to each group translates itself into individual incomes.[13] If the government's objective is to have as big an impact as possible on the national poverty gap[14] then the relevant regional ranking is one by incidence of poverty in each region (*not* by the regional poverty gap). An intuitive account of this result follows from considering the 'poverty alleviation efficiency' of a uniform transfer to a region. If every income in a region is increased by $1, the cost is $1 times the total number of people, while the increase in poor incomes is $1 times the number of *poor* people in that region. The poverty alleviation efficiency is simply the ratio of the latter to the former, which is just the incidence of poverty in that region.

This argument from Kanbur (1986) can apply to any method of classifying the population (i.e., it need not be regional). Household size and composition could be used to condition payments if this was felt to be easy to monitor. For example, the number of children might be chosen as an indicator. In fact, combinations of region, of residence and household characteristics could be used, as was done in Colombia:

> In Colombia areas of poverty were identified as part of the national development plan. Targets of food subsidies were then narrowed to households with children under five years old or a pregnant or lactating woman. This reduced the number of possible beneficiaries and thus lowered administrative and fiscal costs. Little leakage or fraudulent coupon use was apparent (World Bank, 1986a).

If the number of indicators is pushed to the limit, we would be back to a case where every unit was being identified separately. The beauty of using just a few indicators is that administrative costs are kept low while leakage is less than it would be under a universalistic scheme, so that more poverty alleviation can be achieved with the same resources. This suggests a focus for future research on LDCs in which there is quantification of the impact of targeting according to different characteristics. In fact there are three important decision variables on which data should speak:

1. Given a set of partitions of characteristics (e.g., regional boundaries) what levels of benefit are appropriate?
2. Where should the divisions be made between different groups (i.e., where should boundaries be drawn, if targeting is, for example, according to age)?
3. How many partitions should there be (e.g., how many age bands or regional areas)?

These questions provide exciting possibilities for both theoretical and empirical work.[15] As more and more categories are introduced, then the targeting achieved by indicators becomes finer and poverty is reduced. On the other hand, more categories raises administrative costs (a further justification for the position depicted in Figure 5.7). The optimal policy equates the marginal reduction in poverty, from a further indicator being used, with its marginal administrative cost. This is illustrated in Figure 5.9, where 0 to n denotes the number of indicators, $C(n)$ is the marginal cost of more indicators and $P(n)$ is the marginal gain on

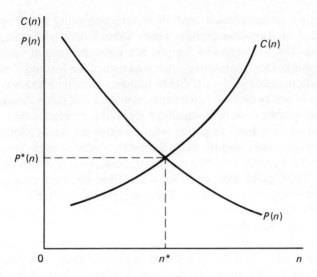

FIGURE 5.9

poverty as a function of the number of indicators. The optimal number of indicators is n^*.

Interesting empirical work has already begun in this area. Ravallion and Chao (1987) illustrate how the benefits of region-based targeting can be quantified. They first of all calculate, for a given budget, the poverty level that could be achieved with optimal use of regional poverty information, following the analysis of Kanbur (1986, 1987b). The gain from targeting is then defined as the amount by which an untargeted budget would have to be larger in order to achieve the poverty level attained through targeting. They call this the 'equivalent gain from targeting'. They present evidence for Bangladesh, the Philippines and Sri Lanka. For the first two countries they distinguish between the urban and rural sectors, for the last they consider urban, rural and estate sectors. Their illustrative exercises show that the gains from indicator-based targeting vary greatly from country to country, ranging from almost 40 per cent in the Philippines to around 2 per cent in Bangladesh. Another interesting conclusion is that the smaller the budget is, the greater are the percentage gains from targeting.

A much more detailed analysis of targeting using indicators is provided in Ravallion (1987), which focuses on land-contingent transfers (i.e., transfers of income are given contingent on land ownership). This is attractive since land ownership is often observable where income is not. Such transfers are almost always a feature of policy decisions, particularly in Asia and Latin America. For the specific case of Bangladesh Ravallion concludes that 'the equivalent gain from targeting with unrestricted land-contingent tax powers is only slightly more than 10 per cent of mean income for rural Bangladesh or 20 per cent of mean poverty deficit of the poor'. These gains have to be set against the administrative costs of land contingent policies. This suggests a further case for studying the administrative costs of poverty alleviation programmes, as outlined above.

Another type of targeting via indicators occurs when certain foods are subsidised because it is thought that they are primarily consumed by the poor. Besley and Kanbur (1988) distinguish between two types of food subsidy programme: (1) where a fixed quantity of food is provided at below market prices and (2) where the market price is subsidised for every unit that is purchased. If resale of rations cannot be prevented, then the first type of programme is equivalent to an income transfer to all those eligible for it. The size of the transfer is equal to the ration quantity times the unit subsidy. The central question then becomes the criterion according to which ration shops are located in particular areas, or according to which ration cards are issued within an area. The second type of food subsidy programme is one which benefits consumers in proportion to their consumption of the commodity in question. Thus, in absolute terms, the rich gain more than the poor if the commodity is not an inferior good. Besley and Kanbur (1988) show that if the objective is to minimise the aggregate poverty gap at the national level, the appropriate indicator to use is the ratio:

$$\frac{\text{Quantity consumed by poor}}{\text{Total quantity consumed}}$$

Commodities should be ranked according to this ratio and those highest on the list should be prime candidates for protection during the period of retrenchment on the food subsidy.[16]

Notice that the above ratio can be calculated using household income and expenditure surveys. Indeed, this is done in Kanbur (1988) to argue that rice in Côte d'Ivoire is not a prime candidate for subsidy. The importance of this ratio has indeed been grasped in the policy literature. World Bank (1986a) notes:

> The main determinant of food's suitability for subsidy is the share of it that goes to the target population. If a food is consumed exclusively by the target group, the subsidy will be very efficient; a dollar's worth of subsidy will provide almost a dollar of added income to the target group. But if the target population consumes only 30 per cent of a subsidised food, the subsidy is much less efficient.

However, it can be shown (see Besley and Kanbur, 1988) that the use of the 'consumption by poor' ratio is strictly valid only when the objective is minimisation of the aggregate poverty gap. Different rules come into operation if the poverty alleviation objective pays special attention, for example, to the poorest of the poor and when Engel curves for food show significant non-linearity.

Finally, we take up the case where individual responses are such as to allow the possibility of changing between the categories being used for targeting. An obvious example is the relocation of families to areas where ration shops are present, or increasing family size if that is being used as an indicator. Roberts (1983) provides a general theoretical analysis of such problems. Clearly, if individuals can respond to the use of non-income indicators by manipulating their indicator to advantage, the policy-maker should take this into account. The central question is whether the incentives for poorer families to do so are greater than those for the richer families. For example, if migration costs are smaller as a percentage of richer household income the 'wrong' households may move in response to the setting up of a ration shop in a distant area. Once again, detailed research is needed to quantify the tradeoffs involved. If these responses are sufficiently adverse, even the use of non-income indicators for targeting comes into question – creating a further argument in favour of more univer-salistic schemes.

5.7   SELF-TARGETING

An alternative approach to targeting involves designing schemes which are based upon broad, self-acting tests which only the truly poor would pass. We shall refer to such schemes as 'self-targeting'. In general, programmes of this kind involve an agent either making a non-monetary payment to receive an income transfer or receiving a payment in kind rather than·in cash. We shall first discuss two paradigmatic examples of such schemes before drawing some general conclusions from their design.

Workfare

A workfare scheme operates by making a claimant of poor relief give up labour time in exchange for an income transfer. There are two reasons for doing that.[17] First, those who are poor may have a lower opportunity cost of labour time relative to others and hence, for a given income transfer, are prepared to give up more labour time. A work requirement may thus serve to screen the truly deserving from the rest. Such a test of eligibility has figured centrally in Indian famine relief policy (see Drèze, 1986). Its efficacy depends crucially upon whether the hypothesis that the opportunity cost of time is lower for target groups is valid. Holding other things equal, it seems likely that this would be so. If, however, poorer families have greater household commitments, for example to child rearing activities, then work requirements would be a poor targeting device. Alderman (1987) presents evidence suggesting that having to wait in line for food is a discouragement for many consumers. His evidence also questions the view that the poor gain disproportionately from using such allocation mechanisims.

A second reason for wishing to impose a work requirement is that it encourages certain kinds of behaviour. It may encourage agents to invest in skill formation which makes it less likely that they will require poor relief in future. Whether this argument works depends upon whether there is a link between key investment decisions and the avilability of relief to poor. In the context of the United States, this has proved to be a controversial issue (see, for example, Murray, 1984). There seems however to be very little research on this issue in the context of LDCs.

Transfers in kind

Targeting of certain groups in the population can also be achieved by making transfers in kind, a point first clearly explained by Nicholls and Zeckhauser (1982). Consider, for example, a good which is demanded discretely such as an educational qualification or a course of medical treatment (see Besley and Coate, 1989 for a detailed analysis of this problem). Such goods are typically available at different quality levels. If the state provides a certain quality level free of charge, then a consumer must choose between public and private provision, weighing up the cost of buying the good in the private market. If the government can find a quality level such that the demand for the publicly provided good is only from the poor, then quality choice provides a self-acting test, on the basis of which the poor can be targeted. Moreover, such targeting is consistent with the government having limited information about the poor population.

There are three main principles behind this argument. First, quality must be a normal good. Note that when taste variation is brought into the picture, then matters are somewhat complicated; for example, religious affiliations may be an important determinant of a consumer's propensity to use certain kinds of medical services. The correlation between tastes for quality and incomes then becomes important, and the present story overlaps with the statistical targeting story of section 5.6. Second, there must be a private market for the publicly provided good at the higher quality level. This certainly inhibits the applicability of this sort of targeting in the context of LDCs since often the only private sector alternatives are of a kind that only those with very high incomes can afford. Third is the related point that one must be able to find a quality level at which only some fraction of the population make use of the publicly provided good. This is required since otherwise, in kind transfers are dominated by transfers of cash of the same value. This is because transfers in kind carry a dead weight loss due to the fact that cash can be spent upon whatever a consumer wishes. In general, this deadweight loss can be tolerated only if there is a gain from targeting particular groups.

Both kinds of self-targeting schemes that we have discussed require the effective prohibition of a secondary market in the publicly provided good. For example, it must be impossible for a rich consumer to get a poor consumer to undertake his work requirement in order for him to get his benefit. Similarly, those who do not wish to consume public education should be unable to sell their right to a school place to another. In practice, there are many commodities on which this restriction can be enforced. However, this requirement does suggest that, in general, food will *not* be an acceptable commodity for a self-targeting scheme. Typically, it would be impossible to prevent unwanted food allocations from being claimed by consumers who were not poor and then sold. Hence, the gains from the programme would cease to be targeted.

The two theories of targeting under limited information which we have identified here are best viewed as complementary to each other. For example, a workfare scheme located in a particular region draws motivation from both statistical and self-targeting considerations. We believe that many thoughtfully designed targeting schemes will have this property.

5.8   CONCLUSION

In the wake of recent calls for finer targeting of poverty alleviation expenditure in developing countries, we have investigated some of the principles of targeting. We posited an 'ideal solution', where transfers went to the poor and only to the poor, as the benchmark for discussion and as the rationale for current trends in the policy debate. But the ideal solution fails to take into account three crucial aspects of the real world: (1) administrative and informational costs of implementation, (2) individual responses and incentive effects, and (3) the political economy of the problem. It has been argued that each of these militates against the ideal solution. The optimal strategy will probably lie somewhere between the two extremes of the ideal solution and complete universalism mediated by each of the three considerations above.

All of the above suggests the need for more country-specific research which quantifies the costs and benefits of targeting using the variety of micro-level data that has increasingly become available for many developing countries; research which is also sensitive to the political feasibilities of reform.

6 The Macroeconomics of External Shocks[1]

DAVID BEVAN, PAUL COLLIER and JAN WILLEM GUNNING

6.1 EXTERNAL SHOCKS, ECONOMIC THEORY AND THE CRISIS OF THE 1980s

Until the 1980s the predominant concerns of development economists were sectoral: problems of agriculture, problems of industry, or the interactions between them such as migration. During the 1980s the predominant concern shifted to macroeconomic issues. This shift was not because the sectoral problems had been solved, but because they were suddenly swamped by even more serious macroeconomic shocks. In some countries, for example Tanzania, living standards fell by half in just a few years.[2]

The development agencies switched a substantial part of their lending and advice from a sectoral to a macroeconomic focus, and the IMF, an agency with an exclusively macroeconomic brief which had played virtually no role in development before the mid-1970s was, by the mid-1980s, a central actor. IMF plans were adopted in much of the developing world.

Unfortunately, at the start of the 1980s the economic theory needed to analyse the type of macroeconomic events being experienced had not been formulated. The macroeconomic theories used for developed countries were not directly applicable: they were often closed economy models and their concerns were aggregate unemployment and inflation. Most developing economies, and especially the African ones most in trouble, were highly open. The problems of the 1980s were not predominantly unemployment and inflation but how best to respond to the shock of a (probably temporary) fall in foreign income. Further, these economies were usually festooned in government controls which could be (and had been) ignored in models of developed economies. This essay describes some of the macroeconomics which has been formulated to fill this gap.

Macroeconomic crises are the result of shocks. Shocks – or large, rapid unanticipated changes – can occur either because constraints upon agents alter or because the preferences of agents alter. Constraints may suddenly alter because of changes either in productivity or in world prices. For example, in the early 1970s Sahelian Africa suffered a productivity collapse in agriculture as a result of drought. Preferences may also suddenly alter. Traditional Keynesian economics was built on the notion that the 'animal spirits' of the business community were volatile so that the investment or savings propensities might shift. However, a more credible example of a shock due to volatile preferences is when the agent in question is the government. While the macroeconomic crisis of the 1980s had more than one cause, external shocks were undoubtedly central. In much of Latin America the accumulated disposition of assets and liabilities was such that the sudden rise in world interest rates compressed imports. In Africa the structure of income was such that the sudden fall in commodity prices had the same effect. In many countries these negative external shocks had been preceded by temporary positive shocks, such as the coffee and tea booms of the late 1970s. Often these opportunities had been so badly mismanaged that by the early 1980s these countries would have been in serious difficulties even without the additional problems of negative shocks.[3]

An economic theory of external shocks had been formulated during the 1970s by economists working on developed countries in response to the increase in the oil price in 1973, the theory being known as 'Dutch Disease'.[4] According to this theory, a foreign exchange windfall will (usually) raise demand for non-tradable goods and thereby lead to an increase in their relative price, causing a contraction in the non-booming tradable sector. In developed economies the latter is likely to be industry, in developing economies it is more likely to be agriculture. As far as it goes, this theory is as applicable to developing countries as to developed ones. It has been used, for example, to analyse the impact of the Indonesian and Nigerian oil shocks and the Egyptian remittance boom.[5]

Unfortunately, the theory is essentially comparative static: it treats the shock as if it were a once-and-for-all permanent change (as many people saw the oil shock at the time). Yet most of the external shocks which hit developing countries are in some sense temporary so that we should expect short-run dynamic effects to be crucial. For example, they might give rise to large fluctuations in domestic savings. Except in the special case of a perfect world capital market, these fluctuations in savings will be reflected in fluctuations in domestic investment. Since investment usually requires non-tradable capital goods ('construction'), windfall savings will then cause a temporary construction boom. The advance from the Theory of Dutch Disease to the analysis of temporary external shocks we call the Theory of Construction Booms,[6] and it will be the focus of this essay.

The first key relationship in the Theory of Construction Booms is between an external shock and investment. The theory argues that there are two routes by which a trade shock will affect investment. It will usually alter the propensity to save. Temporary positive shocks are especially likely to raise savings; in the presence of capital market imperfections, this will lower the cost of funds for domestic investment. Further, it will usually (whether permanently or temporarily) directly alter the marginal efficiency of investment. These routes are considered in turn in sections 6.2 and 6.3 and their net effect in section 6.4. The second key relationship is between investment demand and the sector which supplies non-tradable capital goods. This is discussed in section 6.5, the comparative static predictions of the theory being contrasted with those of the Theory of Dutch Disease. Section 6.6 describes the short-run dynamics implied by the model. Section 6.7 introduces a government regulation common to most developing countries, namely exchange control, which prohibits citizens from holding foreign assets. We show that the regulation has the undesirable effect of amplifying the impact of the shock, inducing private agents to respond in a socially inefficient way. Finally, section 6.8 considers another role of government, as a resource-using agent in its own right.

6.2   THE SAVINGS EFFECT OF A TRADE SHOCK

The once-and-for-all shock considered by Dutch Disease Theory turns out to be an unsuitable special case, in that it has no implications for the propensity to save. Permanent income and current income both change by the same amount so that transitory income (that component of income which should be saved if changes in consumption are to be sustained) is unaffected. Most shocks do have implications for the savings propensity because they are in some sense perceived as temporary. We may classify shocks by whether they are regarded as being consistent with past expectations and by whether they cause expectations to be altered. If the shock is regarded as consistent with prior expectations those expectations are termed 'inclusive'. This does not mean that the timing of the event was correctly predicted. If the shock is inconsistent with prior expectations they are 'exclusive'. If expectations are inclusive then the shock gives no cause to alter them in the future, so expectations are necessarily 'unrevised'.[7] However if expectations are exclusive the shock might lead to a revision of expectations but need not: the event might be regarded as unrepeatable. The permanent shock of Dutch Disease Theory involves exclusive and revised expectations: the change was not anticipated but is expected to persist. However, many shocks are inclusive and therefore unrevised: the rise in the copper price in the late 1980s was similar to those of previous decades. An exporting country such as Zambia should expect such fluctuations (though not, of course, know when they will occur). Finally, events which are regarded as once-in-a-lifetime might lead to no revision in expectations even if they were not consistent with prior expectations. The massive increase in coffee prices in the late 1970s was probably so perceived by many coffee growers.[8]

In both the unrevised cases, permanent income rises to the extent that the extra saving out of the windfall income yields a sustainable flow of income. For example, permanent income will rise by 9 if there is a 10 per cent rate of return and a windfall of 99 (of which 90 would be saved). These three cases[9] are summarised in Figure 6.1. In practice most trade shocks (positive or negative) will lie somewhere between them, giving rise not only to some change in permanent income but also to some change in transitory income.

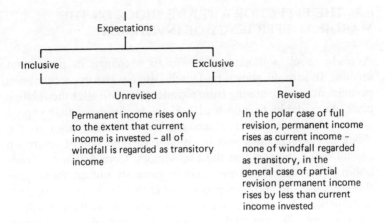

FIGURE 6.1   Income effects of trade shocks

A change in the propensity to save need have no effect upon domestic investment, but only if it leaves the cost of funds unaltered. This would be the case if the country had access to a perfect world capital market so that it could borrow and lend at a given world interest rate. In this case, all savings out of windfall income would be invested abroad and would leave the world interest rate unaltered. Domestic investment would be unaffected. The typical developing country is, however, capital scarce and so normally a capital importer. Borrowing for investment is financed at the margin from foreign funds. Because there is increasing country risk, firms face a rising cost of foreign funds. They therefore pay an interest rate well above that which savers could get on the world market. Windfall savings are then invested domestically: at the margin domestic investment is financed from domestic savings. The interest rate is now endogenous: it falls until (if the increase in savings is large) it reaches the rate on foreign assets. Any further domestic savings will then be temporarily invested in foreign assets. Hence, except in the special case of a perfect capital market, an increase in domestic savings increases domestic investment by lowering the cost of funds.

6.3   THE EFFECT OF A TRADE SHOCK ON THE MARGINAL EFFICIENCY OF INVESTMENT

A trade shock will generally lead to a change in permanent income. In turn, as shown by Dutch Disease Theory, a change in permanent income arising from a trade shock will alter the relative price of tradable to non-tradable goods. Suppose that capital goods, once installed, are sector-specific but that prior to the shock the capital stock was in equilibrium, the rate of return on capital being the same in the two sectors. Consider first a trade boom. This will raise the relative price of non-tradables and thereby raise the marginal product of capital in the sector in units of tradables. If labour is mobile between sectors then it will be attracted into the non-tradable sector. This will raise the marginal physical product of capital in the sector. Thus, prior to investment, the trade boom will have increased the marginal product of capital in the non-tradable sector both in units of tradables and in units of non-tradables. Given our assumption that prior to the shock capital was efficiently allocated, the marginal efficiency of investment was the same in both sectors. If financial capital markets are efficient, so that investment occurs in those activities where risk-corrected returns are highest, the return on investment will always be the higher of the returns to capital in the two sectors. Post-shock investment will thus be directed to the non-tradable sector. The marginal efficiency of investment will have risen in units both of non-tradables (because of the fall in the capital–labour ratio) and of tradables (additionally because of the fall in their relative price). Now consider a negative shock and a consequent fall in the relative price of non-tradables. The analysis goes through as before except that it is the tradables sector into which investment is attracted. The marginal efficiency of investment rises in units of tradables (because of the fall in the capital–labour ration) and in units of non-tradables (additionally because of the fall in their relative price). Hence, whether the trade shock is positive or negative, there is some stimulus to investment via changes in its marginal efficiency.[10] Which direction of shock produces the larger stimulus depends upon the capital–labour ratios in the two sectors. Denoting the favoured sector by X, then the more capital-intensive is X the more will the marginal physical product of capital be increased by a given migration of labour from the other sector. Hence, if the tradable sector happens to be the more capital-intensive, a negative trade shock will generate a larger stimulus because then the tradable sector is the favoured sector.[11]

6.4 THE EFFECT OF A TRADE SHOCK ON INVESTMENT

Table 6.1 sets out the combined effects of positive and negative shocks on investment via the two routes discussed above. If expectations are exclusive and fully revised there is a positive marginal efficiency of investment (MEI) effect, but no savings effect. Provided depreciation is sufficiently slow, the net effect on investment is positive even in the case of a negative shock. Note that in general expectations revision may be only partial. Full revision is a special case which happens to be the implicit assumption underpinning the theory of Dutch Disease. With unrevised expectations, investment is affected by both the MEI effect and the savings effect. The MEI effect is weaker than the exclusive revised expectations, but remains positive. In the case of a positive shock both effects work in the same direction, stimulat-

TABLE 6.1 Investment effects of trade shocks

Type of shock	Type of expectations	MEI effect	Savings effect	Net effect
Positive	Unrevised	Small positive	Positive	Positive
	Exclusive Fully revised	Large positive	Zero	Positive
Negative	Unrevised	Small positive	Negative	Ambiguous
	Exclusive Fully revised	Large positive	Zero	Positive

ing investment, but with a negative shock the savings effect is negative so the two are opposed, the net effect on investment being ambiguous.

To summarise, of the four types of trade shock, three give rise to investment booms, while in one case the effect is ambiguous. We now turn to the consequences of a change in the propensity to invest for relative prices.

6.5   INVESTMENT AND CONSTRUCTION BOOMS

A key result of the Theory of Construction Booms is that a trade shock is likely to raise the relative price of non-tradable capital goods. A change in the propensity to invest alters the demand for capital goods relative to consumer goods. That is, trade shocks have asymmetric demand effects requiring a disaggregation into capital and consumer goods. From the Theory of Dutch Disease we know that trade shocks also have asymmetric supply effects: a foreign exchange windfall enhances the supply of tradable goods but not that of non-tradable goods. Hence, the analysis of a trade shock requires both disaggregations, as set out in Table 6.2.

To make the distinctions more concrete, each aggregate has been labelled with a representative item. Although there are four distinct aggregates, the two tradables can be treated as a composite as long as the country is 'small' (unable to influence world prices). That is, the relative price of 'manufactures' to 'machinery'

TABLE 6.2   **Commodity aggregation for trade shocks**

	Tradables	*Non-tradables*
Consumer goods	'Manufactures'	'Services'
Capital goods	'Machinery'	'Construction'

is given on the world market, so the distinction between capital and consumer goods is critical only within the set of non-tradables. An increase in the demand for capital goods will generally be partly for 'machinery' and partly for 'construction'. The supply of 'machinery' is perfectly elastic at the world price, but that of 'construction' depends upon bidding away resources from other uses within the economy and so the extra demand will usually tend to increase the relative price of 'construction'. As this happens, firms will attempt to substitute 'machinery' for 'construction', but the two types of capital are assumed not to be perfect substitutes.[12]

The Theory of Construction Booms thus predicts that positive trade shocks will tend to lead to an increase in the relative price of 'construction' as a result of extra demand being skewed towards capital goods. The Theory of Dutch Disease predicts that positive trade shocks will lead to an increase in the relative price of all non-tradables as a result of extra foreign supply being skewed towards tradables. The two theories are complementary, as we now show. As demonstrated formally in Bevan *et al.* (1989), it is possible for a temporary boom to lower the price of non-tradable goods through a Rybczynski effect. Here, however, we abstract from such longer-term general equilibrium effects on output and assume that relative price changes in the goods market can be directly inferred from the changes in demand and the increased foreign supply of tradables. That is, we are abstracting from the subsequent effects of investment on output. We assume that the country cannot invest in foreign assets and that substitution effects dominate income effects. We also assume that the construction sector uses no capital.

The relative price implications of the different types of shock are shown in Figure 6.2. The vertical axis depicts the relative price of 'construction' to tradables and the horizontal axis the relative price of 'services' to tradables. The C–C locus shows equilibrium for 'construction'. Along a ray from the origin the price of 'construction' would be rising relative to tradables and constant relative to 'services'; hence, there would be an increasing tendency to excess supply so the C–C locus must be flatter than such a ray. The S–S locus shows equilibrium for 'services'. By an analogous argument it must be steeper than a ray through the origin.

Temporary positive shocks (Figure 6.2a) shift both the C–C locus (upward) and the S–S locus (to the right). Hence, the prices

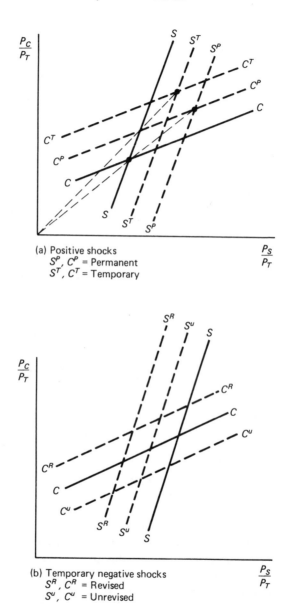

(a) Positive shocks
S^P, C^P = Permanent
S^T, C^T = Temporary

(b) Temporary negative shocks
S^R, C^R = Revised
S^u, C^u = Unrevised

FIGURE 6.2   Relative price effects of trade shocks

of non-tradable goods rise relative to tradables. However, because the demand for 'construction' rises relative to that for 'services', the price of the former (P_C) will rise relative to the latter (P_Z) unless this demand bias is offset by different elasticities of supply.

Temporary negative shocks (Figure 6.2b) shift the S–S locus to the left. If expectations are fully revised, the C–C locus unambiguously shifts upwards (recall from Table 6.1 that the net effect on investment is strictly positive). The price of 'construction' rises relative to tradables and also relative to 'services'. The change in the relative price of 'services' to tradables is ambiguous, as is the change in the weighted average price of non-tradables relative to tradables. If expectations are unrevised, the direction of shift of the C–C locus is ambiguous (see Table 6.1), so all relative price changes are ambiguous.

TABLE 6.3 The prediction of Dutch Disease and Construction Boom Theories compared

Direction of change in price of non-tradables relative to tradables.			
Type of shock	*Type of Expectations*	*Dutch Disease Theory*	*Construction Boom Theory*
Positive	Unrevised	Not considered	Rises P_C/P_S also rises
	Exclusive Fully Revised	Rises	Rises P_C/P_S also rises
Negative	Unrevised	Not considered	Ambiguous P_C/P_S also ambiguous
	Exclusive Fully revised	Falls	Ambiguous P_C/P_S rises

The relative price changes predicted by Dutch Disease Theory and Construction Boom Theory are compared in Table 6.3. Since Construction Boom Theory has the more disaggregated commodity set it includes some relative prices missed by Dutch Disease Theory, but the set of non-tradables can always be reaggregated so that the predictions of the two theories concerning its price relative to tradables can be compared. Recall that only exclusive fully revised expectations are considered in Dutch Disease Theory, the case in which current and permanent income change by the same amount; its predictions are limited to two of the four types of trade shock considered here. In one case (a positive trade shock with exclusive revised expectations) the two theories agree on the direction of change of this relative price: in the other (the negative analogue) Dutch Disease Theory makes a firm prediction which Construction Boom Theory suggests may sometimes be falsified.

So far, we have considered only the comparative statics of the Theory of Construction Booms. This has made it directly comparable to Dutch Disease Theory. However, unlike that theory, its main message is in the dynamics.

6.6 THE SHORT-TERM DYNAMICS OF CONSTRUCTION BOOMS

Although the formal dynamics of construction booms can be quite complicated,[13] some of the basic ideas can be depicted in simple diagrams for an important special case. Assuming capital to be sector-specific, we consider a positive trade shock with unrevised expectations. We further simplify the analysis by abstracting from any change in the marginal efficiency of investment, leaving only the savings effect.

The trajectory of the shock is depicted in Figure 6.3: the windfall lasts from time t_0 to $_1$ and for its duration is of a constant magnitude. Some or all of this windfall is added to assets, and this is depicted in Figure 6.3b.[14] We assume that in normal times the rate of return on domestic capital is above the world interest rate paid on financial assets, so that in the long run it is efficient for windfall assets to consist entirely of domestic capital. However, during the trade boom the price of capital goods is abnormally high due to the construction boom, so it may be efficient temporarily to hold some windfall savings as foreign financial assets. By building up foreign financial assets during the trade boom and then running them down subsequently the investment boom can be spread out over a longer duration than the construction boom, moderating the rise in 'construction' prices. Denote the time at which windfall foreign financial assets are exhausted as t_2.

The implications for the cost of funds for domestic investment are shown in 6.3c. While foreign financial assets are being held, the opportunity cost of funds is only the world deposit interest rate (r_W), at other times it is assumed to be higher.[15] The domestic interest rate is lower after the construction boom than before because of domestic asset accumulation in the interim.

The resulting stimulus to investment if firms correctly perceive this temporary reduction in the interest rate is shown in Figure 6.3d. The temporary investment boom has as its counterpart a temporary rise in the weighted average price of capital goods ('machinery' and 'construction'), shown in Figure 6.3e[16] and a reduction in the marginal efficiency of investment, shown in Figure 6.3f. The rational agent will equate the returns to foreign financial assets with those on capital goods net of losses resulting from the fall in their price as the price of 'construction' gradually reverts to normal:

$$r_W = \text{MEI} + \dot{P}_K$$

where r_W = world interest rate

$\dot{P}_K$ = the proportional rate of change in the price of capital goods

With r_W constant and the MEI inversely monotonic in investment, this entails an accelerating decline in the price of capital goods back towards their normal level after an initial leap. The difference between the windfall and the path of domestic investment yields the path of foreign financial assets depicted in Figure 6.3b.

These dynamics are both normative and positive: that is, they show the efficient path for the economy, and this path will be followed if agents are well informed, rational and unconstrained. Just as Dutch Disease is not a disease (unless additional assumptions are introduced) so as a construction boom is the appropriate

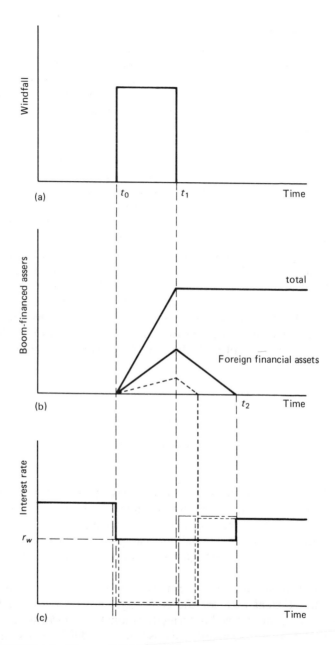

FIGURE 6.3 The time path of a construction boom

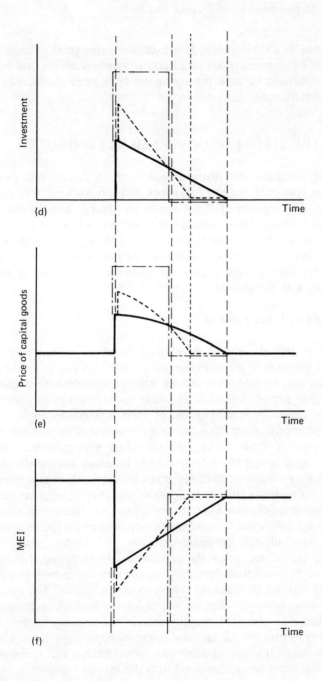

(d)

Investment

Time

(e)

Price of capital goods

Time

(f)

MEI

Time

response to a trade shock. However, there are good grounds for suspecting that many actual effects of construction booms have been excessive because private agents have been constrained by government controls.

6.7   THE EFFECT OF GOVERNMENT CONTROLS

So far, we have not distinguished between private and public agents. However, the external shock may directly bear upon these groups differentially. Even if the shock directly accrues only to private agents (such as a change in world prices which is not offset by taxes or subsidies) the behaviour of public agents is important. Public agencies perform a dual role: they are resource-using, and they regulate private agents. We consider each role in turn, starting with the second.

Foreign exchange controls

In most though not all developing countries citizens are not permitted to hold foreign financial assets. This produces various effects, but the one on which we will concentrate here is that in aggregate private agents must either match savings to domestic capital formation continuously, or vary their claims on the only other domestic agent, namely the government. Consider the case of a positive trade shock with unrevised expectations. Private agents wish in aggregate to save their transient income. In many developing countries the only financial asset which the government offers to its citizens is domestic currency. The government now has three choices. First, it must choose whether or not to meet this temporary extra demand for money. As private agents convert their windfall into domestic currency, the money supply will automatically rise unless the government takes action. Indeed it will rise by more than demand since the increase in high-powered money enables the banking system to expand credit. The government can, however, sterilise the inflow of foreign exchange by increasing the required liquidity ratio of the banking system. If it chooses to prevent the increase in the money supply then private agents have no way in aggregate of rephasing the investment boom: it must be synchronised with the savings boom.[17]

If the government does choose to increase the money supply to match the extra demand, it then has a further choice, namely whether to retain or to spend the foreign currency which it receives from private agents in exchange for the domestic currency it issues. If the investment boom is to be stretched beyond the savings boom the government must retain these resources in the form of foreign financial assets so that as private agents attempt to convert their financial assets (money) into capital goods, government holdings of foreign exchange can be run down to enable investment to exceed savings. Foreign exchange reserves would thus temporarily be accumulated and then run down as the government held foreign currency on behalf of private agents. However, instead of this custodial role, the government may choose to spend these resources. In this case, the extra financial assets of the private sector are in aggregate illusory, for when the sector attempts to spend them there are no resources to finance an excess of investment over savings and so the price level will be bid up, dissipating the assets in real terms. The public sector will therefore have preempted the attempt by the private sector to defer investment. The government now has a third choice, namely whether to spend on capital goods or consumer goods. If it chooses to spend entirely on capital goods then aggregate investment is not reduced by its policy, but the investment boom is again synchronised with the savings boom. If it chooses to purchase consumer goods then the aggregate savings propensity is lowered.

Figure 6.4 sets out the resulting decision tree and describes the consequences for investment. The consequences of the unregulated case have already been described in section 6.6 above. The consequence of both the No Monetary Accommodation case and the Monetary Accommodation → No Reserve Accumulation → Investment case is that the investment book is synchronised with the savings boom. The consequences of this synchronisation are depicted by the dashed lines in Figure 6.4. The time path of investment (Figure 6.3b) now coincides with that of the income windfall (6.3a). As a result, the price of capital goods and the MEI reflect the investment path. The marginal efficiency of investment is markedly lower than in the unregulated case as agents grow into unrewarding projects. We have assumed that in these cases government behaviour does not rebound upon the private propensity to save out of windfall income. However, this

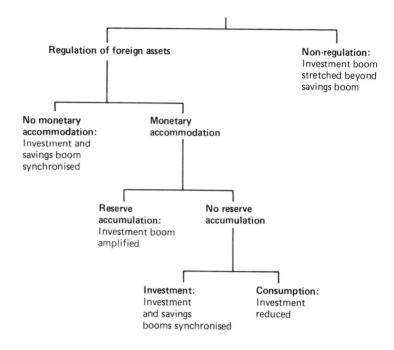

FIGURE 6.4   The government decision tree and its consequences

assumption is implausible. For example, savings which take place just prior to t_1 have a heavily negative return because there is an immediate and substantial capital loss as the price of 'construction' falls. It seems likely that faced with this, private agents would choose to consume more and invest less. Hence the aggregate savings propensity out of the windfall would fall. This is, of course, also the direct consequence of the Monetary Accommodation → No Reserve Accumulation → Consumption decision.

Now consider the consequences of the Monetary Accommodation → Reserve Accumulation decision. Although in this case the government merely acts as a cypher for private agents, in the process in effect it imposes a 100 per cent tax on the interest earned on foreign financial assets. Private agents hold domestic currency and so earn no interest. With some underlying inflation, domestic currency will typically carry a heavily negative rate of interest in real terms. As a result the opportunity cost of investment falls below the world deposit rate of interest. This is shown by the dotted line in Figure 6.3. The jump in investment is therefore more pronounced (Figure 6.3d) than in the unregulated case but the investment boom then fades more rapidly. The boom in the 'construction' sector is amplified (Figure 6.3e). Finally, reflecting the investment path, the marginal efficiency of investment is lower during the boom. Again, because the return on windfall savings is lower, it is likely that the propensity to save will be reduced.

To conclude, given this regulation the economy will commit two types of error in responding to an external windfall. First, by crowding more investment into the period of the windfall it will reduce the marginal (and hence the average) return on windfall investment. Second, the propensity to invest out of windfall income will be reduced. Both of these errors have the effect of reducing the capacity of the economy to convert a temporary gain into a substainable increase in consumption. In economies particularly subject to external shocks, temporary windfalls will account for a large part of the net investment effort. Hence, the Theory of Construction Booms tells us that the regulation of foreign assets in such countries may be highly detrimental.

Trade controls

The consequences of an external shock are also affected by government trade controls. Such controls may take the form of tariffs but more commonly take the form of import quotas. Both increase the domestic price of importables relative to the world price, and for any quota there is some equivalent tariff which would have the same effect on prices. So far we have argued that the construction boom effects of an external shock require a disaggregation of the non-tradables sector into capital and consumer goods because the relative price of the two will change. Once trade controls are introduced it usually becomes necessary for the same reason also to disaggregate the tradable sector into its protected and unprotected components. The only circumstance in which such disaggregation is not needed is if the rate of tariff (or tariff equivalent) is invariant with respect to the shock. We now consider two possible rules which the government might use to determine trade policy, in both of which the tariff (or tariff equivalent) is endogenous to the shock. Under the first rule the equivalent tariff rises due to the shock, under the second it falls. Each rule generates unintended and undesirable side effects.

Under the first policy rule, which might reflect inertia, import quotas are kept constant despite the external shock. The only way in which the economy can then benefit from a favourable shock is if the volume of exports is reduced. The same volume of imports can be purchased by a smaller volume of exports due to the terms of trade improvement, and this releases resources for the production of import substitutes. This resource movement out of the export sector is induced by a change in relative prices. With fixed quotas importables behave as non-tradables at the margin. Increased demand drives up their price until it has risen relative to the export good, for only then will resources be induced to reallocate into the sector, enabling the extra demand to be met. Under this policy rule an increase in the world price of exports thus causes a decrease in their domestic price and a decline in export volumes. Such a trade policy is highly inefficient: resources move out of the export sector at precisely the time when they should move into it.

Under the second policy rule the government adjusts import quotas so as to maintain balance of payments equilibrium on current account with a fixed exchange rate and a fixed money supply. In effect, whenever foreign exchange earnings increase the government relaxes quotas. We refer to such a rule as an endogenous trade policy. Under such a rule, starting from a pre-shock equilibrium, a favourable external shock will give rise to a reduction in the rate of the equivalent tariff. This can be seen as follows. The policy rule will be breached if the balance of payments moves into surplus. Given the money supply, the balance of payments will move into surplus if the demand for money increases (since there will be an excess demand for money). But the shock tends to increase the transactions demand for money for two reasons. First real income (and hence expenditure) is increased. Second, the relative price of non-tradable goods is increased. Since if tariffs are constant the domestic price of importables is constant, this relative price change must involve a rise in the nominal price of non-tradables. The current account will thus remain balanced only if there is some offsetting decrease in the transactions demand for money. This is achieved by a reduction in the equivalent tariff which lowers the nominal price of importable goods. So far the second policy rule appears to have had opposite effects to the first: the first raised protection, whereas the second reduced it. The first worsened resource allocation and so it might appear that the second would improve it. However, we will now see that this need not be the case.

If the favourable external shock is temporary, then the trade liberalisation is reversed when the shock ends. Once the private sector has learned that the government is determining its trade policy in such a way, then if it recognises the shock as temporary, it can predict the subsequent increase in the equivalent tariff rate. Such an anticipation of tariff increases will raise the demand for imports of durable goods. Calvo (1987, 1988) has shown that in such situations there is a build up in inventories of imported goods. This is inefficient: there is a private return from storage but no social return. Hence, the net welfare effect of such a policy rule during a favourable temporary shock is ambiguous when compared with a policy of keeping tariffs constant. A permanent reduction in tariffs would improve resource allocation, but one which is perceived to be temporary also gives rise to behaviour which is socially costly.

6.8 GOVERNMENT TAX AND EXPENDITURE POLICIES

The more direct part played by government in determining the overall response to the trade shock is considered in this section from three perspectives. The first examines what tax and expenditure choices may be appropriate when the shock initially accrues to the private sector and when the private sector is itself capable of responding optimally. The second poses the same question, but relaxes the assumption of optimal private response. The third is concerned with public responses in the case where a windfall accrues directly to the government.

Government taxation and spending in response to a private windfall

Since a well managed private windfall requires no custodial intervention from government, it might appear that a relatively passive or laissez-faire public response would be appropriate.

Matters are more complicated than this, however, for three different sets of reasons. These involve, respectively, the long-run level of public expenditure and taxation, the marginal cost of public funds and the nature and composition of public expenditure. The first relates to the new long-run equilibrium following adjustment to the shock, the others tend to affect the trajectory of adjustment to this equilibrium. Each is considered in turn.

Permanent national income is higher following the boom, so that tax revenue will rise at existing tax rates. There is no equivalent mechanism ensuring an automatic rise in public expenditure, so a passive response will generate an arbitrary fall in the public sector deficit. However, it is plausible to assume that the elasticity of desired public expenditure with respect to permanent national income is positive, so that there should be discretionary increases in planned public expenditure. If this elasticity differs from the corresponding elasticity of tax revenue at existing rates, some change in the level and/or structure of tax rates will also be necessary. In effect, the size and shape of the public sector will automatically change, but there is no reason to suppose that these automatic changes will correspond to what is wanted.

We do not consider this question of long-run design further here. The properties of the short-run adjustment path will be compounded from the changes required to implement the new long-run equilibrium and those of a purely transitional nature. In the rest of this section we concentrate on the latter.

One reason for supposing that the appropriate short-run fiscal response should differ from the long-run response is that the marginal cost of public funds may temporarily drop during the boom (see, for example, the round table discussion in Neary and Wijnbergen, 1986). The usual argument is that the windfall is rather like an economic rent, so that it can be taxed away with minimal incentive effects. Whether this is so depends on the type of income instability involved, and the informational content attributed to the increment in income.

The principal determinant of the marginal cost of public funds is the deadweight cost of the tax system, reflecting disincentive effects. The marginal costs will be low when these disincentive effects are small because the relevant private substitution elasticities are low. The question, therefore, is whether these elasticities are likely to be low in respect of incremental income. For the unrevised exclusive case, this does appear to be likely. The increment is truly a windfall in this case; it was anticipated neither in fact nor probabilistically, and it has no implications for future supply decisions. If the windfall could be gathered with no increase in current labour supply, it would then be pure profit or rental income, and taxation of it would have no incentive effects.

Now suppose that one of the inclusive cases holds. Taxation of the incremental income at an enhanced rate now lowers mean expected net income, unless it is accompanied by correspondingly reduced taxation during periods of low income. No general conclusions can be drawn about the implication of either approach for the level of the marginal cost of public funds. In principle this could rise or fall, depending on the nature of preferences, the form of the distribution and the structure of taxes. Hence there does not appear to be any general presumption in favour of a high effective tax rate on the increment in cases where this is perceived to be part of the normal ups and downs of economic life.

This discussion may be summarised as follows. If a windfall is commonly perceived as both temporary and once-and-for-all, then there are powerful arguments that a high proportion of the incremental income should be taxed at source. If it were perceived as unusual, but part of the normal pattern, these arguments do not go through.

Finally, the appropriate fiscal response may be influenced by the nature and composition of public expenditure, particularly by the allocation between tradable and non-tradable goods on the one hand, and that between capital and consumption goods on the other. The sharp movement in the relative price of non-tradable goods will imply some shift in the optimal allocation of public expenditure between tradable and non-tradable goods, more markedly in the short than in the long run.

It may also have implications for the level of government spending, as opposed to its allocation. For example, if the major part of public services are non-tradable, these will become relatively more expensive during the windfall and contraction of public expenditure might be desirable. Expenditure on goods from the non-tradable sector during this period will be relatively inefficient from the government's point of view. In the worst case the rise in non-tradable prices reflects real increases in resource costs, so there is a social loss arising from excessively bunched spending.

But even if the price rises constitute pure transfers to factor owners, there is no reason to suppose that the government would value these unintended transfers high enough to match the marginal costs of public funds.

The flow of current government services can be sustained in two quite different ways. The government may simply purchase part of current final output and then supply this in the form of public services. Alternatively, it may create and operate capital facilities which generate output directly (as with government owned factories) or in cooperation with privately owned factors (as with much infrastructure).

Assume, for simplicity, that the government wishes to increase the flow of public services in line with changes in permanent national income. Then if public services constitute only purchases of final output, public expenditure will also rise in line with permanent national income. However, to the extent that public services are provided by public capital, the actual pattern of incremental expenditure will exhibit an early peak followed by a decline. As a polar case, suppose that the government's main activity was building infrastructure with very low maintenance costs and depreciation rates. Then virtually all the incremental government expenditure would occur as a short surge of capital expenditure very soon after the windfall.

While intertemporal considerations indicate that a stable deficit is unlikely to be optimal during the windfall, this discussion demonstrates that even the direction of change is ambiguous. Consider the following polar cases. In the first, the windfall is external to expectations, so it is optimal for the government to obtain a large share of it as incremental revenue. Meanwhile public expenditure exclusively takes the form of purchases of final output. In these circumstances, expenditure rises in line with government permanent income which increases relative to permanent national income following the boom. During the boom, the government runs a large surplus, and has the task of lending this to the private sector and attempting to ensure that it is all invested in private capital.

In the second polar case, the windfall is internal to expectations, so the government's revenue rises only proportionately. Meanwhile public expenditure exclusively takes the form of infrastructure investment (non-tradable goods are ignored). Public services are planned to rise proportionately to permanent national income. Hence the government undertakes a massive capital expenditure programme equal to the sum of its windfall tax income and the present value of taxes on incremental permanent national income. In consequence, the budget goes heavily into deficit during the boom.

A realistic pattern would lie somewhere between these extremes; but it does not appear possible to sign the transitional budget changes.

Stabilising taxation

So far, we have assumed that the private sector responds optimally. Leaving aside considerations of the control regime itself, there are two principal reasons why this may not hold. The first involves market imperfections that constrain private choices, the second involves faulty private perceptions of events.

If private sector agents' spending decisions are constrained not by their permanent income but by – for example – their marketable assets and current income, then the government has to correct for these constraints. Its fiscal stance must be chosen in such a way that the paths of private sector current assets and disposable income permit spending decisions which are appropriate to the underlying permanent incomes. This problem is likely to be acute in the case of a long-lived windfall – for example, the discovery of oil reserves. It may then be necessary for the government to run a large deficit to generate a sufficient relaxation of private sector current constraints to enable the sector to increase spending appropriately. In the case of a very short-lived windfall, this complication is likely to be much less serious, and will be ignored here.

Both public and private sectors may misunderstand what is happening during the windfall. For example, either or both may get the duration of the windfall, and hence its magnitude, wrong. For concreteness, suppose that the government gets it right, while the private sector is over-optimistic. The private sector is likely to attempt to consume too high a proportion of the windfall, and the government must attempt to prevent this. Ideally the government would raise a forced loan, returning the money when the windfall was clearly over or, equivalently, temporarily raise taxes, subsequently to lower them. However, all this is predicted on two assumptions – that the government has more accurate perceptions than the private sector of the underlying instability, and that it is capable of exercising the required custodial function. Even if the first assumption holds, the obvious response is to disseminate the superior information rather than to act on the assumed ignorance of private agents. In any case, the second assumption requires substantiation.

Public windfalls

Sometimes trade booms automatically accrue to the government without any tax decision because it owns the asset (for example, oil). The government then faces a difficult problem of how to pass the benefits on to the population. This is particularly marked in the oil states of the Middle East. If it is administratively impossible to make direct transfers to the population, the government can either subsidise private consumption or purchase goods and services on behalf of the population. In the case of subsidies, private agents benefit partly by lower prices and partly by higher factor incomes consequent upon the increased demand. Two special cases are revealing: that in which the subsidy is non-tradable and is just sufficient to keep its relative price to consumers unaltered by the boom-cum-subsidy; and that in which the subsidy is tradable and is just sufficient to keep its relative price to producers unaltered by the boom-cum-subsidy. In the former case, since consumer prices are unaffected by the trade shock the only transmission mechanism is via factor incomes. In the latter case, since producer prices are unaltered, the only transmission mechanism is via lower consumer prices.

If, instead of subsidies, the government purchases goods and services, the effects upon the population depend partly upon whether they are desired and partly upon whether they are tradable or non-tradable. If the goods are both undesired and tradable, such as armaments, then the windfall yields no benefits to the population. If they are undesired but non-tradable, such as pyramids, then the population gains because the government must purchase the factor services of its population in order to build them. Factor services will be willingly only supplied if the government offers incomes higher than those available in other activities.

If the goods are both desired and non-tradable, like roads or schools then the population gains both through higher factor incomes and through the benefits directly provided by the expenditures.

6.9 CONCLUSION

Many developing countries are prone to substantial trade shocks. In the 1950s the response of many economists was to devise public stabilisation schemes, national and international, to shield private agents from the shocks. Commonly, these schemes were either never implemented or failed because they required an implausibly high capacity on the part of public agents. More recently, the attention of economists has shifted to the study of how well informed private agents will respond to shocks. This analysis began with the theory of Dutch disease which showed that for such events it is important to distinguish between tradable and non-tradable goods. More recent theoretical developments have emphasised that because of their effects upon investment, trade shocks also require a distinction between capital and consumer goods. A trade shock will usually give rise to a large change in the demand for non-tradable capital goods. This is why export booms commonly lead to construction booms. The government influences the outcome of shocks in two ways. First, through its control regime it regulates the behaviour of private agents. We showed how foreign exchange and trade controls might reduce the capacity of well informed private agents to respond to a shock in a socially efficient manner. Second, through its fiscal policy the government raises and spends money. Even without the complications of a control regime, the design of an appropriate fiscal response to a shock is likely to be difficult. In the presence of the type of control regimes common in developing countries, private responses are likely to be socially sub-optimal and the problem of identifying an appropriate public response insuperable.

7 Explaining Industrial Success in the Developing World

SANJAYA LALL

7.1 INTRODUCTION

Developing countries vary greatly in their experience of industrialisation (Weiss, 1988, Chenery *et al.*, 1986). At one end of the spectrum are the 'newly industrialising countries' (NICs) of East Asia, which have enjoyed high, sustained growth of their manufacturing industries and are competing in world markets in a broad range of sophisticated industrial products. Industrial development has been the engine of their income growth and the structural tranformation of their economies. At the other end are the 'least developed countries', (LDCs) largely in Africa and some in Asia. These have rudimentary industrial sectors, producing a narrow range of mainly simple consumer goods. Their industries display little dynamism, export little, have few linkages (apart from primary inputs) with the domestic economy and often act as a drag on their economic growth. In between the two extremes lies the rest of the developing world, with greater or lesser success in building efficient, dynamic modern industry.

What explains this enormous diversity of experience? Much of the recent literature on industrialisation in the Third World has focused on one set of explanations for industrial success: trade policy. It has been argued that export-oriented strategies are more conducive to rapid, efficient and sustainable industrial development than inward-looking, import substituting strategies (Balassa, 1989; Balassa *et al.*, 1982; Bhagwati, 1978; Chenery *et al.*, 1986;

Krueger, 1983; Little, Scitovsky and Scott, 1970; World Bank, 1987). The evidence of the East Asian NICs (in particular that of Korea and Taiwan) has been widely used to demonstrate the superiority of outward-looking strategies.

The superiority of outward-orientation has been traced to the neutrality of government interventions in the incentive structure facing manufacturing enterprises. The most neutral of regimes is free trade, but others also qualify for neutrality if biases in favour of domestic markets are offset by compensating measures to make exports attractive. It is, however, generally argued that regimes that have achieved neutrality are also liable to lower and less variable incentive biases (i.e., be generally more liberal and open to international competition) than regimes that are predominantly inward-looking. The combination of lower protection and export incentives is supposed to produce both static benefits (from better resource allocation, greater efficiency in operation, full realisation of scale economies and lower rent-seeking) and dynamic benefits (faster internal technical progress, greater receptivity to world changes in technology and markets). This is usually called the 'neoclassical approach' to industrialisation strategy (Wade, 1988).

This general case for trade strategy as the main determinant of industrial success is based on the assumption that incentives are the most important determinant of performance. It is assumed, in other words, that market prices provide correct signals for economic activity and that the ability to respond to those signals is present: stated simply, product and factor markets are supposed to be efficient in developing countries. There are, however, some variations on this theme, depending on *how* efficient markets are taken to be. The more extreme version (what may be termed the strong neoclassical approach) tends to assume that all markets are highly efficient in developing countries. There is, in this version, rarely any instance of market failure (or, at least, explicit consideration of this is not taken): free trade is supposed to provide the ideal set of incentives, with no need for interventions on the supply side to ensure adequate response. The 'weaker' or moderate versions of the neoclassical approach admit that there may be market failures, in both product and factor markets (see Pack and Westphal, 1986). *Some* intervention is thus considered permissible, in the form of infant industry protection or 'functional' interventions in factor markets. However, such intervention must not be 'selective' (promoting chosen activities over others) in either factor or product markets. It must be limited in scope and duration, especially for infant industry protection (which must be uniform across activities). It must take cognisance of the risk of 'administrative failure' (if such failure is more harmful than market failure, it may be better not to intervene).

The neoclassical analysis of industrialisation leads to a clear set of policy prescriptions. In the 'strong' version, the immediate ideal is free trade, sound macro policies and minimal economic intervention (apart from the provision of basic infrastructure). In the moderate version, the case for low, uniform and temporary effective protection of infant industry may be accepted, as well as non-selective support of supply-side factors, in particular education and technology. Much of the current literature seems to veer between the two versions. The overwhelming emphasis given to trade strategy and, more generally, to 'getting prices right' generally leads many writers to appear to adopt a fairly 'strong' position. The need for low, uniform protection is accepted by the more moderate analysts, but on a specific interpretation of the process of infant industry maturation (of which, more below). The case for intervention on the supply side is generally not taken up explicitly in discussions of national industrial performance. The portrayal of successful industrialisers as having 'neutral' (and implicitly fairly liberal) regimes conveys the impression that all factor markets were able to respond efficiently to incentives. 'Getting prices right' thus ends up as not merely a necessary, but also a sufficient, requirement of industrial success. The neoclassical concern with efficient resource allocation as determined by market prices tends to override other possible concerns.

There is no doubt that the neoclassical analysis of industrialisation has a great deal of validity. It has helped move policy-makers in developing countries away from earlier fears of gross and widespread failure of markets to a greater reliance on market forces. It has drawn useful lessons from the performance of the East Asian NICs, which are now regarded as role models not just by economists but also by practically all governments in developing countries. However, in terms of providing a comprehensive framework for understanding industrial development the neoclassical approach has certain deficiencies. These arise largely from its assumptions about the functioning of markets and the nature of industrial efficiency, which lead it, in turn, to simplify or misinterpret the experience of the East Asian NICs.

This essay draws upon the important contributions of the neoclassical approach, but extends it by providing a more realistic analysis of industrial competiveness. It suggests that other factors (besides outward-orientation) are necessary for successful industrialisation to proceed. Incentives are a necessary but not sufficient condition for industrial development. 'Correct' incentives may, moreover, well deviate from prices thrown up by free markets, and incentives by themselves may not produce the 'supply-side' factors needed for industrialisation. The possibility of market failure has thus to be addressed clearly in any theory of industrialisation, and its remedies may lie in interventions of a kind currently regarded undesirable by the 'strong' neoclassical approach. A more comprehensive and realistic framework than exists in the received literature is needed in this field. This essay provides the beginning of such a framework.

7.2 SUCCESSFUL INDUSTRIALISATION

Before launching into the analysis of industrial success, it would be useful to describe briefly in what 'success' consists. Industrial development may be taken to consist only of the growth of manufacturing capacity or production. However, successful industrialisation implies more than simply adding physical capacity or increasing production (over a brief period). It implies also that the capacity is built and untilised efficiently, and that growth is sustained over the longer term by increases in productivity and competitiveness. It implies, in other words, a certain *efficiency and dynamism* in the industrialisation process, which distinguish it from a process where investments are set up at high cost, output is unable to compete internationally, productivity stagnates over time, activities fail to diversify and linkages with the rest of the economy are limited. In the developing world, in particular, it is useful to separate output growth from genuine industrial development.

There are several possible indicators of dynamism and efficiency in industrial development. In a static sense, industrial investments should, by some international norms, be carried out at reasonable cost; operating costs and product quality should be competitive, by reference to 'best practice' technical standards; and local resources, competitively priced, should be drawn upon to every possible extent. In a dynamic setting, where technologies are constantly evolving and new products and processes appearing in world markets, 'efficiency' in developing countries also involves a parallel rise in productivity and diversification in industrial technologies.

For individual manufacturing firms in developing economies to display static and dynamic efficiency over time, the environment in which they function must also necessarily undergo structural transformation (Chenery *et al.*, 1986). For instance, the nature of activities undertaken will tend, in all the smallest economies, to 'deepen', with more complex, skill and technology activities being launched, and a larger proportion of manufactured inputs, capital goods and supporting services being procured locally. Inter-industry linkages will thus tend to grow, with the involvement not just of manufacturers but also of consultants, service firms, traders, research establishments and specialised financial intermediaries. In addition, successful industrial development will generally entail a growing proportion of the skills and technologies required for manufacturing growth being generated locally. A great deal of technology will continue to be imported – in developed as also in developing countries – but a larger share of routine, and some specialised advanced, technological work will be conducted locally if costs are to be kept low and diversification sustained. Reliance on foreign skills and technologies over a broad front is not merely very expensive; it also inhibits the absorption of new manufacturing activities and their spread through the economy. A successful industrialising country will, therefore, display increasing depth and complexity of manufacturing activity, with growing local content in physical, human and technological inputs.

The most convenient way of assessing industrial success would thus be to examine the growth of manufacturing value-added over a long period, and such indicators of efficiency and dynamism as incremental capital–output ratios, growth of total factor productivity, export growth and diversification, and levels of protection afforded to domestic industry. Taking these various criteria together, and allowing for the size of the economy, it is generally agreed that the most successful industrialisers in the developing world are the four East Asian NICs, Korea, Taiwan, Singapore and Hong Kong (World Bank, 1987; Lall, 1990). These differ significantly among themselves, with the first two, being much larger, having attained much greater depth and diversity than the latter. Brazil and Mexico would probably count as the next tier, with larger industrial sectors but lower levels of efficiency and dynamism. Argentina, Yugoslavia and India may come next (and China, if one included non-market economies), but these are being rapidly overhauled by the 'new NICs' of South-East Asia (Thailand, Malaysia and, to a lesser extent, Indonesia), which have smaller and shallower industrial structures but are displaying rapid growth of exports and competitiveness. Then comes the whole range of other developing countries, with the rear brought up, as noted at the start, by the poorest economies of sub-Saharan Africa (SSA).

With this simple map to guide us, let us turn now to the basic building block of industrial success: the *attainment of static and dynamic efficiency at the firm level*. The micro-phenomenon of achieving efficiency is often ignored in general discussions of industrial performance in developing countries. This is natural, given the theoretical (neoclassical) tradition of assuming that firms are small and homogeneous, with equal access to skills and technology, and with the instantaneous mastery of technology that is implicit in the production function analysis (Nelson, 1981). But this tradition is misleading. Firms do not instantaneously and costlessly gain static efficiency even with 'right' prices. Over time, they do not have free access to the skills and knowledge needed to achieve dynamic efficiency. This is true of all firms, but the process of achieving efficiency is more complex and difficult for firms in developing countries. Section 7.3 explains why.

7.3 EFFICIENCY AT THE FIRM LEVEL

It is almost a truism to suggest that efficiency in setting up, operating, diversifying and expanding an industrial operation requires specific knowledge and skills to technology and organisation ('capabilities' for short) on the part of the firm. Yet this truism, if considered further, has important theoretical and practical implications. When industries are started, the necessary capabilities do not exist within the firm. If they cannot be obtained 'off the shelf' from factor markets in the economy or abroad, industry cannot be operated efficiently unless they are generated by the firm itself. In developing countries, a few capabilities may be hired from the local economy or imported. But when a technology or a form of work organisation is introduced to the economy for the first time, a significant proportion of the necessary capabilities necessarily has to be created within the enterprise. The efficiency of its operations then depends on its ability economically to mobilise external capabilities, to integrate them into its organisation, and to generate its own set of technological, managerial and other capabilities.

The acquisition of industrial capabilities is not an easy, automatic or costless process (see, among others, Bell *et al.*, 1984; Katz, 1987; Lall, 1987; Dahlman *et al.*, 1989; Fransman, 1986; Pack and Westphal, 1986; Teitel, 1984). It cannot be assumed, as in simple theoretical models, that firms start by operating on a production function where such capabilities are already fully formed and evenly distributed. The concept of a neoclassical production function is itself a misleading representation of how firms operate, even in advanced industrial countries (Nelson, 1981; Nelson and Winter, 1982). Individual firms display persistent differences in productivity even when using the same technologies, largely because of differences in the efforts they have made to acquire the relevant capabilities. In developing countries, such differences tend to be much greater, because a new activity is much 'newer' in relation to existing skills and knowledge, and supporting institutions are weak or non-existent. Moreover, firms tend to be unaware of the need for, and returns to, investments in capability creation, and so under-invest, especially when there is a risk that part of the rewards will not be appropriated by them, when finance for such activities is not readily available, or when reaping the full benefits of capability acquisition depends on similar investments by other enterprises in the production chain (Pack and Westphal, 1986).

While every enterprise has to invest time and effort in mastering a set of new skills to reach even a static efficiency frontier (see Bell *et al.*, 1984), the nature and degree of effort is not uniform. The nature of the technology, the level of development of factor markets and skill availability, the support available externally, all determine how much individual firms need to do to reach best practice levels. Different activities have intrinsically different requirements for capability acquisition; some involve more stages of processing or the interaction of a larger number of disciplines than others; some require a large engineering workforce; some need greater inputs of pure science or more linkages with a network of laboratories or testing facilities; and so on. The determinants of firm level competitive advantage are thus far more complex than conventional theory suggests, and there is no given or predictable 'learning curve' down which all firms travel.

The significance of skill and knowledge acquisition goes beyond reaching static efficiency. It is also a major, perhaps the major, determinant of *dynamic* efficiency – i.e., of adaptation to change, of improved productivity performance, and of innovation. The significance of formal R & D efforts for innovation is, of course, well recognised. But technological efforts are also required on a constant basis merely to keep abreast of changing conditions and technologies in factor or product markets. Nearly all industrial technologies evolve and improve over time. Demand patterns change, new competition arises, raw material prices and character-istics change, new products appear, old ones disappear, and so on, all requiring technological responses. The introduction of new products and processes can be undertaken successfully only if the relevant skills and knowledge are developed by the manufacturers. This requires capabilities to search for and create new knowledge, partly by formal research and development and partly by less formal types of technological effort: even the successful deploy-ment of technology licensed from others requires in-house assimi-lative, adaptive and integrative effort (Cohen and Levinthal, 1989). Although the pattern of dynamic change and response varies enormously with the technology, and with the depth of mastery aimed at by the firm, any firm which stops investing in internal technical efforts stagnates, or fails.

The full range of industrial capabilities needed by modern industry is very large. Capabilities can be grouped under three broad headings – entrepreneurial, managerial, and technological. This section concentrates on technological capabilities for ease of exposition, but this is not intended to minimise the significance of other capabilities. Firm level technological capabilities can be categorised in several ways. A functional classification is useful to illustrate the spectrum of skills to manage the various activities involved in setting up and operating an enterprise. Table 7.1 (taken from Lall, 1987, who has a longer analysis) shows an illustrative matrix of technological capabilities by function and complexity. The functions relate to three general sets of activities: investment, production, and linkages.

Investment capabilities are the skills needed to identify, prepare, obtain technology for, design, construct, equip, staff, and commission a new facility (or expansion). They determine the capital costs of the project, the appropriateness of the scale, product mix, technology and equipment selected, and the understanding gained by the operating firm of the basic technologies involved (which, in turn, affect the efficiency with which it later operates the facility). *Production capabilities* range from basic skills like quality control, operation, and maintenance, to more advanced ones like adaptation, improvement or equipment 'stretching', to the most demanding ones of research, design, and innovation. These skills determine how well a given technology is operated (technological mastery), whether it is adapted and improved over time (minor innovation), and whether it is transformed by the introduction of major changes (major innovation). *Linkage capabilities* are the skills needed to transmit information, skills and technology to, and receive them from, component or raw material suppliers, subcontractors, consultants, service firms, and technology institutions. Such linkages affect not only the productive efficiency of the enterprise (allowing it to specialise) but also the diffusion of technology through the economy and the deepening of the industrial structure, both essential to industrial development (Cohen and Levinthal, 1989).

Technological capabilities have to develop both in scope and in complexity over time if a developing country enterprise is to grow and prosper. No firm can or should undertake the whole range of technical functions illustrated in Table 7.1. However, it must master those that are essential to its efficient operation and dynamic growth, while buying-in those capabilities provided more efficiently by specialised agents. Its investment capabilities should thus grow in terms of its knowledge of equipment and technology suppliers and its understanding of basic process design, but generally it may be efficient to leave equipment manufacture, process engineering, and construction contracting to others. In

TABLE 7.1 Illustrative matrix of technological capabilities

		FUNCTIONAL					
		INVESTMENT		PRODUCTION			
DEGREE OF COMPLEXITY		Pre-investment	Project execution	Process engineering	Product engineering	Industrial engineering	Linkages within economy
BASIC	SIMPLE, ROUTINE (Experience-based)	Prefeasibility and feasibility studies; site selection; scheduling of investment	Civil construction; ancillary services; equipment erection; commissioning	Debugging; balancing; quality control preventive maintenance; assimilation of process technology	Assimilation of product design; minor adaptation to market needs	Work flow, scheduling; time-motion studies; inventory control;	Local procurement of goods and services; information exchange with suppliers
INTERMEDIATE	ADAPTIVE DUPLICATIVE (Search-based)	Search for technology source; negotiation of contracts; bargaining suitable terms; info. systems	Equipment procurement; detailed engineering; training and recruitment of skilled personnel	Equipment stretching, process/r.m. adaptation and cost saving; licensing new technology	Product/quality improvement; licensing and assimilating new imported product technology	Monitoring productivity; improved coordination	Technology transfer to local suppliers; coordinated design; S & T links
ADVANCED	INNOVATIVE RISKY (Research-based)		Basic process design; equipment design and supply	In-house process innovation; basic research	In-house product innovation; basic research		Turnkey capability; cooperative R & D; licensing own technology to others

production capabilities, it should master the basic and intermediate levels fully to gain static efficiency; over time it should move gradually into original product or process design, even if it continues to import major innovations from industrialised countries. Passive reliance on others for all aspects of minor or major innovation can be costly and inhibiting; it can prevent the firm from diversifying its product range and from deploying its accumulated capabilities fully. The costs and uncertainties associated with capability building, however, rise with each further stage. The equilibrium established by each firm reflects its perceptions of its own potential and a number of external factors.

What determines the acquisition of firm level capabilities? The process involves a complex interaction between various factors (originating both within the firm and outside it), which may be grouped under three headings: incentives, investment and external support. Let us take them in turn. *Incentives* for undertaking capability-building efforts arise from the need to launch efficient and production and adapt to local circumstances, to meet competition in product markets, to cope with technological and other changes in factor markets, to comply with official regulations, and so on (see Katz, 1987; Dahlman *et al.*, 1989; Lall, 1987). The most important incentives, over the longer term, probably arise from competition and movements in the technological frontier.

Competition, particularly in international markets, provides the most basic spur to 'learning' and innovation, but it is a double-edged sword. Given the higher costs–lower quality that are inherent in the process of developing new capabilities, a full exposure to competition from mature firms can destroy a new entrant, especially from a developing country. The case for infant industry protection has a long and venerable standing in economic theory. It is based on the need to help firms bear their initial costs (when capital markets fail fully to finance these costs or when externalities reduce the full appropriation of the benefits) before they reach maturity. In much of the relevant theory, however, externalities are treated as trivial and 'maturity' merely involves reaching minimum economic scales of production while travelling down a predictable learning curve. This is a fairly mechanistic process, achieved by reaching a certain production volume, with no need for specific effort (or further investments), no uncertainty and no requirements of outside support or of measures to 'internalise' externalities. Given these assumptions, the learning period is brief, costless and foreseeable, and very similar across different activities. Such analysis gives rise to the policy prescription that where developing countries wish to give infant industry protection, the level of protection should be low (because the range of capabilities to be acquired is small), brief (because the process is short and predictable) and uniform across all manufacturing activities (because, by assumption, the process of maturity is the same in all technologies).

This is a misleading representation of the capability acquisition process, and so of the appropriate roles of protection and competition. The process is not mechanistic or predictable. It is based on additional efforts by the firm and calls for interaction and coordination with a host of other economic agents (which may be undergoing similar learning experiences). It does not end with achieving static efficiency (i.e., best practice levels of operation), but also encompasses the dynamic process of broadening and deepening the original core of capabilities. Moreover, the maturing process differs by technology, because of inherent differences in the levels and complexity of skills involved. It also differs by the level of development of the economy, because this affects the extent to which industrial skills, institutions and manufacturing linkaged (external support) already exist.

The need for protection may thus be longer than envisaged in standard theory, and it will vary by industry and country. What is more important, protection by itself may not be sufficient to achieve maturity: the firm itself has to be induced to invest in capability building, and external support and the growth of linked activities have to be adequate to its needs. 'Intervention' is thus a better term than 'protection' to describe what is needed. Protection may be one element of the intervention package, which would *also include some competitive inducements* to capability acquisition and the development of external support (discussed below). Inducements may thus include the threat of international competition, or an appropriate combination of international competition and protection (e.g., export activity with a protected domestic market, as practised by Japan and Korea). Protection by itself may be harmful if it merely removes such inducements and fails to provide other forms of support to uncompetitive firms. As the firm and economy mature, moreover, the need for intervention and protection declines because the base of capabilities expands and support mechanisms become fully institutionalised. Whether the case for intervention completely disappears is, however, an open question.

The *investments* needed for capability acquisition at the firm level involve physical capital, skill creation, technological effort and organisational functioning. Of these, only the first is usually taken into account, but clearly it is the others which allow given physical facilities to be operated efficiently. Skill development arises partly from simple learning-by-doing (i.e., production itself), but largely it is dependent on training. Technological effort covers routine technical activity as well as the search for new information, the integration of bought-in technology and formal R & D. Organisational investments include all the efforts needed to improve management and marketing.

External support for firm level capability development includes the supply of various types of generic as well as specific skills, the provision of physical infrastructure, the development of input suppliers, sub-contractors and service firms, an adequate technology infrastructure (such as industrial standards, quality assurance testing facilities, or basic research), a well-functioning financial system and an efficient administrative structure. Many of these factors are taken for granted in developed market economies, and simply assumed present by neoclassical analysts; they are critical to the efficient functioning of firms in a market setting but, as suggested below, they cannot be taken as given in developing countries.

It is important to note that it is the *interaction* of these three elements that determines firm level capabilities. Incentives without investments in capability acquisition or external support cannot call forth efficient production. Investments in capability development may be worth little if guided by the wrong set of incentives; or their value can be lessened if external support is deficient. Similarly, there is little point in mounting expensive external support systems if incentives are misdirected or if firms do not invest in their own capabilities. Let us now recast these micro factors to macro-level determinants of industrial development, and see how they explain recent performance.

7.4 NATIONAL INDUSTRIAL PERFORMANCE

We noted at the start that industrial success in the developing world tends, in recent literature, to be attributed largely to outward-oriented trade strategies, which are presented as being market driven and non-selective (i.e., non-interventionist in 'strong' or neutral and 'weak' forms). Since the empirical association between export-oriented strategies and industrial success is by and large quite persuasive, is the neoclassical explanation acceptable as presented?

It is argued here that it is not. The 'strong' version focuses only on *incentives*, which are taken to be given by free market prices, and implicitly takes as given the ability to respond to those incentives. The 'weak' version equates export-orientation with a neutral incentive framework, accepting the need for functional interventions but rejecting that for selective interventions. The previous discussion suggests that correct incentives are very important, but may not be given by market prices. Industrial development also depends on two other sets of factors: *capabilities* (at the national levels) and *institutions* that provide support to markets and to firm level efforts to acquire competitiveness. As at the firm level, the performance of industry at the national level is determined by the interaction between incentives, capabilites and institutions. Appropriate industrial policies are those that take account of potential market failures in each set of factors, and in their interaction.

It is relevant to note that this is the approach adopted explicitly or implicitly in explaining differences in industrial performance or productivity growth in the advanced industrial countries (OECD, 1987). Since incentive structures differ relatively little among OECD countries, and all are export-oriented, open market economies, persistent differences in competitiveness are explained with reference to 'supply-side' factors related to capabilities and institutions. Particular note should be taken of work by Nelson and Winter (1982, also see Nelson, 1981) and a recent commission headed, among others, by Solow (Dertouzos *et al.*, 1989), which traces the decline in US productivity to such factors. It is curious that the literature on developing countries, where these factors differ much more than among developed ones, has so far largely ignored supply-side considerations in favour of incentive factors. A sensible approach would be to integrate both.

Incentives

At the national level, the incentives considered most important for industrial development have been those arising from trade strategy and, secondarily, from domestic industrial policies (on internal entry and exit, concentration, ownership, employment and the like). The emerging consensus that outward-orientation and greater internal competition provide a healthier set of incentives for industrial development than inward-looking, competition-stifling strategies seems well founded (Pack, 1988; Bhagwati, 1988). *Ceteris paribus*, export-oriented economies are able to grow faster and achieve greater efficiency because they achieve static *and* dynamic comparative advantage to a greater extent. In initial stages, they can make greater use of their abundant factor (labour); they realise scale economies better as they move into more capital-intensive activities; their acquisition of capabilities is faster and healthier because it responds to international competition; and greater access to foreign markets provides a free inflow of information as well as enhancing the ability to buy new equipment and technologies (see also references given on pp. 118–19 on export-orientation).

However, export-orientation need not imply free trade or the absence of intervention. The earlier discussion suggested that there is a valid case for protection (as part of a larger intervention package) for those activities which had relatively complex technologies and needed exceptional effort and support to master. The need for protection arises because the gains from capability building are unpredictable and dynamic (and so are unlikely to be fully financed by capital markets, especially in developing countries), and also because there may be strong externalities (from technical and skill spillovers) and complementarities with other investments, which markets cannot take into account (Biggs and Levy, 1990; Pack and Westphal, 1986; Westphal, 1982). This furnishes a case for protecting strategic sectors as well as individual activities, since some sectors (like capital goods) may have greater externalities and complementarities than others. Despite the 'weak' neoclassical case, this protection need not be uniform across activities, low or brief. The ideal extent and duration of protection would depend on the technology and other characteristics of each activity. It would also vary by country, depending on the level of development of industry, markets and institutions: uniform prescriptions are not valid. Variable levels of protection are, under these conditions, not inimical to efficient resource allocation: on the contrary, they are (if ideally designed and administered) *necessary to restore efficient allocation*.

This is clearly not an argument for the high, prolonged, haphazard protection of the type afforded by typical inward-looking economies. Protection has to be selective and must be balanced, as far as possible, with the need to provide a competitive spur to capability acquisition. It is possible to combine the needs of protection during the learning period with those of competition, by promoting entry into export markets while sheltering domestic markets. Efficient selective intervention indeed requires that it differs significantly from the usual pattern set by import-substituting regimes. The latter are *not* selective: they protect all activities undertaken locally, for indefinite periods, with no discrimination by technologies or learning periods. They fail to provide competitive spurs to capability acquisition: they thus intervene non-selectively and uneconomically. By contrast, truly selective intervention, geared to achieving efficiency, can be used very successfully to promote industrial growth and diversification.

The experience of the NICs illustrates this nicely. Korea started from a small industrial base and built up a diverse, relatively high-technology industrial sector, with considerable backward linkages and 'deep' local capabilities. Hong Kong started with a long trading experience, a well-developed physical and administrative infrastructure and a large stock of experienced entrepreneurs and technicians. It built up a very flexible, but specialized, light industrial structure with low backward integration and little capability beyond production engineering and easy (as opposed to R & D based) product design. Korea had to use considerable, variable and often prolonged protection at critical stages, of both firms and sectors, to achieve its aims. However, it counterbalanced protection with strong pressures to export, supporting measures to build capabilities and institutions and with interventions to ensure that plants achieved minimum economic sizes

(Pack and Westphal, 1986; Amsden, 1989). Hong Kong managed with free trade. One strategy may not have been better than the other in an absolute sense. However, the Hong Kong strategy is probably not relevant for large economies that do not start with its peculiar advantages and that need to deepen their manufacturing sectors, by going into capital and intermediate goods production, in order to sustain and spread industrial growth. The Korean (and Taiwanese, see Wade, 1988), strategy of intervening selectively to build up new industries that quickly became export-competitive is much more relevant to medium and large developing countries that have to deepen their industrial structures. But the selectivity of protection and the emphasis on world competitiveness sharply distinguishes the East Asian strategy from that of inward-looking countries like Mexico, Brazil or India (or, indeed, most other developing countries). The model that the former followed was well tried and proven: Japan had expanded exactly by combining protection with aggressive export promotion. That of the latter has generally proved costly, inefficient and sluggish (on India, see Lall, 1987).

To conclude on incentives, market signals and competition are very important inducements to healthy industrial growth. However, the presence of dynamic learning sequences, externalities and underdeveloped skills and support systems in developing countries leads to market failure. This creates a case for selective government intervention, with variable, often high, protection of particular activities as one element of a larger package of policies (Biggs and Levy, 1990). The other elements are discussed below, here we merely stress the value of export orientation, but with caveats.

Capabilities

At the country level, capabilities can be divided into three: *physical investment, human capital* and *technological effort*. These three are strongly interlinked with each other, and interact in a way that makes it very difficult to identify their separate contributions empirically (see Nelson, 1981, on the related pitfalls of econometric growth accounting). They do not, however, always go together. Countries often experience imbalances in providing the different components of national industrial capabilities, with detrimental results. If physical capital is set up without the skills to operate it efficiently, production is high cost and productivity does not improve with time. If the skills are created but technological effort lags, the country remains unable to diversify and develop innovations; it becomes highly dependent on imports of technology, which could be expensive and constricting. If the skills and technological effort area increases but physical investment lags, human resources cannot be utilised in production, and so on.

The significance of *physical investment* is evident, and treated so centrally in conventional growth models, that it need not be taken up here at any length. The neoclassical school accords this adequate treatment, stressing the stimulation of healthy investment by the freeing of financial markets and setting of realistic interest rates, a stable and balanced macroeconomic framework and generally allowing competitive prices to guide investment. The importance of sound macroeconomic and financial management for providing the wherewithal and broad incentives for industrial development is evident. Where differences arise between the neoclassical approach and the practice of industrial policy in the NICs concerns selective intervention to guide investment into chosen industries.

The use of protective measures affects resource allocation as discussed earlier, but governments can directly control the flow of investible funds to support sectoral strategies. This would be regarded undesirable by those who believe in the efficiency of markets, but theory and practice again suggest that where prices do not give correct long-term signals because of uncertainty, information gaps, externalities or inadequate institutional development, selective intervention may be necessary to achieve dynamic progress. Investment allocation can then be used to back up promotional policies launched by offering infant industry protection. This is the strategy adopted by Korea, where directed credit and interest rate subsidies were extensively used to build up heavy industry and to share the risks involved with the large firms that were selected to lead the industrialisation effort (Pack and Westphal, 1986; Amsden, 1989).

Let us turn now to human capital and technology. Though there is a broad acceptance that the development of efficient industry requires a constant generation of skills, it is not always easy to trace the direct relationship between specific skills and efficiency or growth. Similarly, it is accepted that the assimilation and deployment of new industrial technologies requires technological effort, even by countries that rely on imports for the basic technological knowledge, but the link between such effort at the national level is diffuse. Nevertheless, econometric connections between skills and technology, on the one hand, and industrial growth and export success, on the other, have been established (see, in particular, Dean, 1984; Fagerberg, 1988; and the classic work of Harbison and Myers, 1964).

Let us consider *human capital* at some greater length (see Lall, 1990, for a longer discussion). The kinds of human capital that are relevant for industrialisation can be created in several ways and have different implications at differing levels of development. Basic literacy and primary schooling creates simple labour skills: this is relevant to all industrial functioning but, by itself, is probably significant only for initial low-technology, small-scale industrial activity (though even such activity requires a core of high-level technical and managerial skills). Higher levels of education, from secondary schooling to vocational training and university level technical–managerial education, become progressively important as the technical complexity of industry rises. More advanced, specialised training in scientific and technical fields grows in significance as industry approaches the frontiers of technology. Needless to say, the *quality* of training and its *relevance* to emerging industrial needs are as important as its quantity.

Formal pre-work education is only part of the story. The creation of human capital occurs also during employment. Some skills are acquired by simple production experience; others are created by on-the-job training and special arrangements for skill enhancement; others call for more formal training of employees in the firm or outside; and some skills are created by technological activity itself. As technologies grow more complex and fast moving, the role of employee training and retraining becomes more important in maintaining competitiveness. Developed countries spend increasing amounts on this function, sometimes (as in Japan) more than on the entire formal education system. Yet there are differences between them in the extent and quality of training which show up in their long-term industrial performance (see OECD, 1987; Dertouzos *et al.*, 1989).

The provision of basic formal education and the maintenance of its quality and relevance are generally accepted as a government responsibility: there is, in other words a strong risk of market failure in generating this capability. Even where private educational establishments are important, the financing of education in adequate quantity, especially in poor countries, involves intervention because individuals tend (due to externalities, risk-aversion and inadequate foresight) to under-invest in their own education. The provision of adequate employee training by firms may also involve intervention where firms under-invest due to appropriability problems (because they lose their trained workers to other firms). This is increasingly emerging as a problem in developed countries like the US and UK. In Japan, by contrast, the far lower rates of turnover enable its firms to have very high training investments without official support (OECD, 1987).

While the moderate neoclassical analyst would readily accept the need for intervention to generate human capital, 'strong' neoclassicals have tended to ignore this factor in their analysis of industrialisation. Even the former would, however, advocate only functional intervention, partly because of a simplified view of the needs of industrial technologies (only 'skills' in some generic sense are considered important), partly because of an assumption that market forces would summon the appropriate skill composition from the education system. In fact, the skill profiles of particular industrial technologies are highly specific and different from each other (Teitel, 1982). To produce the evolving structure and quality of skills required for future development entails information that the market may not possess, and involves uncertainty and investment. There may again be a case for selective intervention to ensure the production of new skills, which is greatly strengthened when the government is also intervening selectively in the pattern of industrial growth.

The association between human capital investments and industrial success can be illustrated from recent industrialisation experience. Table 7.2 gives some data on formal education on the four East Asian NICs, the two major Latin American NICs (Mexico and Brazil), India, two 'new NICs' (Thailand and Indonesia), and one of the most advanced of the SSA countries (Kenya). It shows that the East Asian NICs had a relatively strong human capital base in the mid-1960s, at the start of their export-oriented industrialisation drive. They had nearly universal primary enrolments. In secondary and tertiary education, Korea, Taiwan, and Singapore were substantially ahead of the others, while Hong Kong lagged, at near Indian levels. Over two decades, the East Asian lead, especially in secondary education, increased dramatically, with Korea and Taiwan pulling ahead of the others. Korea, in particular, put on a tremendous spurt in tertiary education, bringing it to OECD levels. Thailand also registered a massive increase in tertiary education, taking enrolments to 20 per cent of the relevant age group, second only to Korea. By contrast, Kenya had only 1 per cent of the age group enrolled in tertiary education, and 20 per cent in secondary education, by 1985: a small base on which to found industrial development. The number of tertiary students per 100,000 population further reveals the extent of the Korean lead (3606), with Taiwan (2080) some distance further behind, followed closely by Thailand (1998). These three, in turn, are far ahead of the other: Kenya's 114 is at the other extreme.

The remainder of Table 7.2 shows enrolments in technical education (at different levels of specificity) and vocational training. The figures are deflated by total and urban populations, since either may be considered the relevant skill base available to industry. In general, the lead of Korea and Taiwan is maintained throughout (except in engineering enrolments only, where Singapore surpasses Korea when deflated by total population). Singapore comes next, while Hong Kong trails the other East Asians, but is otherwise fairly high in the list. Mexico turns out a roughly comparable performance to Hong Kong, and always does significantly better than its neighbour Brazil. India is low in rankings by total population, but performs much better when ranked by urban population: it surpasses Singapore and Hong Kong in general science and engineering as well as the narrower category of natural science, mathematics and engineering education, coming just behind Mexico in the former and ahead of it in the latter. In pure engineering, however, it drops to Indonesian levels. Thailand turns up a startlingly high enrolment figure for general science and engineering, especially in terms of urban population; unfortunately, a more detailed breakdown is not available. Kenya, by contrast, has very low levels of technical training.

TABLE 7.2 Indicators of investments in human capital

	South Korea	Taiwan	Hong Kong	Singapore	Brazil	Mexico	India	Thailand	Indonesia	Kenya
Per cent Age Group Enrolled in:										
Primary Education										
(1965)	101	97	103	105	108	92	74	78	72	54
(1985)	96	100	105	115	104	115	92	97	118	94
Secondary Education										
(1965)	35	38	29	45	16	17	27	14	12	4
(1985)	94	91	69	71	35	55	35	30	39	20
Tertiary Education										
(1965)	6	7	5	10	2	4	5	2	1	0
(1985)	32	13	13	12	11	16	9	20	7	1
No. of tertiary students per 100,000 population (latest year)	3606	2080	1410	1406	1140	1508	776 a	1998	600	114
No. of tertiary students in GSE b_7 (000) (Year)	585 (1987)	207 (1984)	36 (1984)	22 (1983)	535 (1983)	563 (1986)	1443 (1980)	360 (1985)	235 (1985)	12 (1985)
As % of Population: Total	1.39	1.06	0.67	0.89	0.40	0.70	0.21	0.70	0.14	0.06
urban	2.02	1.36	0.72	0.89	0.57	1.02	0.97	3.90	0.53	0.30
No. of students in SMEc_7 (000)	320.6	151.7	27.5	16.2	323.3	336.9	1269.0	n.a.	137.3	4.8
As % of population: Total	0.76	0.78	0.51	0.73	0.24	0.42	0.19		0.09	0.02
urban	1.10	1.00	0.55	0.73	0.34	0.59	0.86		0.33	0.12
No. of students in engineering only (000)	227.6	128.7	21.1	15.4	164.6	281.8	397.0	n.a.	109.5	3.3
As % of population: Total	0.54	0.68	0.41	0.61	0.13	0.35	0.06		0.07	0.02
urban	0.78	0.85	0.42	0.61	0.17	0.50	0.27		0.27	0.08
No. of students enrolled in vocational training (000) (Year)	814.5 (1986)	404.6 (1984)	31.7 (1984)	9.4 (1984)	1481.0 (1985)	853.6 (1985)	397.7 (1981)	288.0 (1984)	1061.3 (1986)	7.8 (1985)
As % of population of working age	3.06	3.24	0.86	0.54	1.83	2.0	0.07	0.96	1.14	0.08

Notes: a 1980.
b General science and engineering fields: natural science, mathematics and computer science; medicine; engineering; architecture; trade; craft; transport and communications; agriculture, forestry, fishery.
c Natural science, mathematics and computer science, engineering.
Sources: World Bank (1988d); UNESCO, *Statistical Yearbook 1988* (Paris: UNESCO, 1989).
Government of the Republic of China, *Statistical Yearbook of Republic of China, 1988* (Taiwan, 1988)
Government of the Republic of China, Ministry of Education, *Educational Statistics of Republic of China* = (Taiwan, 1984).

As far as vocational training enrolments is concerned, Taiwan and Korea lead the group by a large margin, with over 3 per cent of their working populations enrolled. Mexico is next with 2 per cent, followed by Brazil with 1.83 per cent, Indonesia with 1.14 per cent, Thailand with 0.96 per cent, and Hong Kong with 0.86 per cent. Singapore's low figure of 0.54 per cent is misleading, because the government runs a large training programme for workers which is not included under vocational training; the programme is widely regarded as a model of excellence even in developed countries. India is also surprising in having an even lower rate than Kenya.

These data on education are not adjusted for the quality and curriculum content. Nor do they take into account completion or dropout rates. The very important skill creation that takes place by firm level training is also ignored for lack of information. Some scattered indicators suggest, nevertheless, that the general lead of the East Asian NICs (Korea, Taiwan and Singapore) is reinforced by these considerations (Lall, 1990). East Asia in general enjoys high completion rates relative to other countries. Korea emerges as second only to Japan in international tests of numeracy when a large sample of developed, and a few developing countries, are compared. It also enforces unusually high investment by firms (5–6 per cent of sales) in training.

Enrolment figures indicate the current 'production' skills, but do not capture the existing stock. Clearly, countries with larger stocks of technical manpower need smaller current rates of production, though the value of old stock deteriorates rapidly in a period of technological change if old skills are not constantly improved by retraining. Of the sample countries, the largest stocks of scientists and engineers (per million population) are in Hong Kong, 26,600, and Singapore, 14,300. Brazil has around 12–13,000, Korea 9,000, India 1–2,000, Indonesia 1,300, and Thailand and Kenya below 1,000 (these figures, from UNESCO, may be subject to wide margins of error). Recent figures on Mexico and Taiwan are not available, but are likely to be in 15–20,000 range. The combination of stock and flow figures would suggest that the four East Asian NICs are best endowed with technical human capital: of these, Korea has the highest rate of expansion, and, with Taiwan, probably the largest stock of 'modern' technical skills in place. Hong Kong has a large inherited stock, but is lagging in producing skilled workers and technicians. Thailand has a very small inherited stock but is adding to it extremely rapidly. Mexico has a respectable stock as well as creditable 'production' of skills. Brazil has a more modest record, while India has a relatively small stock and a poor 'production' record if the population as a whole is considered.

These inferences are fairly impressionistic, and it is not argued that there is a direct causal relationship from general human capital indicators to industrial performance. Nevertheless, the patterns revealed have interesting implications:

First, the 'star' industrial performers, the East Asian NICs, have a generally higher human capital base than other developing countries. Their formal education levels at the start of their modern industry drive were ahead of the others, and the lead has increased since then, particularly in secondary education. They have intervened both functionally and selectively to develop a base suitable for industrialisation.

Second, there are striking differences between the 'star' performers. Korea is drawing ahead of the others in tertiary education, especially in the general science and technology fields. Its selective interventions have increased over time to provide for specific advanced skills (Amsden, 1989). Taiwan follows it closely in secondary education, and is equal or better in and engineering education and vocational training. Singapore places less emphasis on vocational training but is at Korean levels in technical and engineering enrolments, and invests heavily in worker training. Hong Kong generally has a less technically trained workforce, but is still better qualified than industrial giants like Brazil or Mexico, and far ahead of India or Indonesia; it also seems to possess a large stock of scientists and engineers.

These patterns of human capital formation correspond to the relative strategies of industrial deepening and diversification of the East Asian NICs. Korea leads the developing world in its competitive prowess in heavy industry and high technology fields, with Taiwan a little behind in scale-intensive industries, but abreast (or ahead) in skill-based activities. Singapore is specialised in a few skill- and technology-intensive activities, but with a high dependence on foreign investors for technology (this shows up in its low technological investments, see below). All three need to practise a high degree of selective intervention in education and training to complement interventions in industrial structure. Hong Kong's industrial structure is dominated by technologically simple activities: it needs a fairly high level of human capital to maintain and upgrade its competitiveness, but does not have to add to it at the pace or level of specialisation needed by Korea or Taiwan. Hong Kong can manage primarily with functional interventions, though it does create some specific (e.g., textile design) skills. However, its unwillingness to promote training and provide selective support for new industries means that, according to a survey of its leading businessmen and academics, 'Today, Hong Kong does not have either an adequate skill base or the technology capacity necessary to build new comparative advantage in manufacturing at either the scale or speed that is required' (quoted in the *Far Eastern Economic Review*, 12 October 1989, pp. 64–5).

Third, turning to other large industrialisers, Mexico's relatively high level of human capital is not fully matched by its industrial performance. The explanation for this is likely to lie in its 'old-fashioned' protectionist policies, combined with a neglect of the local capital goods sector (which is the least developed of the large semi-industrial economies) and a heavy dependence on foreign technology unmatched by indigenous technological effort (see below). Brazil has a smaller human capital base but a more diversified and dynamic industrial sector, explained by its policies for developing heavy industry and a more aggressive technological strategy. However, it too suffers large areas of inefficiency and its overall competitiveness is far behind East Asian levels, a necessary consequence of its less selective incentive structure and relatively poor human resource levels. India is a more extreme example of this syndrome, with a far more distorted incentive structure (Lall, 1987) and general skill levels far below that of the East Asians. India does not fully utilise its existing high-level technical manpower in production, a reflection of its legacy of restrictive trade and industrial policies and of the very low skill levels with which a large proportion of small enterprises seem to operate. These countries also intervene in creating industrial skills, but it is the non-selectivity of their interventions and the inadequacy of their investments in skill formation that hold back their industrial performance.

To conclude, the pattern of industrial development in terms of efficiency and structure is clearly related to skill endowments. But skills only permit development: they must interact with an appropriate incentive structure to lead to dynamic growth. Export orientation provides the best set of incentives, if modified to protect and encourage industrial deepening and diversification.

Let us now consider *technological effort*. Trained labour becomes productive in industry only when it is combined with technological effort to master and improve on imported technologies. There are two aspects to this issue. The first relates to extent and direction of local investments in technology, the second to the extent and form of imports of technology.

The ideal measure of *indigenous technological efforts* would include a wide variety of technical, engineering, production, design and experimental work. Unfortunately, no data exist on such effort: the only available measures relate to formal R & D expenditures, which is a small, if significant, part of the total. Formal R & D is important for industrial efficiency and growth at higher levels of industrialisation, even for countries relying on imports for basic innovation. Available data (excluding Hong Kong, on which no information exists) are shown in Table 7.3, with Japanese figures given for comparison.

It is apparent that R & D intensities are strikingly similar to the human capital endowments revealed in Table 7.2. The most successful industrialisers, Korea and Taiwan, have invested heavily in R & D. Korea leads the sample (and the whole developing world) in total R & D deflated by GNP – it has also surpassed OECD countries like Spain, Italy, Austria, Denmark or Finland. By the year 2000 it plans to spend 5 per cent of GNP on R & D, exceeding current levels by Germany, Japan or the US. Its investments explain how it has attained a competitive edge, largely by national enterprises (see below), on a variety of high-technology, large-scale industries.

Total R & D figures include research unrelated to industry. The columns on R & D in the productive sector and financed by productive enterprises are more relevant to our purposes. The latter is perhaps the best indicator of genuine technological effort by industry, in that non-industry financed R & D (in official research centres) tends to be wasteful and largely irrelevant to production needs in most developing countries. These figures accentuate the lead of the East Asians, especially Korea, which has industry-financed R & D ratios over three times that of

TABLE 7.3   Research and development efforts in selected NICs and Japan

Country		Total R & D	R & D in Productive Sector (% of GNP)	R & D financed by productive enterprises	Scientists/ engineers in R&D per m population
South Korea	1987	2.3	1.5	1.9	1283
Taiwan	1986	1.1	0.7	0.6	1426
Singapore	1984	0.5	0.2	0.2	960
Brazil	1982	0.7	0.2	0.1	256
Mexico	1984	0.6	0.2	0.005	217
India	1984	0.9	0.2	0.1	132
Thailand	1985	0.3	n.a.	0.04	150
Indonesia	1984	0.3	n.a.	n.a.	152
Kenya	1975	n.a.	n.a.	n.a.	20
Japan	1985	3.5	2.4	2.7	4569

Sources: UNESCO, *Statistical Yearbook 1988* (Paris: UNESCO, 1989).

Government of the Republic of China, *Science and Technology Data Book* (Taiwan, 1987).

Government of Japan, Ministry of Science and Technology, *Indicators of Science and Technology* (Tokyo, 1986).

Ministry of Science and Technology, *Introduction to Science and Technology* (Seoul, Republic of Korea, 1988).

Taiwan, 19 times that of Brazil or India, nearly 50 times that of Thailand, or 380 times that of Mexico.

The last column shows data on scientists and engineers in R & D deflated by population. Taiwan at present exceeds Korea (and is at the level of France), but Korea's rate of expansion is more rapid. Both countries are severalfold higher than the large semi-industrial countries, and some 60 to 70 times higher than Kenya. This measure of the technical 'intensity' of R & D effort confirms the extent of the technological lead of the two East Asian NICs.

What accounts for this dispersion of technological effort among the sample countries? If export-orientation were the only determinant of R & D performance, the implication would be that governments should focus on trade strategy and let the appropriate technological response follow. The rigours of international competition do seem to call forth greater technological effort by the three East Asian NICs, especially in R & D by productive enterprises. But this is not the full explanation. The three NICs differ sharply among themselves, and Korea is in a class by itself. R & D intensity seems instead to be related to the depth and complexity of the industrial sector, the size of local firms and the emphasis on national ownership (discussed below). The 'heavier', more technology-intensive and nationally owned is manufacturing industry, the greater is the local effort required to achieve competitiveness, and the larger local firms need to be to mount that effort. The relative depth, complexity, ownership and firm size in the industrial structures of the three NICs are largely the result of selective government intervention and not of their outward orientation.

Governments have also intervened in the R & D process itself by providing tax incentives, institutional support, funding and direct guidance. Both Korea and Taiwan have extensive promotion programmes for industrial R & D: this is the functional side of their intervention. But they have also intervened selectively, not just via the promotion of infant industries, but also by investing in specific technologies, setting up research establishments in chosen activities, sponsoring particular research projects and so on (Wade, 1988). As with human capital, the adoption of a selective industrial promotion strategy entails selectivity in all the supporting elements.

Let us now consider *technology imports*. All industrialising countries import large amounts of technology, but their patterns of import differ greatly. In part this is due to differing rules and controls on buying knowhow and services abroad: the international technology market is subject to a spectrum of failures caused by asymmetric information, opportunism, missing or segmented markets and so on, and governments adopt a variety of measures to overcome such failures and help national enterprises to purchase technology on fair terms. In part, however, it is due to a more fundamental difference, on national technological strategy. This concerns the relative roles of foreign and local enterprise in building indigenous capabilities. There are striking variations across the leading semi-industrial countries in the extent to which they have drawn on foreign direct investment (FDI) to provide technology and skills.

FDI can, in appropriate conditions, be a very efficient means of transferring a package of capital, skills, technology, brandnames and access to established international networks. It can also provide beneficial spillovers to local skill creation and, by demonstration and competition, to local firms. Where local skills and capabilities are inadequate, FDI can sometimes be the only means to upgrade technologies and enter high-tech activities.

However, the very fact that FDI is such an efficient transmitter of packaged technology based on innovative activity performed in advanced countries can create problems (Lall, 1985, Ch. 7). With few exceptions, the developing country affiliate receives the *results* of innovation, not the innovative process itself. It, therefore, develops efficient capabilities up to a certain level, but not beyond: in the literature this is called the 'truncation' of technology transfer. Such truncation diminishes not only the affiliate's own technological development (i.e., the acquisition of capabilities classified as 'advanced' in Table 7.1), but also its linkages with the host country's technological and production infrastructure, and so beneficial externalities (Cantwell, 1989). Moreover, a strong foreign presence with advanced technology can prevent local competitors from launching risky, long-term efforts to deepen their own capabilities. For these reasons, countries with technological potential may find it preferable to restrict FDI and import technology in 'unpackaged' forms (including foreign minority-owned joint ventures). The choice of mode of technology imports is thus not neutral – some more beneficial than others for certain strategies and at certain stages of development. A selectively restrictive policy on FDI (this policy *has* to be selective, since it cannot be applied neutrally across all technologies) may be desirable when a country's objective is to develop and deepen its own technological base. If the objective is to develop industrially but not to establish an autonomous technological base, however, a country can pursue an open-door policy while providing functional support in the form of the skills and infrastructure needed continuously to upgrade the quality of FDI inflows.

The sample countries cover the whole range of FDI strategies. Table 7.4 sets out the latest available data on stocks of foreign investment in each country and deflates it by the value of GDP in the relevant year as a measure of the relative significance of FDI. It shows, at one extreme, very low levels of reliance on FDI by India and Korea, and, at the other, very high levels by Singapore and Hong Kong, and fairly high levels, among large countries, by Mexico, Indonesia, Thailand and Brazil. The interesting cases are those of Korea and Singapore, both successful NICs which have opted for opposing strategies on foreign capital.

Korea has developed the most advanced and competitive base of technological capabilities in the developing world, drawing on foreign technology mainly in non-equity forms (i.e., by capital goods imports, licensing and minority foreign ventures). In order to nurture this massive effort it has followed the Japanese example of some decades earlier – protection against imports, upgrading of skills, huge investments in R & D and the sponsoring of giant conglomerate private firms (the *chaebol*) to internalise various markets and so cope with the risks of undertaking advanced technological activity and the rigours of international competition.

TABLE 7.4   Stocks of foreign direct investment in selected developing countries

Country	Year of data	Stock ($ b)	% of GDP	Country	Year of data	Stock ($ b)	% of GDP
Korea	1987	2.8	2.3	Mexico	1987	19.3	13.6
Taiwan	1988	8.5	8.1	India	1984 (est.)	1.0–1.5	0.6–0.7
Hong Kong	1985 (est.)	6.0–8.0	20–26	Thailand	1986 (est.)	4.0–5.0	10.5–13.1
Singapore	1986	9.4	53.8	Indonesia	1987	7.9	11.3
Brazil	1987	28.8	9.6	Kenya	1984	0.6	12.0

Source: World Bank (1989d) Sec. 89–998; Lall (1990) World Bank (1989c); Ministry of Economic Affairs, *Statistics of Overseas Chinese and Foreign Investment* (Taipei, Taiwan, 1989).

The strategy may be characterised as one of 'protecting domestic technological learning', where the strategy is defined to include selective protection against imports and selective restriction of FDI, as well as positive measures to stimulate size of firm, education and R & D activity. Singapore, by contrast, has relied entirely on technology generated elsewhere, but intervened (selectively) to induce investors to move up the technological scale and (functionally) to provide a well-trained workforce. The strategy has worked well for Singapore – but whether it can be emulated by larger economies, and whether it will lead to a broad base for sustained industrial development (*à la* Japan or Korea) is open to question.

The case of 'protecting technological learning' by restricting FDI is relevant mainly for countries in the NIC phase. LDCs without the capabilities to mount a significant technological effort, would gain little technologically, and possibly lose a lot in terms of skills and know-how, by restraining FDI. Advanced industrial countries, which already have developed capabilities and institutions, would also gain little and might lose a lot by restricting capital inflows. In these countries, foreign firms often transfer the innovation function as well as the results of R & D, and competitive benefits and externalities may be strongly positive. As far as NICs with technological potential are concerned, however, the evidence clearly points to a case for restricting FDI to build up indigenous technological capabilities.

Institutions

The term 'institutions' is used here in a narrow sense. It does not include such basic institutions like the government, firms, banks, markets, or the fundamental rules of the game relating to property rights, commercial law and the like. It is intended to refer only to bodies set up to overcome specific market failures in the development of industrial capabilities.

Capabilities development can suffer from a variety of market failures in developing countries, particularly at the start of industrialisation (Stiglitz, 1989). For example, market failures can arise from the 'public good' nature of certain inputs (infrastructure, education, certain kinds of scientific research, industrial standards). They can arise from externalities in private activity (on the negative side, for example, pollution or suppression of capability building; on the positive, spillovers from training or research or technology flows in sub-contracting). They can also arise from imperfections in information markets. Unequal access to information by the two sides in technology contracts, absence of technology brokers, lack of trust or reputation in inter-firm transactions, or lack of information in providing credit can hamper or raise the costs of investments, importing technology or diffusing technology within the economy. The 'lumpiness' (large initial capital costs) of certain facilities like testing, quality control, and some kinds of basic R & D, may prevent their being set up by private agents unless there are institutional mechanisms to provide them or bring firms together on a cooperative basis. Or the unpredictability of dynamic learning sequences can lead private firms to under-invest in technological activity.

As development proceeds, countries tend to acquire solutions to many market failures. In some cases, specialised commercial intermediaries may appear in response to market needs; in others, manufacturers themselves may grow in size to 'internalise' deficient markets (the literature on multinational corporations treats their very existence as the internalisation of market failures in skills and technology). In other cases, however, market-driven solutions of this sort may take too long to develop, or may fail to appear at all. Government intervention may then be called for to provide remedies. Intervention can address the market failure directly, or can proceed by setting up specialised institutions to deal with specific problems. Interventions are probably better suited to one-off problems, while institutions are likely to be more efficient in addressing permanent needs to support markets. Institutions have the added advantage that they can be made autonomous, and can draw the affected private agents directly into their operation.

Scattered evidence suggests that the East Asian NICs, in particular Korea, Taiwan and Singapore, were the most assiduous and systematic in building institutions to support industrial development. They had advanced standards, quality assurance, training, information collection, technology diffusion, testing and research support institutes. They involved private industry in many such institutions, in particular those geared to penetrating foreign markets and importing and generating technology. Korea differed from the other NICs in that it deliberately fostered the growth of giant conglomerates to overcome various market failures in capital, technology and information markets. Taiwan developed largely with small and medium enterprises, but compensated by providing institutional support for technology import, adaptation, generation, and diffusion. Some observers believe now that the Taiwanese model is proving less efficient than the Korean in entering high risk areas of advanced electronics technology (Mody, 1989), but it has proved extremely effective in meeting less rigorous needs.

Other industrialising countries have also provided broad institutional frameworks and direct intervention to support industrial development. Some institutions may have been very effective; their overall impact has, however, been diluted (in comparison, say, to Korea or Taiwan) by several factors: efficient institutions could not achieve the same results for lack of a proper incentive structure for industry; the institutions themselves were not as well conceived or staffed (perhaps reflecting deficiencies in general skill availability); they were not given sufficient autonomy or internal incentives, or were unable to forge the necessary links with industry; or institutional objectives were not clear and consistent. It is difficult, by the nature of the subject, to evaluate institutional performance in this general way. It is even more difficult to distinguish the impact of institution building on the industrial development that resulted, since institutions were only one of the determinants of industrialisation. The main point at issue here is to establish that institutional support is an integral part of industrialisation strategies.

7.5   CONCLUSIONS

This essay has provided a general framework for analysing industrial development and policy. It has suggested that industrial success cannot be explained by a few selected variables, such as outward-orientation or laissez-faire, but only by a combination of several forces that interact with each other in complex ways. Partial explanations run the risk of misinterpreting the evidence and drawing the wrong implications for policy: this has certainly been the case with the literature on industrialisation in developing countries. The emphasis on 'getting prices right' and reducing intervention by the 'strong' incentive-based approach has led analysts to minimise the role of capability and institutional factors, and to ignore the role of the state in *getting* the prices right and in *remedying market failure* in developing capabilities, *both functionally and selectively*. The experience of the East Asian NICs has provided the empirical fuel for the incentives based approach – yet a closer examination of their experience supports a different explanation.

In this explanation, incentives do matter, and export-orientation (suitably designed to protect infant industries and technological learning) does emerge as superior to inward-orientation. But successful industrialisation is the outcome of the interplay between incentives, capabilities and institutions, not simply concentration on one to the exclusion of others. At the firm level, the process of achieving competitiveness is neither automatic nor costless; it takes time, directed technological effort, new skills, the development of complementary activities and an external network of information and support. It involves risk and considerable uncertainty, especially in early stages of development. Incentives affect the pace of capability development and its direction and content.

At the national level, different combinations of incentives, human capital, technological effort and institutional development seem to produce different kinds of industrial performance. One set of factors cannot by itself produce sustained, broad-based, competitive growth. Just getting proper incentives in place will be better, *ceteris paribus*, than having an inward-oriented, uncompetitive regime, but will not promote industrial upgrading and diversification (even if infant industry protection were given) if technical skills, management, technology and institutional support are not simultaneously improved. Kenya cannot become a Korea only by adopting outward-looking strategies. Simply creating skills, performing R & D or setting up institutions will, on the other hand, be counterproductive if the necessary incentives are lacking. And the incentives themselves must be fashioned to remedy market failures that inhibit the development of complex and risky industries and capabilities.

Government policy thus affects all three components of industrial development. Take *incentives*. Many incentives for industrial activity arise directly from macroeconomic policies and the trade and industry strategies adopted. A consensus is emerging on the trade and industry policies that promote healthy industrialisation. These are largely taken to be market-oriented policies that promote competition, specialisation by comparative advantage, and free flows of technology and capital internationally. However, it is recognised that there can be serious failures in the provision of correct signals from free markets (Stiglitz, 1989). The existing configuration of prices and costs may not be a reliable guide to future competitiveness where there are externalities, complementarities, potential learning gains (especially if backed by capability-building efforts) or other market failures. Earlier discussion has pointed to the need for interventions in international investment and technology markets.

This analysis suggests, therefore, that there may be little theoretical or empirical justification for some currently common policy prescriptions. Given inherent differences between technologies and national capabilities, there is no strong reason (except administrative convenience) to recommend uniform, low rates of protection as a standard measure. Some activities, or entire sectors, may need much higher protection and capability-building support than others, depending on their technical requirements and the cost of measures taken to develop necessary capabilities. The ideal extent and structure of protection will differ by country: there is no valid case for proposing general rules applicable to countries at differing levels of development. Similarly, strategies on foreign direct investment, the promotion of heavy industries or the fostering of particular types of industry structures may legitimately differ across countries. There are many grounds for concern about the *efficiency* of actual interventions of this sort; but this may constitute a case for strengthening informational and administrative capabilities, and for instituting safeguards against excessive intervention, not for rejecting selective interventions out of hand. Much of the earlier cost of intervention by import-substituting countries results from the *non-selectivity of there strategies, not from their selectivity*. It is plausible that in an export-oriented framework their efforts to promote activities selected for their economic potential would have borne much greater fruit. 'Picking winners' may not be as difficult as is often made out if governments foster a broadly competitive environment and confine choices to a fairly general level of selectivity (i.e., to industries or sets of activities rather than to particular products or firms). There may be high pay-offs to finer levels of selection, but the capabilities needed to implement such selectivity (as in Korea) may be outside the reach of most developing countries.

As far as *capabilities* are concerned, there is perhaps more agreement on the need for policy interventions to promote physical and human capital development and technological effort. However, the interventions needed may be selective as well as functional if industrial strategy itself is geared to realising specific forms of dynamic comparative advantage. Many developing countries invest heavily in education, training, and ambitious science and technology programmes, but not always effectively. The facilities set up are often of poor quality, irrelevant to the needs of industry, or operated in a way that is totally divorced from productive activity. This is where the setting up of appropriate *institutions*, geared to the specific needs of industrial efficiency, becomes significant. The development of autonomous, specialised institutions, with proper structures of control and incentives, can be critical to the building and deployment of industrial capabilities through the economic system. Governments can play a central role in promoting, encouraging, or directly setting up such institutions. As with capabilities, institutional promotion may be selective as well as functional.

The above is not meant to suggest that there is a single optimal path to industrial development for all developing countries. Some differences in viable strategies are given by the 'state of nature': size, resource endowment or location. Small countries are not, other things being equal, handicapped by their size, but the sorts of industries they can set up and the technological options they can pursue differ from those for large countries. But there are other differences in possible strategies which depend more on choices of policy-makers than on the 'state of nature'. The extent and pace of industrial deepening, for example, is a strategic variable for the policy-maker: this determines, in turn, the pace and content of human resource development, incentives needed via protection or credit allocation, requirements for technical support or infrastructure, and so on. A country which (like Hong Kong) chooses to specialise in light industry needs to invest heavily in (generic) human capital, infrastructure and some (selective) support for likely export activities, but it needs to intervene less (and less selectively) in other ways than one which aims for heavy industry of particular types. Similarly, the desired extent of national ownership or indigenous technological capability (the two are closely linked) determines the need for efforts on local skill creation and R & D.

The four East Asian NICs thus represent four different models of industrial development because of their differing choices on certain strategic variables: the promotion of selected industries or of selected enterprises, fostering of particular types of industrial structures, reliance on domestic as opposed to foreign ownership of industry, and development of an indigenous base of technology and skills. It is an open question which set of choices constitutes an ideal long-term development strategy. What is evident is that *many strategies are viable*, each based on a different combination of incentives, capabilities and institutions, and each carrying its own set of concomitant interventions. Accepting that efficient markets are the optimum all developing countries should aim at, there are many ways that different countries can 'plug into' markets effectively, depending on their ability to alter their endowments of skills, technology, knowledge and institutions.

The choice of a less selective set of interventions (*à la* Hong Kong) reduces the risks of backing expensive losers, but it has its own demands and drawbacks. To achieve something approximating the industrial success of Hong Kong, a government would need to intervene to build up a comparable base of skills, entrepreneurship, trading knowhow and infrastructure. To enable competitive new activities to emerge without selective promotion, furthermore, the government would have to intervene to create new skills, technologies and institutions. If the objective is to establish a deep and diverse industrial structure (as is relevant for medium to large economies), such functional measures would have to be very extensive indeed. It may even be the case that dynamic industrial development with non-selective interventions would place *greater* demands on administrative capabilities (to mount functional interventions) rather than less. If such capabilities were lacking, the process of development may be slower or more lopsided than with a package that included careful selective interventions. The achieving of static comparative advantage with minimum of interventions is not an objective any policy-maker would opt for – achieving dynamic growth has no simple or easy (e.g., just 'getting prices right') answers.

In the final analysis, therefore, a large role remains for government policies in promoting each of the three determinants of industrialisation. How well or badly governments perform this role depends on the availability of administrative skills, the nature of political ideology and the play of political forces in each specific case. In some instances, a market solution may be more efficient than intervention where 'government failure' is more damaging than market failure (Biggs and Levy, 1990). The evidence suggests, however, that *well directed intervention is not just compatible with sustained development, it is necessary*, and that such intervention should be *selective as well as functional*.

8 New Trade Theories and Developing Countries

DAVID GREENAWAY

8.1 INTRODUCTION

Conventional wisdom has it that international trade is driven by inter-country differences in factor endowments or factor productivity. The former is formalised in the celebrated Heckscher–Ohlin–Samuelson Theorem (HOS), the latter in the equally important (but less influential) Ricardian Theorem. Although these theorems are often discussed in general terms, one senses from the literature a presumption that they are particularly applicable to explaining the trade flows of less developed countries (LDCs). It can be readily seen why this presumption emerges. After all, many LDCs depend heavily on exports of primary products which tend to be natural resource-based. Moreover, some empirical evidence suggests that the trade flows of LDCs, particularly north–south trade flows, are driven by differences in factor endowments or factor productivity, (see for instance Leamer, 1981).

The 1980s, however, saw an extraordinary transformation in the way in which economists think about international trade. A vast literature has emerged which emphasises the role of market imperfections such as oligopoly, non–constant production costs, product differentiation and so on (for an overview, see Greenaway and Milner, 1986). Theories have been developed to illuminate the circumstances under which these factors will be important. Again this work tends to be 'anonymous' in nature, but the implicit presumption tends to be that these factors will be more important in explaining the trade flows of developed market economies

(DMEs) than those of LDCs. Empirical evidence has focused primarily on DMEs, and does suggest that a substantial proportion of DME trade may be explained by these factors.

Is this 'paradigm specialisation' by country type justified? Is it appropriate to link HOS and Ricardian theory largely to LDC trade, and the new theories largely to DME trade? This essentially comes down to two questions, the role of HOS–Ricardian theory in DME trade, and the role of the new theories in explaining LDC trade. This essay concentrates on the latter, and it is organised as follows. Section 8.2 briefly outlines the principal characteristics of the new theories and considers whether, in principle, they could explain trade flows of LDCs. Section 8.3 examines the evidence currently extant on intra-industry trade (IIT) in LDC trade flows. This is necessary since it is presumed that intra-industry trade is driven by the factors explored in the new theories. Section 8.4 is more normative in orientation and addresses the policy implications of the new theories in a LDC context. Section 8.5 offers some concluding comments.

8.2 THE NEW TRADE THEORIES

It has long been recognised that market imperfections like monopoly, scale economies and product differentiation are pervasive features of the real world. Since HOS and Ricardian theories assume these away it has been recognised that alternative theories incorporating these features of the real world are necessary. In the late 1960s and early 1970s, there were a number of attempts to model these features, (e.g., Corden, 1967; Gray, 1973). These and other attempts were however model-specific and not readily generalisable. But it was the later contributions by Dixit and Stiglitz (1977) and Lancaster (1979) which provided the foundations for the subsequent extraordinary growth of the literature dealing with these and other features. The importance of these contributions was in providing a theoretical framework for dealing with scale economies and product differentiation in a general equilibrium setting. Since then a truly vast literature has emerged. It is impossible, and in fact unnecessary, to summarise this literature in the space constraints available. Instead we shall simply pick out its main features.

Before we do pick out these features, however, one important point should be noted. This is as follows: 'new trade theories' for our purposes refers to the post-1979 literature on imperfect competition and international trade. We are therefore quite deliberately excluding the literature associated with the neotechnology models associated with the work of Posner, Vernon and others. This is not because it is unimportant; on the contrary these models, particularly Vernon's product cycle model, yield important insights into the trade flows of developing countries. The factors stressed by the recent imperfect competition literature are, however, qualitatively different to those associated with the neotechnology models. Moreover the latter have been more extensively explored.

'Imperfect competition' is a term which describes a very wide range of states. One way of categorising such states is by reference to whether the market in question sustains a 'small' or a 'large' number of firms. 'Small' and 'large' are used here in an economic rather than any absolute sense. 'Smallness' in the number of firms thus implies market power and interdependence; 'large' numbers implies price-taking behaviour. One advantage of this distinction is that we can then think of the small numbers cases as short-run or blocked entry scenarios, and the large number cases as long-run or free entry scenarios. Both settings can then be refined to incorporate different kinds of scale economies and different kinds of product differentiation (see Greenaway, 1987).

Predictions regarding the commodity composition and direction of trade flows clearly depend upon the precise features of the models being used. Some factors are, however, very robust with regard to model specification. Economies of scale is one such factor. Decreasing costs in production are an important determinant of trade across a very wide class of models; decreasing costs allow producers located in different countries to specialise in different varieties/model ranges and thereby gain comparative advantage in these varieties/model ranges. The nature of the production function determines the extent of the scale economies, and this in turn has an important bearing on market structure. Production conditions thus dictate a small number of large producers of wide-bodied jets, but a large number of small producers of running shoes. This obviously has a bearing on the way firms interact with each other. The important point, however, is that scale economies offer a potentially important source of gains from trade.

Another factor emphasised in the new theories on trade is product differentiation. Products may be horizontally differentiated (pens with blue and red ink), or vertically differentiated (plastic pens with blue ink and gold pens with blue ink). If consumer preferences differ across economies, there may be a potential basis for trade in vertically differentiated commodities. As with scale economies, the nature of the product differentiation will have a bearing on market structure. Again, however, the important point to note is that product differentiation offers another potentially important source of gains from trade.

In addition to scale economies and product differentiation other features which are more model-specific also have the potential to influence the evolution of trade flows. For example, strategic interaction between producers located in different countries can under certain circumstances result in trade *independently* of scale or product characteristics; the presence of multinational firms may also stimulate such trade; and the ability of firms to price discriminate may be relevant. We must ask, however, what is the relevance of all this to developing countries? Much of the interest in the new theories stems from the fact that their trade policy predictions are heterodox – they evidently provide new arguments for protection which may be applicable in LDC context. These arguments need to be assessed on their own merits. Clearly, however, the empirical relevance of the new theories also needs to be assessed, in order to evaluate whether these are explanations of trade which are likely to have wide applicability. We will first review trade policy aspects, and then evaluate the empirical evidence.

8.3 STRATEGIC PROTECTION

A whole host of arguments for intervention/protection have emerged from the new trade theories. Inevitably, given the structure of the underlying models, many of the arguments are model-specific and not robust to variations in these assumptions. Since many of the arguments are likely to have limited applicability in the context of most LDCs (like gains from protection that appear to be driven by greater product variety, Lancaster, 1984), we will concentrate on the two arguments which have circulated most widely, and which some commentators have claimed may have applicability in the context of LDCs. These are the external economies and rent-snatching arguments.

External economies

The first of these arguments is predicated on the assumption of positive externalities – that is, beneficial spillover effects in an industry. Where such external economies are important significant benefits go unpriced, reliance on the market is likely to result in underprovision of the good or service in question. Now the idea of externalities being an important market imperfection necessitating government intervention to counter the distortion is not a new one; economists have long accepted the validity of such a case. Nor is the use of external economies as an argument for intervention in the traded goods sector in a LDC new. Johnson (1968) articulates a 'new view' of the case for infant industry protection, which is also developed by Baldwin (1969). This goes beyond the mere presence of scale economies, the existence of which is not in itself sufficient to make a case for intervention, to examine the role of first-mover disadvantages. Specifically, potential investors to an industry benefiting from scale economies may be deterred from entry by fears of non-appropriability of their returns on investment in human and physical capital. Thus the first mover may for instance invest in training industry-specific labour; once fully trained, a new entrant could 'poach' this labour from the first mover. As a result, the first mover bears all the costs of training the labour, but reaps none of the benefits. If this is a widespread perception among potential investors then it constitutes a case of systemic risk, and the infant industry may not emerge.

In the context of LDCs this has been widely accepted as a possible market imperfection. As Baldwin (1969) correctly concludes, however, although it may be a valid argument for intervention, it is *not* a valid argument for protection. Import protection would have several byproduct distortions, and would not necessarily counter the imperfection. Some alternative intervention, like a training subsidy, would be more efficient.

What, then, is 'new' about the external economy argument in the new theories? Basically, this: there are many human capital-intensive, knowledge-based industries/sectors which are potentially strategically important, which may make this particular line of argument more widely applicable than hitherto thought. The sectors most often mentioned in this regard are information technology, semiconductors, artificial intelligence, and biotechnology. These are industries where learning effects are crucially important, and where the benefits from investment are spread widely in society. There may be first-mover disadvantages: even where investment takes place, the industry size could be sub-optimal due to externalities (in other words, an insufficient number of firms will enter the industry); if overseas producers enjoy the benefits of government support for their activities whilst home firms do not, this will provide them with a strategic advantage in both the home *and* overseas market – import protection results in export promotion (Krugman, 1984). Government support allows the firm to expand output and thereby move down its scale curve. As a result, average costs fall providing it with a competitive advantage at home and abroad. For any one, or some combination, of these reasons, it can be argued that government should intervene to promote the industry in question.

It can be argued that the knowledge-based, human capital-intensive industries which analysts have in mind are crucial sectors in the development process in LDCs in general, and NICs in particular. Moreover, the success with which new technology is absorbed has a crucial bearing on comparative advantage. Some LDCs and NICs have already established an international presence in such activities. Korea, for instance, not only assembles microprocessors, but also manufactures semiconductors. Moreover, Korean manufacturers reportedly have research programmes under way to establish a presence in the next generation of semiconductors – dynamic random access memory chips (DRAMs). India has established an international market presence in the provision of software services. In both cases these activities confer wider benefits on society at large; in the Korean case, the rapid evolution of the industry to one where it can conceive of competing at the frontier may, it can be argued, be attributable (at least in part) to government support for the industry. Such support should therefore be more widely available in LDCs. The validity of this line of argument will be considered later.

Rent-snatching

The so-called rent-snatching argument is, superficially at least, a new argument for protection arising from the work of Brander and Spencer (1982; 1984). As we shall see, however, it too has a familiar ring to it. This argument begins with the existence of rents, or supernormal profits, in a market. The simple theory of monopoly tells us that we can expect to find rents in highly concentrated markets. This is well known and empirical evidence suggests that rents are indeed a common feature of highly concentrated markets.

What do rents have to do with protection? After all intuition suggests that the presence of rents in domestic markets most probably provides a case for trade liberalisation – competition from imports is a very effective mechanism for constraining the market power of a domestic monopolist. This is one mechanism by which rents are dissipated in a competitive economy. More generally, one could argue that so long as governments ensure that barriers to entry do not arise, there is no need to worry about rents, the market takes care of the problem.

Suppose, however, that rents cannot be competed away. There may be circumstances where this is the case; production technology may be such that the market can support only a small number of producers operating profitably. Call this number n. If entry occurs and we have $n + 1$ producers, *all* make losses. This could be the case in technologically advanced sectors where product development costs are enormous, and learning economies important. Sunk costs and learning economies create a market structure which is naturally duopolistic or oligopolistic. If such a market were confined within given national frontiers then regulation could be used to secure some of the rents. Suppose, however, that the relevant market is international. In these circumstances intervention could be used to redistribute rents from one country to another.

The basic idea behind this kind of intervention is quite simple. Suppose we have an international market which can support only one firm operating profitably. Suppose further that there are two potential entrants to this market, A and B. Which one of them will survive depends upon the outcome of the competitive process. In duopoly situations, outcomes are difficult to predict because of the problems created by strategic interdependence. In the simplest of game theoretic settings where the firms behave according to Cournot rules, Brander and Spencer (1982) demonstrate how government intervention can have a decisive impact on the eventual equilibrium. Thus, the government of the country in which '*A*' resides could provide its firm with a production subsidy which ensures that whatever firm *B* does, *A* survives operating profitably. Whereas both *A* and *B* make losses if both enter in the absence of intervention, with intervention only *B* makes losses if both enter. The subsidy therefore allows *A* to pre-commit itself to production whatever *B* does. Clearly this increases the probability that *A* will be the successful survivor. If this were so, rents will accrue to the home country which exceed the value of the subsidy. The intervention has succeeded in redistributing income internationally, raising real income in *A* and lowering real income in *B*.

It can be argued that where LDCs have the opportunity to enter markets with these kinds of characteristics, governments should be willing to consider intervention as a basis for helping the firms in question to pre-commit. Baldwin and Flam (1989) have argued that just this kind of intervention has been successfully implemented by Brazil in the market for 30–40-seater aircraft where its national producer (Brazilia) competes with firms from industrialised countries – Saab from Sweden and De Havilland from Canada.

The applicability of these new arguments for protection/ intervention in LDCs can be evaluated in two ways, first by considering how applicable the new trade theories are to the explanation of trade flows in LDCs; second, in the light of this, by evaluating the intrinsic merit of the arguments themselves.

8.4 INTRA-INDUSTRY TRADE IN DEVELOPING COUNTRIES

Assessment of the relevance of the new theories to LDCs requires identification of the widespread presence of scale economies and product differentiation. This, however, is easier said than done. One can, however, get some idea of the existence of these characteristics by evaluating the extent of intra-industry trade in these countries.

There does not exist an exact correspondence between the potential for imperfectly competitive market structures to result in trade and recorded intra-industry trade. This is so for the simple reason that factors like scale economies and strategic interaction can also result in inter-industry trade. However, theory suggests that scale economies and product differentiation are more likely to be associated with intra- than inter-industry trade. Moreover the econometric evidence on the determinants of intra-industry trade currently extant suggest a causal relationship between product differentiation, scale economies and market concentration and intra-industry trade. In evaluating the evidence on intra-industry trade and developing countries, and intra-industry trade and development, we can thus draw some inferences about the relevance of the new theories to LDCs.

Studies of intra-industry trade fall into two broad categories, documentary and econometric. The former simply records the incidence of IIT at a given level of aggregation whilst the latter attempts to identify the determinants of a given level, or change in, IIT. A number of documentary studies have concentrated on LDCs, including Willmore (1974), Balassa (1979), and Havrylyshyn and Civan (1985). The last of these is the most recent and most comprehensive. Table 8.1 reports information on IIT in some 41 LDCs. For purposes of comparison these are broken down into NICs and non-NICs. In addition, for comparative purposes, information on IIT in 18 industrial countries is also included. Several features of Table 8.1 are notable. First, average levels of IIT are highest in the trade of industrial countries (almost 60 per cent). Since scale economies and product differentiation are common characteristics of manufacturing activity in these countries, this is much as one would expect. Second, IIT in some NICs has reached levels in excess of the industrial country average – Singapore and Israel for instance. However, the average IIT for NICs is significantly less than that for the industrial countries. Third, average levels of IIT are lowest for the non-NIC LDCs, coming out at under 15 per cent. This gradation has been confirmed by other bilateral studies. Lundberg (1982) found that Swedish IIT with NICs in 1977 was 17 per cent, whilst that for non-NIC LDCs was 8 per cent. It would seem, then, that IIT is relatively unimportant in non-NIC LDCs but of growing importance in the trade flows of NICs.

TABLE 8.1 Intra-industry trade indices by country, 1978, %

Non-NIC developing countries				NICs		ICs	
Algeria	1.5	Kenya	13.9	Argentina	42.3	Australia	25.3
Cameroon	6.1	Malawi	6.6	Brazil	37.8	Austria	74.1
Central African Rep.	0.7	Malaysia	32.4	Greece	21.1	Belgium-Lux.	79.2
Chile	10.1	Morocco	10.9	Hong Kong	40.8	Canada	66.9
Colombia	20.0	Nigeria	0.2	India	37.4	Denmark	67.0
Costa Rica	32.4	Pakistan	14.8	Israel	61.9	Finland	45.4
Dominican Rep.	6.9	Peru	10.3	Korean Rep.	34.9	France	80.3
Egypt	6.8	Philippines	15.0	Mexico	31.9	Germany	62.7
El Salvador	33.0	Senegal	18.7	Portugal	32.8	Ireland	61.3
Ghana	4.3	Sri Lanka	4.8	Singapore	66.9	Italy	59.0
Guatemala	32.7	Sudan	0.8	Spain	52.1	Japan	26.0
Guyana	19.6	Thailand	17.3	Taiwan, China	34.7	Netherlands	74.2
Haiti	46.3	Trinidad	14.3	Yugoslavia	50.7	New Zealand	25.9
Ivory Coast	13.4	Tunisia	17.3			Norway	44.4
Jamaica	14.4	Turkey	7.9			Sweden	68.3
Jordan	14.9					Switzerland	59.5
						UK	81.0
						USA	59.4
		All non-NICs	14.5	NICs	42.0	All ICs	58.9

Source: Havrylyshyn and Civan (1985) p. 260.

The finding that IIT is more important in NICs than non-NIC LDCs implies that the importance of IIT increases as development takes place. This certainly is what intuition would suggest. As we have already noted, scale economies and product differentiation tend to be features of the manufacturing sector, which grows in relative importance as development takes place. In addition, the demand for manufactures in general, and differentiated goods in particular, tends to be income elastic. Econometric evidence tends to back up this intuition; a range of studies have provided evidence to support a link between *per capita* income and IIT in LDCs, for example Tharakan (1984) and Balassa and Bauwens (1988). This suggests that as LDCs move up the 'ladder of development' the scope for intra-industry specialisation and trade increases both in their 'North–South' and 'South–South' trade. This has certainly been the experience of the NICs. With human and physical capital accumulation, the structure of their trade has altered; they have evolved from being predominantly exporters of natural resource-intensive manufactures (like textiles, clothing and footwear), to more capital and skill-intensive manufacturers (like consumer electronics and engineering products). It is this latter stage which has created the most potential for IIT growth. Since the new generation NICs, or NECs (new exporting countries), appear to be following a similar pattern of evolution we can expect to see IIT become increasingly important to developing countries. Havrylyshyn and Civan (1985) further examined the link between factor intensity and IIT and found that in the NICs in their sample IIT was more likely to be recorded in capital-intensive than labour-intensive product lines.

We have commented parenthetically on the direction and commodity composition of IIT in developing countries. This is worthy of further comment. With regard to direction, IIT figures in both North–South and South–South trade. The former is particularly prevalent in NIC trade and to some extent is a reflection of trade in vertically differentiated commodities (i.e., commodities differentiated by quality). It is also a reflection of increasing trade in parts and components. South–South intra-trade is partly trade in primary commodities (see Greenaway and Milner, 1986), and partly trade fashioned by integration arrangements. A number of analysts have noted the tendency for IIT to be higher among countries which are party to some kind of integration arrangement, in both industrialised and developing countries (Willmore, 1974; Balassa, 1979; Balassa and Bauwens, 1988). This phenomenon has been linked to the lowering of trade barriers and the resulting ability to exploit scale economies. Much of the trade which occurs is in foodstuffs, but also includes some trade in parts and components.

To summarise then on empirical evidence: it would seem that IIT is less important in developing countries than in industrialised countries, as we would anticipate from economic theory. However it is of growing importance in the trade of NICs. Among non-NICs some portion of what is recorded as IIT is trade in primary products and foodstuffs; by contrast, recorded IIT in NICs appears to be predominantly trade in intermediates and finished manufactures produced by relatively capital-intensive methods. Finally, the evidence suggests that as industrialisation proceeds and *per capita* income rises, IIT becomes increasingly prevalent. This clearly suggests that this is a phenomenon which will become more important in the trade of developing countries.

8.5 THE RELEVANCE OF THE NEW TRADE THEORIES

What, then, is the relevance of the new trade theories to developing countries? The new trade theories provide us with a framework for systematically incorporating factors like scale economies and product differentiation into models of trade. This is important since we know these to be common features of the real world. Both theory and evidence relating to IIT suggest that these tend to be characteristics of the markets for manufactures. We would not therefore expect these determinants to be of paramount importance in the trade of the least developed LDCs. By contrast, we would expect them to become more important as industrialisation proceeds. Empirical evidence suggests that this is indeed the case. The new trade theories do have an increasingly important part to play in explaining the direction and commodity composition of the trade of the more developed developing countries (i.e., the NICs), and will have an increasingly important part to play in the future determination of the direction and commodity composition of those economies which are currently non-NIC developing countries.

This being so, what is the relevance of the new theories for protection? Are they likely to provide a widely applicable justification for intervention in LDCs? The answer to this is probably not, for several reasons. First, the new arguments for protection suggest that there may be net benefits from protection in particular circumstances. These circumstances are, to say the least, specific, particularly in the case of rent-snatching intervention. Notwithstanding the fact that one empirical analysis suggests gains from rent-snatching in a NIC (Baldwin and Flam, 1989, the market for 30–40 seater commuter aircraft), this argument is probably wholly irrelevant to the vast majority of developing countries. In fact, a cynic would say that this particular argument has been custom built for the aerospace industry. External economies, the other argument for protection, may however be a more prevalent feature of the real world. But as earlier analysis has demonstrated, these typically do not provide a justification for protection, but for some other form of intervention (such as R & D or training subsidies). Moreover, these arguments ignore the more general benefits of free trade. A number of studies have now addressed the issue of the gains from free trade in an imperfect competition setting (albeit in the context of industrialised countries). Many of these studies suggest that the gains from trade in a setting of imperfect competition may be significantly in excess of those typically associated with the 'conventional' gains from trade – largely due to the influence of scale economies (see Cox and Harris, 1985).

A second set of reasons for being cautious about these new arguments for protection revolves around political economy factors. For example, how does one identify sectors where the most important external economies exist, or where the greatest potential for rent-snatching is available? This is a serious practical problem, and since many developing countries do not have a happy record when it comes to picking winners, it is a problem which is not to be taken lightly. In addition, the evolution of protectionist regimes in many developing countries confirms that demonstration effects are extremely influential. One may find that many industries claim potential external economies, or a potential for rent-snatching (in just the same way as many industries the world over appear currently to suffer problems of 'dumping'). Governments do not always find it easy to resist such pressures.

Moreover, once protection/support is granted, it may not result in industry expansion, but rather in higher rents to the industry incumbents. The prevalence of rent-seeking behaviour in many developing countries suggests that this is certainly a realistic possibility. Rent-seeking, as we know, serves to increase the costs of protection.

Overall, then, there are compelling reasons for doubting whether the new arguments for strategic protection are likely to be widely applicable in developing countries. There are grounds for suspecting that they may provide another case for intervention which simply serves to encourage rent-seeking behaviour, and incrementalism in the formation of policy. Since a growing amount of evidence suggests that this kind of policy posture is damaging to economic performance, this gives grounds for caution (see Greenaway and Nam, 1988). Note, however, that this is *not* to argue that there are no convincing arguments at all for *intervention* in developing countries; there no doubt are such arguments. Of the new arguments one, rent-snatching, does not add to the list of persuasive arguments; the other, external economies in knowledge-based–human capital-intensive infant industries may do. When it does, however, it is likely to provide a case for some kind of intervention other than protection.

8.6 CONCLUDING COMMENTS

In this chapter we have examined the new theories of international trade, the new arguments for protection which appear to be associated with these theories, and the relevance of these developments for developing countries. We have seen that these new theories emphasise common features of real world industrial structures, like scale economies and product differentiation. The new arguments for protection suggest that these features of industrial structure may give rise to potential gains from intervention hitherto unrecognised. Our examination of the empirical evidence suggests that whilst these new theories are of less relevance in developing countries than in industrialised countries, they are not totally irrelevant to developing countries. Moreover, as development proceeds they will become increasingly relevant. As we saw, however, this does not imply that the new arguments for protection are, or will become, valid in developing countries. The potential gains from such protection are realisable only in very specific circumstances, whereas the potential gains from trade in imperfectly competitive markets may be both substantial and widespread. If anything, the new trade theories thus reinforce rather than undermine the case for open trade policies in developing countries.

9 Managing the Debt Legacy: Approaches to Resolution

P. N. SNOWDEN

9.1 INTRODUCTION

By the end of 1987 the total external indebtedness of developing countries exceeded $1 trillion, or half of their combined GNPs. Associated debt service payments amounted to roughly one-fifth of annual earnings from the export of goods and services. After allowing for new lending, LDCs were making *net* transfers to private and official creditors of between $9 and $10 billion annually after 1984 (World Bank, 1988d).

Sections 9.2 and 9.3 examine the origins of this burden, and its culmination in the 1982 debt crisis, while sections 9.4 and 9.5 trace containment policies to 1987. Section 9.6 is devoted to subsequent events with a focus provided by the 'Brady initiative' of March 1989. The initiative advocated debt reduction, and thereby implied official recognition that LDC commercial debt may not be sustainable on the contracted terms. The potential and limits of debt reduction will be noted in conclusion, in section 9.7.

9.2 THE POLITICAL ECONOMY OF EXTERNAL DEBT

Data on the stock of debt and associated ratios are presented in Table 9.1[1], for all LDC debtors, Sub Saharan Africa (SSA), comprising 43 countries, and for Latin America (LA), representing 27 countries in the Americas and the Caribbean. These two

TABLE 9.1 Outstanding debt, selected years

US $ million.	1970			1975			1982			1987		
	ALL	SSA	LA	ALL	SSA	LA	ALL	SSA	LA	ALL	SSA	LA
1. Outstanding public and guaranteed debt *	49536	5374	15992	126151	13932	45275	460201	52603	176078	905851	103,874	338,506
Of which												
(a) Official	33449	3644	8253	71732	8934	16203	203420	30674	39983	436572	73804	97472
(b) Private	16087	1730	7669	54420	4998	29072	256781	21930	136095	469279	30071	241034
Of which												
Financial markets	8325	695	4559	40237	2863	24146	230175	18270	129969	430469	24886	233128
2. Non-guaranteed debt	16641	308	11873	35878	790	22707	102262	3900	62271	90429	5437	34551
Ratios (%)												
Outstanding debt ÷ Exports	83.5	61.2	83.9	69.2	58.1	95.7	98.0	137.8	141.06	164.3	292.2	275.0
Official debt ÷ Outstanding debt *	67.5	67.8	52.0	56.9	64.1	35.8	44.2	58.3	22.7	48.2	71.1	28.8
Concessional terms debt ÷ Outstanding debt *	55.8	58.5	37.7	42.0	49.5	17.4	24.9	37.7	7.0	21.6	37.0	5.5
Variable interest debt ÷ Outstanding debt	1.7	0.9	4.0	19.5	10.1	37.7	38.9	20.9	62.3	43.6	21.7	68.3

Note: ALL = All LDC.
SSA = African South of Sahara.
LA = Latin American and Caribbean.
Source: World Bank (1988c)

regions represent the geographical foci of the 1980s' debt problem. While Latin America's debt is of far greater magnitude, African figures are similar in relation to exports or GNP. There are, nevertheless, major differences between the principal creditors.

Even in 1970 almost half of Latin America's outstanding debt comprised private loans; bank loans (dominating the financial market category) were already important (Table 9.1). This category expanded dramatically until the early 1980s with the result that less than a quarter of Latin America's debt by 1982 was accounted for by official bilateral and multilateral borrowings. The declining relative importance of the official sector also occurred in SSA, although much less markedly. The figures suggest that whereas the rapid build-up of private market debt in Latin America occurred throughout the 1970s, Africa experienced similar rates of accumulation only after 1975.

It is noteworthy that the accumulation of private market debt was not closely linked with the oil price shocks of 1973–4 and 1979–80. Although bank lending had been growing rapidly until 1973, especially to Latin America, there was a pause in 1974 (Stanyer and Whitley, 1981, ppp. 191–2). After 1975 growth of bank intermediation resumed, coinciding with improvements in the terms of trade of LDCs. This was certainly a key factor in the growth of private market lending to SSA, for which it is estimated that the terms of trade improved by 74 per cent between 1972 and 1981 (World Bank, 1989a p. 11). Although most of this improvement was enjoyed by the five oil exporting countries the beverage exporting economies also experienced some gains in these years. The result was that some countries found themselves able to borrow substantial sums from the commercial banks in the late 1970s and early 1980s (Green, 1988, p. 247). The optimistic reappraisal of African export earnings appears to have affected official flows as well. Non-concessional export credits involving interest rates based on the borrowing costs of the official export credit agencies were especially important in the growth of African debt at this time (World Bank, 1988d).

This brief interlude of enhanced African creditworthiness was to have a substantial effect on the *terms* as well as the quantity of the accumulated debt. Table 9.1 shows a significant decline in the proportion of public and publicly guaranteed debt that attracted concessional terms between 1970 and 1982. The proportion involving market related (generally variable) interest rates accordingly increased. Although the experience of the more developed African economies largely accounts for these developments, 'Low Income Africa', experienced a weaker version of the trend.[2] For Latin America, the hardening of the terms of credit arose primarily from that continent's longer-lived access to the private capital markets, rather than from a change in the nature of official financing. This general shift towards non-concessional variable rate debt was to be the key development in triggering the 1982 debt crisis (World Bank, 1985, p. 20).

While improved terms of trade enhanced the developing countries' ability to service debt, other factors connected with developments in international financial markets increased the supply of external finance in the 1970s, albeit at commercial rates. The development of loan syndication allowed 'syndicates' of commercial banks to share in individual loans, thereby avoiding the need for any one institution to absorb an uncomfortably large, risky, asset on its balance sheet. Subdued economic growth following the oil price-induced recession in the OECD economies in the mid 1970s coincided with high bank liquidity and produced pressure to seek out new lending opportunities. Given the floating interest rate nature of their wholesale deposit liabilities, however, the banks were obliged to advance their loans on similar terms; the risk that interest rates would rise over the duration of the loan was passed on to the borrowing country, and was to materialise in an intense form in the early 1980s (World Bank, 1985, esp. Ch.8).

On the demand side of the loan market, countries borrowed for complex reasons. Green characterises SSA borrowing during the period 1973–5 as initially designed to ameliorate the economic effects of drought as well as oil import and other terms of trade shocks (Green, 1988). The increasing recourse to commercial borrowing in 1976–9, he suggests, was intended primarily to finance the enhanced rate of economic growth which took place in those years. Borrowing in 1980–2 was again motivated by oil price-related shocks for importing countries. However, although external shocks had a role in determining African credit demand, domestic policy deficiencies were probably prolonged by the temporary availability of external finance. Throughout much of the 1970s, SSA's share of worldwide exports of the ten non-oil primary commodities thus declined almost continuously (World

Bank, 1989a, p. 10). The key policy influence on this trend was an unwillingness to depreciate the exchange rate in line with relatively high domestic inflation (World Bank, 1989a, p. 20).

The net effect was to discourage production for export by fixing the local currency value of exports (sold at world market prices) in the face of rising domestic costs. The oil and mineral exporting economies were particularly negligent of the interests of farmers as their exchange rates became increasingly overvalued. In consequence, declining agricultural exports, as well as food imports in some cases, exacerbated external payments deficits and the associated need for finance. From a political economy viewpoint, it has been argued that the urban support base of many African regimes produces an imperative for low food prices; a reluctance to devalue the exchange rate would be consistent with this interpretation (Bates, 1981).

Retrospective studies of Latin American borrowing strongly suggest the supremacy of political determinants of country demand for external credit rather than oil-related factors. Oil exporting Mexico and Venezuela have, for instance, experienced external debt crises. The characteristic inflation of the continent has been argued to reflect a perennial struggle between competing socioeconomic groups for shares in national product (Baer, 1987). Governments have only tenuous legitimacy and seek to placate the groups which support them by spending programmes, despite severe constraints on the raising of tax revenue. In this context, money creation is used to 'close' the budget deficit and the resulting inflation acts as an unlegislated tax on money holdings. The largest third world debtor, Brazil, provides an appropriate illustration.

In the face of the oil import price increases of 1974, the Brazilian authorities shrank from imposing the terms of trade loss directly on politically important groups of oil product consumers. Consumption subsidies therefore contributed to a widening budget deficit which had to be financed by foreign borrowing and traditional money creation (Baer, 1987; Dornbusch, 1985a). High levels of domestic spending, combined with cruzeiro overvaluation, exacerbated external deficits and associated foreign borrowing in the late 1970s. A particular priority of the Brazilian authorities appears to have been to avoid unleashing violence in the *favelas* of Rio de Janeiro and São Paulo. When the finance minister Simonsen proposed a contraction of domestic activity in 1979 he was sacked and replaced by the expansionist Delfim Netto (Berg and Sachs, 1988).

Political factors of this type seem to have fuelled much of the Latin American borrowing. Mexico, (the second largest debtor), which preceded Brazil into debt crisis in 1982 had sought to avoid social conflict through heavy government spending during the 1970s. Populist programmes combined with an inability to tax powerful and rich elites to produce budget deficits when oil revenues weakened in the early 1980s. In this case, also, the deficits were financed by foreign borrowing. Such domestic policy constraints, rather than differential vulnerability to external disturbances, seem to distinguish Latin America and the successfully adjusting economies of eastern Asia.

Whereas Korea's debt to GNP ratio was greater than that of Brazil in 1981, far more of the Korean borrowing financed investment in the export sector. Asian governments appear to have avoided the large-scale public sector deficits so commonly a reason for external borrowing and inflation in Latin America. With domestic finance under control, Asian currencies were managed to maintain external competitiveness. In contrast, Latin American exchange rate overvaluation discouraged export expansion and aggravated the need to protect domestic industries against import competition. This exchange rate policy orientation could be explained by the relative importance of rural rather than urban interests in Asian politics. The former gain both as exporters and through more favourable access to imported inputs (Sachs, 1985).

The Sachs study stresses that the smaller budget deficits did not occur as a result of a smaller *size* of the public sector in Asia; the important difference was the willingness of Asian countries to raise the tax revenues necessary to finance public expenditures without excessive inflation. It is suggested that such fiscal prudence was facilitated by relatively egalitarian income distributions in East Asia which minimised distributional conflict over the financing of public expenditures. These, in turn, were often used to expand the capacity of the export sector.

In Korea, as earlier in Japan and in contrast to much of Latin America, pervasive import controls and preferential access to credit were used to shelter and finance nascent export sectors rather than to protect profits of chronically inefficient domestic producers (Dornbusch and Park, 1987). The consequence of this interventionism was a decline in the ratio of external debt to exports and the avoidance of a debt crisis despite the external shocks which were to be administered in the early 1980s.

9.3   DEBT DYNAMICS AND THE 1982 CRISIS

The endemic fiscal crises outlined above suggest that an external debt crisis would have been likely whenever foreign resource inflows were interrupted. To explain why this latent crisis materialised in 1982, it is useful to clarify the factors which help to determine the stability (or otherwise) of the process of debt accumulation. If a country is to sustain a net inflow of resources, it must receive finance to cover both the interest payments on its current debt and an excess of imports over exports; these together comprise the current account of the debtor's balance of payments:

$$\text{Current account} = iD + (M - X) \tag{9.1}$$

where i is the average interest rate, D the debt stock outstanding, and the bracketed term reflects the excess of imports over exports. If the country is experiencing an excess of foreign direct investment inflows (FDI) over capital exports (CE) on the capital account of the balance of payments, not all of the current account deficit will have to be covered by new borrowing. The stock of debt will therefore rise each year as follows:

$$dD/dt = iD + M - X + CE - FDI \tag{9.2}$$

Simonsen (1985) defines the 'resource gap' as $G = M - X + CE - FDI$. Thus:

$$dD/dt = iD + G \tag{9.3}$$

Dividing this expression throughout by D yields the growth rate of nominal debt:

$$\dot{D} = (1/D)(dD/dt) = i + G/D \tag{9.3a}$$

From the creditor's point of view, the debt to export ratio ($r = D/X$) was commonly regarded as an indicator of a country's creditworthiness. Differentiation of this ratio, r, with respect to time yields the following expression:

$$dr/dt = (D/X)(\dot{D} - \dot{X}) \tag{9.4}$$

Substitution of equation (9.3a) above into (9.4) yields an expression for the evolution of the debt–export ratio as shown in Table 9.1:

$$dr/dt = (i - \dot{X})(D/X) + G/X \tag{9.5}$$

The intriguing feature of expression (9.5), in terms of the sustainability of debt accumulation, is that an *indefinite* positive resource inflow is compatible with a *constant* debt–export ratio. Net repayments may not be necessary if the rate of growth to export earnings (X) exceeded the average interest rate on loans (i). If this condition is specified in 'real' terms it suggests that the real resource inflow (positive G) will ultimately be financed from a growing stream of export earnings which the borrowing country is generating. Expressing the same relationship in nominal terms, however, can lead to a quite different interpretation. In this case, growth of export earnings may simply reflect a rate of world inflation to which loan interest rates have not fully adjusted. On this view, the resource inflow reflects a real gain to the borrower financed by an unanticipated erosion of the real value of existing debt in the hands of the creditor. Whereas the former basis could indeed justify an indefinite inflow of resources, the latter would be sustainable only until financial markets had fully adjusted to inflation.

However interpreted, the condition specified was temporarily met in the inflationary global circumstances of the 1970s. Between 1970 and 1979 representative interest rates averaged 10.3 per cent, whereas the export earnings of non-oil LDCs grew at an annual average rate of 20.2 per cent in $ terms (Dornbusch, 1985b). Inflation, by cutting interest rates in terms of the growth of export earnings, ensured that the 1970s provided excellent conditions for external borrowing. This era was ended, however, by the shift towards contractionary monetary policies in the USA, and other major economies, after 1979. The associated rise in world interest rates (to around 12 per cent) was transmitted through floating rate loan contracts to the debtor countries. So was the ensuing world recession with the three categories of countries identified in Table 9.1 experiencing *falling* nominal export earnings in 1982 and 1983.

In these changed circumstances continuing net resource inflows (a positive G) were not compatible with stable debt ratios, as expression (9.5) makes clear. Creditors responded by refusing to renew maturing loans and Mexico, particularly affected by declining oil export receipts, inaugurated the debt crisis by declaring her inability to make principal repayments due on her debts. While the transition to disinflationary monetary policy in the major economies was therefore the key external element in the 1982 crisis, continuing inflation within the borrower economies was to make a significant contribution. Domestic inflation, and the eventual exchange rate devaluation which it presaged, represented a tax on wealth denominated in domestic currency and a consequent inducement to the export of capital. Foreign currency denominated assets do not face such risks; nor do foreign *lenders* whose claims are also denominated in external currencies (Dooley, 1988a).

This incentive structure suggests that external borrowing and debt accumulation may continue alongside capital export initiated by residents. Usually described as 'capital flight', (*CE* in expression (9.5)), one estimate suggests that the outflow may have amounted to around $113 billion between 1977–87 for the four major Latin American debtors (Morgan, 1988, p. 9)[3] This sum would amount to a significant fraction of the accumulation of Latin debt displayed in Table 9.1 with the bulk of the outflows occurring between 1976 and 1982 (Morgan, 1986, p. 13).

With lenders unwilling to 'roll over' the principal on maturing debt, the 1982 crisis reflected the inability of countries to maintain the service payments to which they were contractually committed. Creditor fears of *insolvency* were behind the *illiquidity* crisis of 1982. Insolvency would arise when the present value of the future foreign exchange receipts available to service external debt fell short of the present value of the contracted obligations; on this interpretation, continued new lending could lead only to an indefinite rise in ratios such as that determined by expression (9.5). Conversely, lower world interest rates and improved export earnings prospects could end insolvency as defined above.

9.4   CRISIS MANAGEMENT 1982–7

Debt–export ratios deteriorated until 1987 with export earnings growth and interest rates clearly significant in the trend. Table 9.2 indicates stagnation or decline in the former and only a slow decline in the latter during the 1980s. In these adverse circumstances debt–export ratios could have been stabilised only by the generation of sufficiently large trade surpluses, a need accentuated by continuing capital flight and the stagnation of foreign direct investment inflows (FDI) which was almost certainly associated with the debt crisis itself (OECD, 1988, Table 111-1). In the absence of such surpluses, new loans would be needed to finance some of the contractual interest charges. The ratio in equation (9.5) would therefore rise suggesting, in effect, a partial capitalisation of interest payments due.

This was to be the strategy of creditors following the 1982 crisis; an especially appropriate strategy if debtor difficulties were thought to arise from a temporarily hostile external environment. The view that the major Latin American debtors were in this position receives some support from Table 9.2. The figures show *actual* flows and reveal that Latin America made substantial *net* transfers of funds in the years since 1983 (with net repayments on non-guaranteed private debt particularly significant in the initial two years). While trade surpluses financed part of the loan service payments (the true 'debt burden') new lending also ensured that debt–export ratios continued to rise. It is also clear from Table 9.2, however, that SSA was only able to make positive net transfers in

1985. In consequence, and despite the greater importance of concessional funds in this case, debt–export ratios continued to deteriorate severely. For the 34 Low Income countries, external debt amounted to approaching 500 per cent of exports in 1987 (World Bank, 1989a, p. 16). Many of the countries in this group have solvency problems beyond those imposed by world conditions (Green, 1988, p. 248).

Why did lenders allow this situation to arise? In retrospect, the ready access of African countries to private and official non-concessional finance in the late 1970s and early 1980s was based on an excessively optimistic view of the prospects for the continent's export earnings. The effect of the change in world monetary conditions in the early 1980s was to provoke a belated reassessment of this view and, consequently, a severe restriction on access to new financial resources in 1982–5. The response of bilateral and multilateral donors was to shift more of their concessional aid flows towards the African countries, and to reschedule concessional and non-concessional debts through 'Paris Club' negotiations.[4]

Typical negotiations in the 1970s and 1980s offered countries 10 years to repay their rescheduled loans with a five year grace period. In 1987, some countries became eligible for 20 year repayment and 10 year grace periods (World Bank, 1988d, p. xliv). Rescheduling agreements covering concessional loans were at concessional rates with the longer repayment periods adding to the concessionality. In the case of non-concessional debt, however, interest rates on the rescheduled loans remained non-concessional. Even the growing willingness of some donors to forgive some or all of their concessional loans was insufficient to resolve the underlying insolvency of many of the African countries. Between 1980 and 1988, 25 SSA states, being unable to sustain the previously agreed terms, rescheduled their debts 99 times (World Bank, 1989a, p. 17).

While reschedulings do not generally add to the volume of debt in the statistics of Table 9.1, arrears of payment are incorporated as an increase in debt outstanding, and this element was to become highly significant in the 1980s. Whereas the data of Table 9.2 imply that new official inflows were helping to fund net transfers from Africa to private overseas creditors for much of the decade, it is equally true that the figures reflect *actual* rather than *contractual*

TABLE 9.2 Debt-related financial flows in the 1980s

	1980	1981	1982	1983	1984	1985	1986	1987
SSA US $ millions								
Disbursements of public and guaranteed debt	9,673	9,856	11,185	9,207	7,057	6,476	7,642	7,699
– Principal repayments	2,153	2,375	2,569	3,085	4,062	4,954	3,643	2,793
= Net flows	7,521	7,481	8,616	6,122	2,994	1,523	3,999	4,906
– Interest payments	1,920	2,120	2,415	2,531	2,878	3,101	2,239	2,442
= Net transfers	5,600	5,361	6,202	3,591	116	–1,578	1,760	2,464
of which								
Official	3,173	3,243	3,541	3,621	2,311	1,420	2,458	2,871
Private	2,428	2,118	2,660	–30	–2,195	–2,997	–698	–407
Reference items								
Exports goods and services	57,445	46,926	38,182	35,641	38,926	38.609	33,181	35,543
% Average interest rates (new loans)	7.1%	8.3%	7.6%	7.0%	5.5%	6.0%	5.2%	3.4%
Latin America (US $ millions)								
Disbursements of public and guaranteed debt	30,955	37,138	38,540	28,567	24,606	18,631	17,925	18,604
– Principal repayments	14,202	14,455	13,457	11,240	10,592	9,939	11,468	11,454
= Net flows	16,753	22,683	25,083	17,328	14,013	8,691	6,456	7,151

− Interest payments	12,873	15,494	18,841	18,611	20,528	22,739	22,038	19,852
= Net transfers	3,879	7,190	6,242	−1,238	−6,515	−14,048	−15,582	−12,701
of which:								
Official	2,376	2,969	2,996	1,909	2,825	2,076	1,892	−190
Private	1,504	4,220	3,247	−3,192	−9,340	−16,124	−17,473	−12,511
Reference items								
Net transfers *including* non-guaranteed debt	5,526	16,262	2,140	−10,002	−16,431	−22,143	−21,935	−18,611
Exports of goods and services	128,176	140,463	124,355	118,846	132,028	125,790	110,024	123,085
% average interest rates (new loans)	11.6	13.9	12.6	10.7	11.1	9.1	8.4	7.6

Source: World Bank (1988c)

flows. In the later 1980s, some African governments were easing their foreign exchange shortages by deliberately accumulating arrears of principal and interest to private as well as to official lenders. By 1987, these arrears were obstructing the provision of new official finance by preventing the conclusion of economic stabilisation programmes with the IMF, a precondition imposed by creditors for rescheduling or the provision of new loans.

These circumstances induced a significant shift in the position of official lenders from the end of 1987 when both the IMF and the World Bank launched programmes specifically tailored for the needs of poor African countries. In July 1988, at their Toronto 'summit' meeting, the G-7 countries adopted a new programme towards low income debtors which included provision for forgiveness of debt, the refinancing of non-concessional loans on concessional terms and longer maturities (World Bank, 1988d, p. xxxxciii).

Whereas these changes recognised an African 'solvency' problem, the international community had a clear interest in choosing not to draw the same conclusion for Latin America. At the end of 1982, nine major US banks had loans outstanding to Latin America which represented 176.5 per cent of their combined shareholders' capital and reserves (Sachs, 1986). Were these loans to be written off as unpayable, the statistic implies that some major banks would themselves have been technically insolvent. The spectre of an international banking crisis produced a swift response to the Mexican announcement and the fluctuating fortunes of that country were to be central to the later development of international policy on debt management.

9.5   COMPROMISE AND CONFLICT: FROM MEXICO TO BRAZIL

The US and European governments provided $14 billion of emergency funding to Mexico while the IMF supplied a $4 billion credit. In this, and later cases, the Fund had a key role in dealing with a potentially serious market 'failure': the reluctance of individual banks to commit new funds. General failure to do so would have obliged Mexico to default on *existing* loans as service payments could not be met out of current surpluses. The solution was for the Fund to insist on rescheduling and the provision of new funds from banks in proportion to their existing 'exposure' (loans) to Mexico (Gurria, 1988). The reward for the banks of this regimentation was that the Fund agreed an economic stabilisation programme with Mexico which would allow all external debt to be serviced on commercial terms. The Mexican debt would therefore be regarded as 'performing' by bank regulators, avoiding the need for heavy loan loss provisions out of current profits. Moreover, interest payments received would be counted as profit earned.[5]

The IMF programme sought to produce the necessary external surpluses by curtailing the rate of growth of Mexican credit. The Fund has traditionally emphasised the connection between domestic monetary expansion and external payments deficits which, in the LDC context, focuses attention on the monetary financing of government budget deficits. The Mexican programme accordingly attacked the budget deficit by a cut of one-quarter in real public spending between 1982 and 1985. Partly by rationalising (raising) the prices of goods and services supplied by the public sector, the budget deficit was brought down from 17 per cent of GDP in 1982 to 'only' 6 per cent by 1985 (Villarreal, 1988). Further policy actions included the continuous devaluation of the peso in an effort to promote non-oil exports. In producing the required external surplus the policy was highly successful; Mexico generated a trade surplus of $13.8 billion in 1983. With export earnings unchanged, however, this result arose from a collapse in imports as GDP fell by 5.3 per cent in real terms during that year (Villarreal, 1988).

Notwithstanding these internal costs, Mexico was to persist throughout the 1980s with structural reforms and a cooperative stance towards her creditors. Indeed, at the height of the 1982 crisis, the country continued to pay interest due despite the opportunity taken by creditors to raise the latter on the new and rescheduled amounts noted above. Cooperation was rewarded by reduced borrowing costs following a major multi-year rescheduling arrangement in 1984 (covering $48 billion of loans due for repayment between 1985 and 1990). 'Enhanced surveillance' over Mexico's economic policies by the Fund was the basis for new 'concerted' bank loans. The expectation was that these would help Mexico to resume economic growth with non-oil exports making a key contribution on the basis of a competitive peso exchange rate. Although such exports grew rapidly, the recovery in 1984–5 depressed the trade surplus below the necessary interest payments. Moreover the depreciation of the currency contributed to inflation and the latter helped to boost fiscal deficits. By September Mexico breached the IMF targets as Mexico City suffered two devastating earthquakes (Gurria, 1988, p. 88).

Despite these extraordinary complications the authorities planned a contractionary budget for 1986 only to experience a collapse of oil export prices in February. The period until July was devoted to negotiating new finance from the commercial banks as well as from the IMF on the basis of a further agreement with the Fund. With the shortage of foreign exchange helping to cut GDP by 3.8 per cent during 1986, Mexico sought to obtain an agreement which would finance a resumption in economic growth. The July agreement with the Fund was a landmark in explicitly recognising a growth objective for GDP of 3–4 per cent per annum for 1987–8. In addition, the objective was to be insured against Mexico's vulnerability to oil price fluctuations by compensatory financing inflows if the oil price fell below $9 per barrel (Villarreal, 1988, p. 56). Additional provision was made for 'pump priming' public sector expenditures if the economy failed to reach the growth targets. Internally, and in recognition of its domination of budget deficits since 1984, the agreement adjusted the Fund's fiscal objectives for Mexico to allow for the impact of inflation on government interest payments. The agreement was worth over $12 billion in new funds with the contingent elements adding a further $2.4 billion. The commercial banks were to provide over half with the balance from the IMF, the World Bank and other official sources.

Final success for the agreement was achieved only after considerable pressure from the American authorities had been exerted on the reluctant commercial banks. The latter were disquieted by the magnitude of new finance involved and the apparent slackening of IMF fiscal disciplines. Although concluded only in March 1987, the agreement was seen by the Americans as the first manifestation of the 'Baker initiative' which had been launched by the US Treasury Secretary in Seoul in October 1985. This plan had envisaged the provision of $25 billion of new money from the World Bank (together with the Inter-American Development

Bank) and an equal amount from the commercial banks to support a resumption of economic growth in fifteen major debtor countries over a three year period. The initiative had been provoked by the mounting political resistance in these countries to IMF stabilisation measures which had been widely associated with the recessionary consequences of the type noted above for Mexico (World Bank, 1988d, p. xviii). Instead, the Baker approach had envisaged 'adjustment with growth' in which debtors would receive the new capital to support their external payments as growth resumed. In return, borrowers would carry out structural adjustment reforms intended to improve domestic economic efficiency. Liberalisation of the trade sector through tariff reform and the maintenance of competitive exchange rates were key elements of the 'supply-side' programme envisaged.

In terms of the debt accumulation model discussed in section 9.4 the Baker approach implied a temporary further rise in outstanding debt, in the belief that countries would be able to stimulate the growth of net export revenues. Solvency, and the associated return to creditworthiness, would be achieved by a combination of efficiency enhancing domestic reforms and a more promising world environment for debtor export expansion. It was envisaged throughout that debt service payments would continue as before. Notwithstanding this post-1985 'consensus', the Baker proposals foundered on the reluctance of the commercial banks to provide the appropriate level of financing. Accordingly, the period was to be characterised by substantial reverse flows from the major debtors to the world financial markets noted in Table 9.2. With lenders unwilling to supply adequate new funds, therefore, interest was to switch to the alternative means of reducing this burden: a reduction in the outstanding debt stock. A central catalyst for this change in emphasis arose from events in Brazil.

Following the 1982 crisis Brazil, like Mexico, submitted to an IMF approved programme (agreed in November) which provided the key to new bank finance and a rescheduling of principal due (see Dias, 1988 for details). A substantial cut in imports was to result as real GDP fell by 3.2 per cent. Nevertheless, a 30 per cent devaluation of the cruzeiro in February 1983 had prepared the ground for later strong growth in Brazilian exports in 1984 and a resumption of economic growth (Dias, 1988, p. 156). Despite Brazil's growing trade surplus in 1984, which had permitted the full payment of interest due on her external debt, the IMF internal targets for the last three months of the year were not met. The following year was to pass without further agreement but with Brazil continuing to pay all interest due. The election of the Sarney government imposed further political constraints on agreement with the Fund and the new Finance Minister favoured domestic 'heterodox' policies aimed at stabilising Brazil's accelerating inflation. The intention was to cut inflation, without the recessionary consequences of 'orthodox' Fund supported policies, by a programme which relied on deindexation of domestic wage contracts and a price freeze. Although the programme was a dramatic initial success in cutting inflation and avoiding recession, it was undermined by the monetary consequences of an uncorrected public sector deficit.

To avoid the domestic political opprobrium of seeking an agreement with the Fund in the face of declining external surpluses, the Sarney administration decided on confrontation with the country's commercial bank creditors. Interest payments on external debt were suspended in February 1987, initiating a default which ended in June 1988 when Brazil reluctantly accepted an IMF approved programme in return for an extensive loan rescheduling. Loss of access to trade credits during the default period was one factor in the change of course. Moreover, the costs of future reconciliation with creditors were being increased by the accumulation of interest arrears on terms more onerous than those achieved by the more conciliatory Mexican negotiators. While the refinancing agreement signed in September 1988 resembled established practice, the temporary Brazilian default was probably more significant as a turning point with attention moving away from the Baker approach to the issue of debt reduction.

The Brazilian default provoked the largest bank, Citicorp, into allocating $3 billion to a loan loss reserve in May 1987. This represented 25 per cent of its outstanding LDC loan portfolio and the decision triggered a general trend. By September 1989, one major bank (J.P. Morgan) had made provisions for 100 per cent of its medium- and long-term loans. Such provisions were financed from accumulated profits and, therefore, represented a considerable success for the crisis management strategy outlined in section 9.4. These balance sheet developments, however, contained no direct benefit for the debtor nations *as banks continued to demand loan service payments on the contracted terms.* Nevertheless, loan losses could now be absorbed without undue consequences for current reported profits. The provisions, therefore, paved the way for Voluntary Debt Reduction (VDR), the approach which was to be endorsed and promoted by US Treasury Secretary Brady as a means to resolving the debt crisis in March 1989.

9.6 THE BRADY INITIATIVE AND VDR

Following Brady's initiative, 'voluntary' debt reduction has developed into a more or less *concerted* decision by creditors to grant debt relief (defined as a reduction in the contractual claims to principal and/or interest due on a loan). These latest agreements must therefore be distinguished from earlier VDR actions initiated by country debtors to exploit the discount at which their debt was trading in the secondary market. A recent example involved the cash buyback of Bolivian debt in March 1988 using money provided by donor governments. Another market-based scheme is the debt–equity 'swap'. Here the country offers a holder of its discounted debt *national* currency which must then be used for investment in local businesses. A purchaser of the country's *discounted* debt receives in exchange approximately the original *face value* of that debt in local currency. The purchase and swap therefore effect a *preferential* exchange rate for external (often multinational) investors in local enterprises. Chile pioneered this strategy in 1985 and 30 per cent of debt had been converted by the end of 1988 (Morgan, 1988, p. 11).

Although these programmes reduced outstanding debt, they do not represent a joint decision by creditors to offer debt *relief.* They involve a voluntary exchange of one kind of financial instrument for another. While it may be beneficial to exchange an obligation to pay interest for one to pay dividends which vary with the profitability of the underlying enterprises, debt holders will make the exchange only if they expect to benefit from it. Debt–equity swaps effectively comprise a 'package' of transactions, with one element being equivalent to a simple cash buyback of the country's debt (Bulow and Rogoff, 1988). Financially swaps are identical to a direct inflow of foreign investment into the debtor country with the foreign exchange proceeds used to buy outstanding debt

(Bulow and Rogoff, 1988, p. 691). As with a cash buyback, this latter element may well benefit creditors rather than debtors (Dooley, 1988b; 1988c).

The difficulty resides in the floating claim nature of outstanding debts when full repayment is not probable. In these circumstances, the secondary market value of a country's debt reflects the present value of anticipated repayments which the country *will* make (see, however, Snowden, 1989; Dooley, 1989a). Whether these reflect what the country will *be able* to pay (Dooley) or simply what it can be *coerced* into paying (Bulow and Rogoff), there is no reason to expect that the change in the pattern of external claims will make any difference to the future payment capacity which the market is valuing. The market price per dollar of outstanding debt will be equal to the present value of the anticipated payments to holders divided by the nominal value of debt claims outstanding. While the country must pay this price representing the *average* value of the debt, the *marginal* value of the debt retired in the course of a debt–equity swap or buyback is almost zero when full repayment on the remaining claims is unlikely. The effect will be to raise the value of these claims, with the implication that the country's debt burden will be little affected. While debt–equity swaps may therefore offer little financial benefit, they may still be worth pursuing for their real effects. In particular, the reduced discount on remaining debt may generate foreign investment inflows which would not otherwise have been forthcoming.[6]

In order to assess the contrasting merits of 'concerted' VDR, it is necessary to establish that bank creditors would collectively wish to take part, since there is a strong reason to expect many of them to be reluctant to grant relief. Although countries may currently be unable fully to service their contracted debt, creditors have a claim over any foreign exchange surpluses likely to be generated: there is a 'debt overhang' (Krugman, 1988). A future improvement in circumstances could still allow creditors to recover a larger fraction of their outstanding claims *up to the full contractual amount*. A decision by banks to cut their claims eliminates the possibility of full repayment whereas the previous practice of loan rescheduling maintained their claims to full repayment intact (Krugman, 1988).

While this 'ceiling' effect may seem to rule out *voluntary* debt reduction there are several influences which may prompt creditors to be more positively inclined to it. The basic point in all of these arguments is that, paradoxically, debt reduction or relief may *increase* the returns enjoyed by creditors over a situation where no reduction is granted. The simplest case is where the debt reduction is motivated by the same desire to forestall default as was present in the era of rescheduling; without relief, countries may fail to pay anything. This provides a *default forestalling* argument in favour of debt relief.

Two other motivations for creditors to grant relief are more subtle. A distinction has been drawn between an *investment capacity* effect of debt relief and an *investment incentive* effect, both of which (by raising investment spending in the debtor country) may raise future output facilitating more complete repayment of the remaining claims (Corden, 1988a). The capacity effect arises because the debt overhang is 'contaminating' investment prospects in the country from the point of view of new foreign lenders and investors (e.g., Sachs, 1988). The effect is to limit the ability of the country to finance new investment projects which could generate a rate of return above the opportunity cost of the funds. Debt relief which reduced current payments on the existing debt would free resources for investment and raise future output potential.

The investment *capacity* argument does not, strictly, require debt relief as defined above; the same could be achieved by rescheduling and 'new' concerted lending aimed at offsetting the burden of current interest payments.[7] However, these approaches involve mounting external claims and lead to the possibility that the country may not be willing to pay. In contrast, the investment *incentives* argument for debt relief recognises a need to create incentives for the debtor to act in the creditor's interests. This argument can be illustrated with reference to Figure 9.1 (see Corden, 1988b; Dooley, 1989b).

The country has initial resources of P_1 in the first period shown on the vertical axis. Inherited debt D is repayable with interest in the second period shown on the horizontal axis. The transformation curve P_1P_2 indicates that by reducing present consumption below P_1, resources can be invested to yield output in period 2. With the debt D, however, the amount available for period 2 consumption when debts have been repaid is shown under the curve P_1P_2 (= P_1P_2 shifted left by the amount of debt to be repaid

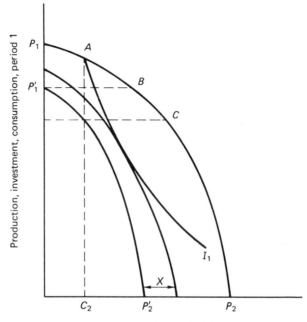

FIGURE 9.1   Debt relief and investment incentives

in period 2). Suppression of period 1 consumption from P_1 to P_1' would thus not augment consumption in the second period after debt repayment. The country faces a 100 per cent marginal rate of 'tax' on its investment returns up to this point.

Only if consumption can be compressed further, to a point below B on the outer curve, will the country gain anything from investment in period 1. In addition, a tolerable minimum of consumption may then require compression at least to C if debts are to be repaid in full. If it is assumed that creditors could coerce payment out of period 2 resources up to this minimum consumption level, it is probable that the country would choose default at A. Creditors would therefore receive nothing and the country would just sustain its minimum consumption requirement. In this simple model, the solution is to offer debt relief of X in the first period so that the country chooses a point at or below C. Creditors then are paid in full on their remaining claims and the country gains in future consumption as a compensation for current sacrifice. This result has been equated with moving the country up the 'wrong side' of a 'debt relief Laffer curve', so that a reduction in contractual claims actually increases the creditors' expected returns.

Although a distinct argument, Figure 9.1 suggests that the investment capacity justification for debt relief could contribute to the same end. By providing more resources in the first period so that investment can be increased, the consequent outward shifts of the transformation curves imply that debt repayment may be rendered more attractive.

These arguments for debt relief, therefore, must be set against the ceiling effect mentioned earlier to suggest that relief could be in the collective interests of creditors. Unfortunately, while creditors as a whole may benefit from such relief, *individual* creditors would be inclined to let *other* creditors grant it while holding on to their original claims; relief granted by others would make full repayment of their own claims more likely. Since all creditors would reach the same conclusion the relief would not be granted. This 'free rider' problem may be addressed by having the relief coordinated by an outside agency like the IMF and this is the logic of concerted agreements under the Brady initiative (Froot, 1989; Dooley, 1989b).

As with the earlier Baker initiative, the Brady adoption of debt reduction seems to have been partly provoked by a deterioration in the position of Mexico. While the country had continued with contractionary policies and export promotion following the 1986–7 agreement with the IMF, collapsing oil prices during 1988 were reversing the external gains she had made. The incoming Salinas government was under domestic pressure to promise resumed economic growth. Accordingly, it became committed to ending the net transfer of resources abroad, (which had reached 6 per cent of GNP in 1988), and to reducing the outstanding debt both absolutely and as fraction of GDP. The Brady endorsement of debt reduction was an attempt to achieve such an outcome. In April 1989, a further IMF agreement with Mexico seemed to offer the first tangible result of the new approach.

The agreement covered nearly $53 billion (over half) of Mexico's medium- and long-term bank debt. Banks currently have the choice of providing *new money* over a four year period equivalent to 25 per cent of their existing exposure *or* to swap their loans for one of two types of new bond. The choice here is between new bonds carrying a face value discounted by 35 per cent, but carrying market-related rates, or *par value* bonds carrying a below market rate of 6.25 per cent. The purpose of offering two types of bond is to allow banks to choose the most appropriate instrument given the preferences of the regulatory and tax authorities in their country of domicile. These 30 year bonds have their principal, together with 18 to 24 months' interest, collateralised (guaranteed) by $7 billion of resources from the IMF, the World Bank, Japan and from Mexico's own reserves. The mechanism employed involves the purchase with these funds of US Treasury 'deep discount' bonds. While such securities pay no interest, they are bought at a substantial discount to their value on maturity. It is this maturity value which will support the principal of the new bonds issued. A similar agreement is being negotiated with Venezuela.

9.7 CONCLUSIONS: THE LIMITS OF VOLUNTARY DEBT REDUCTION

The Mexican agreement is the first test of the Brady approach and the key concern for the future is whether debt reduction offers a major opportunity for resolving the difficulties of the debt over-hang. With the Brady emphasis on *voluntary* programmes, it is clear that the free rider problem will remain a significant impediment. In the Mexican case, it is ameliorated by the attraction of new bonds partially guaranteed by donor provided funds. In addition, participating banks have succeeded, for the first time in significant agreements, in obtaining seniority for the new over the old claims.[8] The importance of seniority is that it undermines the value of old securities since the new instruments receive priority in repayment. This further encourages banks to swap old debt for the new bonds and the greater the proportion of old loans that are swapped the less significant becomes the remaining free rider problem. While the Mexican bond exchange discount was negotiated in bank steering committees, an agreement by creditors to allow 'senior' bonds to be exchanged for debt by open auction would also undermine free riding in the same way (Froot, 1989).

Beyond voluntary approaches lie various degrees of compulsion aimed at improving the terms on which the exchanges can be conducted. One possibility recently proposed would be for the tax deductibility of bank loan loss provisions to be made conditional on banks participating in debt reduction schemes. Loss of this tax privilege would raise the cost of free riding and, by increasing the supply of old debt for exchange, pass some benefit to the country debtor. In practical terms, while VDR will be valuable, the ultimate outcome for countries and their creditors probably depends far more directly on the evolution of world interest rates and trading conditions than it does on financial engineering.

10 Economic
Development and
Services

BRIAN HINDLEY

10.1 WHAT IS A 'SERVICE'?

'Economic development' might be defined as an increase in the command over goods and services of the members of a community. But to give meaning to the phrase 'goods and services', and to start connecting the provision of services with economic development, the notion of 'services' first needs elaboration.

A preliminary way of conveying an idea of what services are is by a list. A typical list of services might include the transport of goods and persons by land, sea or air; banking, insurance and other financial services; communications; wholesaling and retailing; franchising; education; health care; engineering, architecture and constuction; accounting; advertising; consultancy; legal services; recreation and entertainment; and tourism.

The provision of services accounts for a very large part of economic activity. The United Nations Commission on Trade and Development (UNCTAD Secretariat, 1985, p.13) comments that:

> In terms of its contribution to gross domestic product, the service sector is the largest in the world economy . . .services comprised 64 per cent of world GDP, 67 per cent of the GDP of developed market economies and 51 per cent of the GDP of developing countries in 1979.

These fractions vary with what is counted as a service.[1] The more relevant point, for present purposes, is that services are not on any definition trivial.

The activities included in the list above also give a basis for suposing that services, even apart from their sheer bulk, are an important and even crucial element in economic development. Economic development is often discussed in terms of expanding industrial or agricultural output – that is, in terms of increasing the output of goods. Yet lumps of output at the end of a production line or in a field do not have value to anyone. And all of the activities involved in transportation, marketing, communications, design, financial arrangements and risk-sharing, and improving techniques of production (i.e., technology transfer) are services.

Quite apart from the direct value of services to their final receivers, services are essential inputs into the production of other goods and services. Unreliable transportation, poor communications, poor product or production design, or bad financial or legal advice can diminish or destroy the otherwise favourable prospects of industries of all kinds.[2]

Generalities of this kind are a useful introduction to the issues. On the basis merely of a list, however, it is difficult to move far beyond such generalities. To go further, a definition of 'services' is needed.

Probably the most useful and certainly the most intellectually stimulating effort to define 'services' is that of Hill (1977). In Hill's basic definition (p. 318), a service is:

> a change in the condition of a person, or of a good belonging to some economic unit, which is brought about as a result of the activity of some other economic unit, with the prior agreement of the former person or economic unit.

Two elements in this definition are crucial. The first is that a service brings about a *change* in condition. That carries the implication that services are not, as is sometimes asserted, like goods that perish especially quickly. Rather, they are in a different logical category from goods.

The second condition is that a service occurs *between* economic units. Among other things, that condition prevents the definition of a service expanding to include the entire economic universe. The difficulty can be seen in a statement such as 'the production processes of all goods consist of services (including the services of labour and capital), and goods are purchased for the services that they provide (for example, transport, appeasing hunger)'.

There is a sense in which such statements are true. Nevertheless, to analyse the service sector – that is, for example, the activities of people who sell taxi rides, as opposed to those who make taxis, a boundary line between services and other activities is necessary. Hill's boundary is the form of the transaction.

This same boundary is used in national income accounting, and it can give rise to substantial problems of measurement. The same *activity* might sometimes be classified as a service and sometimes as something else. If households start washing their clothes themselves, for example, rather than taking them to a commercial laundry, the activity will vanish from the national accounts. Painting a car might sometimes be part of a manufacturing process, sometimes a service, and sometimes nothing (so far as the accounts are concerned).[3]

10.2   POLICY ISSUES – A FIRST LOOK

An alternative way of approaching services is to look directly at the differences between goods and services. One difference is that goods are tangible, so that, with more or less trouble or cost, they can be shifted from place to place. Goods have simple and relatively homogeneous delivery systems; services, on the other hand – being, as Hill remarks, a *change* in the condition of a good or person–cannot themselves be shifted from place to place. The outcome of a service can often be shifted from place to place, and so can the signifiers of property rights generated by a service – for example, an insurance policy. Moreover, and of central importance, the *means of producing* a service can be moved. A service as such, however, can neither be stored nor moved.

Services therefore often cannot be traded in the same way as goods. A good can usually be sold by a firm located in country A to a person in country B, and shipped from A to B, without relocation of either the supplier or the buyer. The provision of a service, on the other hand, often requires physical proximity of the service provider and the good or person receiving the service. The provision of services by a firm located in country A to users located in country B will thus often, though not inevitably, require the A firm to shift factors of production to B – to engage in inward investment in B (Sampson and Snape, 1985).

The connection between the provision of services and inward investment raises problems of policy towards international service transactions. Over the past few years, there has been much discussion of whether services should be 'brought into the GATT' – that is, of whether the actions that a government can take with respect to international transactions in services, and therefore with respect to its domestic service sector, should be subject to some form of international control.[4] The proposal that services should be brought into the GATT has been sponsored by developed countries (in particular the United States) and has been strongly opposed by many developing countries (Bhagwati, 1987b; Hindley, 1987a). Part of the reason for the opposition of the developing countries is that international service transactions often entail foreign investment. Hence, any meaningful GATT agreement on services requires restrictions on the ability of a government to control such inward investment – a restriction to which many developing countries strongly object.

A second major difference between goods and services is the extent and form of government regulation of service industries. It is widely accepted that government regulation is essential to the efficient supply of a service. However, regulation of the provision of services by governments links with a more fundamental difference between goods and services, which is that services are often more customised than goods. A lawyer or doctor advises you on one problem and one set of circumstances, and me on another. Such customisation means that regulation of the *output* of service industries is difficult. It is less costly for governments to regulate the quality of *inputs* into the provision of services. Such regulation, however, readily translates into controls on the entry of competitors.[5]

There are competing theories of regulation. One theory is based upon the notion that the outcome of unrestricted competition between providers of a service will produce results that are undesirable from the standpoint of users of that service. It therefore holds that regulation is necessary to correct these deficiencies in the competitive process. This is the public interest theory of regulation. On this view, the purpose of regulation is to improve the conditions of *buyers* of a service, and that is what regulation does in fact – save, perhaps, for errors by the regulators.

Providers of a service, however, are also likely to see ways in which the outcome of purely competitive processes can be improved upon. In particular, they will prefer the higher incomes that would derive from control of entry into their occupation, or from restrictions on competition between those who are admitted to it.

Once regulators are given powers to avoid competitive outcomes, therefore, there is likely to be a conflict over how those powers are used. Regulatory powers can as well be used to achieve anti-competitive goals of the *providers* of a service as to protect the *buyers* of the service from lazy or predatory service suppliers. In this conflict, service providers have several clear advantages. They are well informed about the nature of the service and are consequently better able to assess the effects of regulatory actions than users of the service. They will frequently be fewer in number than users, and this, combined with their greater interest in the conditions of their occupation, makes it easier for them to organise themselves and the expression of their views, and to press for the adoption of those views by regulators. Finally, regulation requires a knowledge of the industry to be regulated. Such knowledge will often be found only among practitioners or potential practitioners. Regulators may therefore have an inherent sympathy for the views of the ostensibly regulated.

These factors lead to a theory of regulation that is an alternative to the public interest theory of regulation. It is widely known as the 'capture' theory (Stigler, 1971; Peltzman, 1976. Rottenburg, 1980, provides a useful survey of the theory and tests of it). It conjectures that members of a regulated industry will often succeed in capturing the powers of regulators and in using them for their own purposes. The capture theory thus suggests that regulation will be good for the profits or life style of providers of a service, but less good for users of it. Users might in fact, be better off with no regulation at all than to have the provision of the service controlled by captured regulators.

These two differences between goods and services – the difficulty of international transactions without factor movements in many services, and the pervasiveness of regulation – interact with one another. When services can be internationally traded, their 'invisible' properties mean that it is difficult, and often impossible, for governments to protect local producers by means of tariffs on imports. Regulation then can act as a substitute for protection by tariff or quota. When a service cannot be traded directly, regulation often impedes the establishment of the subsidiaries or branches of foreign firms that are then necessary if the service is to be provided by them. A consequence is that many service industries live in a state approaching autarky – protected from foreign competition to a degree that is rarely approached in industries producing goods. Indeed, in the economic literature, 'non-traded goods' and 'services' are frequently identified with one another.

The effects of these autarkic conditions are easy to guess at but less easy to prove. Theory predicts that there will be large differences in the price of a service in different markets. There is, however, a major difficulty in collecting statistical evidence of that outcome. The problem is that it is difficult to correct for differences in the *quality* of the services offered in different markets. For some services, prices are available and quality can reasonably be assumed to be constant or corrections made for the difference in quality. Transport services is one area in which price comparisons have been made. The results suggest that the effects of protection are substantial.

The United States provides one striking example in its policies towards the shipment of PL 480 agricultural aid. Until early 1986, US law required at least 50 per cent of such shipments to be carried in US flag ships (in 1986, the percentage was raised to 75 per cent). The remaining shipments were open to competition by ships flying other flags. Hence, there are two prices for such shipments: one for US ships and the other for other ships. The latter presumably is an approximation of a world price.

One study (White, 1988), correcting for type and size of cargo and distance shipped, comes to the conclusion that 'as a conservative estimate, we can say that the U.S. flag rates for the protected shipment were about double those of foreign flag carriers'. This conclusion is consistent with those of previous studies of the differential (US GAO, 1982; US GAO, 1984; Binkley and Harrer, 1981).

Studies of another protected US maritime market show even greater differentials. For the shipment of petroleum, the data suggests that the price per ton-mile of US tankers operating in the protected environment of shipments for the Strategic Petroleum Reserve is about four times that of the international rate (Morgan, 1980; Congressional Research Service, 1983; Roush, 1984).[6]

Other instances of the effect of protection and regulation come from civil aviation. The price of flying in the regulated European market, for example, is often several times the price of flying the same distance in the deregulated US market. Even when differences in operating costs are taken into account, large differentials remain (CAA, 1983).

Airline costs and revenues appear to be related to regions. The International Civil Aviation Organisation (ICAO, 1983) has commented on this as follows:

> The differing revenue/cost ratios achieved by European airlines appear to be determined by the competitive situation on each route group in 1982. On routes between Europe and Asia–Pacific the competition was such that neither the European nor the Asia–Pacific airlines achieved profitability.

On Europe–Middle East routes the European airlines could earn a profit because they were able to maintain a higher average revenue field than the Middle East airlines. On the Europe–Africa route group, the European airlines were also profitable because they had much lower cost levels than the African airlines.

An interesting aspect of the deregulation of airlines in the United States is the failure of advocates of regulation to anticipate the extent of the downward pressure on wages in the industry that deregulation created; they had not appreciated, that is to say, the extent to which labour in the industry had captured the rents created by regulation.

Regulation may have produced similar effects elsewhere. European airlines frequently object to comparisons of their own fares with those in the United States. They say that their costs of operation are higher. Pryke (1987, pp. 29–30) comments on this that:

The main reason for this disparity in costs was that the maintenance costs of West European airlines were 27 per cent greater, their expenditure on ticketing and sales was 52 per cent higher and their general administration costs were 112 per cent more than for American airlines.

This raises another issue. This is the difficulty of assessing the outcome of protection or liberalisation in the service sector. For example, on the facts and figures currently available, it seems quite clear that airlines based in the United States have a comparative advantage over airlines based in Western Europe. It is easy to conclude that open and unsubsidised competition between the two groups would result in the domination of the field by US airlines. But to reach that conclusion, it is necessary to assume that such open and unsubsidised competition will not affect wages and effective labour inputs in Europe. That is a dubious proposition, as the analysis and figures cited above suggests. The extent of US comparative advantage is therefore almost certainly over-estimated by any exercise based upon current statistics for the industry. Perhaps there is no US comparative advantage that would survive competition. Protection of other service industries may raise the wages or lower the effective input of workers in the industry. Estimates of the chances of survival and success of such currently-protected industries in the face of international competition that do not take account of this fact may be much too pessimistic.

The Cecchini Report on the effects of integration of the internal market of the European Community (Cecchini, 1988, Table 6.1, pp.38–9) provides data on the price of financial services in member states of the EEC. It is presented in a recalculated form in Table 10.1. Table 10.1 gives the price of the service in the member state with the lowest price as 1 and expresses all other prices as a multiple of that price. Line 1 of Table 10-1, for example, shows that Belgium has the lowest cost of consumer credit and that the German price is 4 times the Belgian price.

There are no doubt many questions to be asked about this data. They range from the methods by which it was collected, and the actual equality of the services whose price is being compared in different countries, to underlying differences in the cost of supplying a service in different jurisdictions (for example, there may be

TABLE 10.1   Prices of standard financial products in EC member states, prices expressed as a multiple of the lowest member-state price

	Bel.	Ger.	Spa.	Fra.	It.	Lux.	Neth.	UK
Consumer credit	1	4	2.4	n.a.	3.7	1.3	2.3	7
Credit cards	2.6	2.3	1.8	1	2.7	1.3	2	1.6
Mortgages	1.6	2	2.7	2.2	1.2	n.a.	1.2	1
Letters of credit	1.4	1	1.8	1	1.2	1.4	1.3	1.2
Drafts	2	2.4	5.5	2.9	2.3	2.5	1	2.1
Travellers' cheques	1.5	1	1.4	1.5	1.3	1	1.4	1
Commercial loans	1	1.1	1.3	1	1.2	1.1	1.5	1.6
Life insurance	2.7	1.5	2.0	1.9	2.6	2.4	1.3	1
Home insurance	1	1.2	1.7	1.8	2.2	1.9	1.4	2.3
Motor insurance	1.6	1.4	2.4	1.3	3	2.1	1.1	1
Commercial fire and theft	1.1	1.7	1.5	3	4.1	1	1.2	1.5
Public liability	1.3	1.8	1.9	2.6	2.1	1.3	1	1.1
Private equity transactions	1.6	1.2	1.9	1	1.1	1.2	2.5	2.6
Private gilts transactions	3.1	5.1	8.6	3.3	1	3.4	7	3.7
Institutional equity transactions	2.4	3.2	4.8	1.8	2.8	3.2	2.4	1
Institutional gilt transactions	6	1.5	2.5	2.5	3	1	1.9	n.a.

Source: Cecchini (1988) Table 6.1.

more automobile accidents in one country than another, so that the cost of insuring against the risk of automobile accidents must be higher). Nevertheless, it is difficult to believe that the very large differences shown in Table 10.1 can be entirely explained in such terms.[7]

10.3 SERVICES AND DEVELOPMENT

Most of the figures cited above refer to developed countries. But what about the provision of services in developing countries? How do services and policies affecting the provision of services affect their development prospects? Two facts that are relevant to answering this question have already been cited.

One fact is that services bulk very large in national incomes. The second is that where comparisons have been made between markets with different degrees of protection (which is all too infrequently, especially in developing countries), the price of a service often varies enormously. The first fact suggests that substantial economic damage can be caused by a deterioration in the price–quality combinations of services that are available to domestic firms and residents. The second fact suggests that poor policy towards the service sector is capable of causing large deteriorations in the price and quality of the services on offer.

Moreover, many services are used as intermediate inputs in other production processes. Evidence from input–output tables for Malaysia and the Philippines suggest that roughly half of all services provided in those countries are intermediate inputs (Arroyo, 1984, p.14).

The effect of high-price and/or low-quality services will therefore spread across the economy as a whole. To take a simple example, a country that has an inherent comparative advantage in the production of cut flowers (or some other perishable item, for example) may neither produce nor export flowers if it lacks an internal and external transport system that is sufficiently well organised to supply prompt or reliable delivery. Inadequate transport may make the flower industry unviable, so that it simply fails to appear. Poor communications or an inadequate financial system may similarly mean that industries that would be viable fail to appear or, if they exist, have a different structure than they would have had had better services been available.

A third relevant fact is that the available evidence suggests that many developing country governments' policies towards their service sectors are a very long way from being optimal. The evidence that is currently available is patchy and anecdotal; moreover, much of it comes from developed country sources, such as USTR (1985), so that it is strongly biased towards restrictions on international transactions. It would be of great value to have detailed studies of the policies of developing country governments towards domestic service providers, together with an analysis of their consequences.[8] In many service industries, however, and for many developing countries, the largest source of potential competition with incumbent providers comes from abroad.

Official restrictions on international transactions in services can be divided into three groups.[9] First, there are general restrictions, such as foreign exchange controls, that limit the possibility of purchasing foreign services. Second, there are policies that directly limite the possibility of domestic residents receiving services that are provided abroad. Third, there are policies that effect the possibility of service providers from abroad locating in a particular country in order to provide services to residents of that country. Here, I shall focus on the direct restrictions.

Restrictions affecting cross-border trade in services

An excellent illustration of a service that is in principle tradable is cargo insurance. Cargo moves from country A to country B. It can in principle be insured in either A or B (or, indeed, in any third country).

Frequently, however, governments insist that imports should be insured domestically; some require that exports should be insured domestically; and some governments require both imports *and* exports to be insured in the domestic market (for example, in Bangladesh; Burundi; Cuba; Dominican Republic; Italy; Malta; Mexico; Rwanda; Senegal; Tanzania; United Republic of Cameroon). An interesting question is what happens in – or to – trade between countries both of which insist upon exports and imports being insured with domestic insurers. Preumably the hapless traders must insure in both markets.

Trade in other forms of insurance is in principle possible, but is impeded. The purchaser of a policy from a non-admitted insurer is subject to fines in some countries. Insurers and agents who sell insurance policies without being admitted to the market are sometimes subject to fines and sometimes to imprisonment (the Philippines; Singapore; Thailand; Turkey). In a number of countries, insurance purchased from foreign-based companies does not qualify for tax concessions that are available on policies issued by domestic insurers.

Insurance trade can take place at two levels. Direct insurance transactions entail sales from the insurer to an agent or direct to the final purchaser of the insurance. Reinsurance, on the other hand, involves transactions between insurers, with the reinsurer accepting all or part of the risk insured by the direct insurer. The international reinsurance business is subject to some restrictions, mainly in the form of rules as to the amount of reinsurance that local insurers must cede to local reinsurers – typically a single state-owned firm. Kenya and Turkey, for example, call for the cession of 25 per cent. The Philippines, on the other hand, permits no more than 20 per cent reinsurance with foreign companies, and Brazil requires all reinsurance to be with the state corporation.

Nevertheless, international reinsurance is still relatively unrestricted. This opens the possibility that protection imposes lower costs than would otherwise be the case, since it implies the possibility that local insurers in some degree act as agents of the international reinsurers who, in turn, are operating in an extremely competitive and open global market. By the same token, however, it also puts in question the rationale of the very heavy protection given to local insurers. (Hindley, 1982, discusses protection of the insurance industry in developing countries in detail.)

Another service that is tradable in principle is maritime transport. Traditionally, the industry has been largely free of official restrictions (leaving aside cabotage – that is, regulations concerning coastal shipping *within* a country, which has often been reserved for domestic carriers). Nevertheless, a bilateral system similar to that in aviation has made inroads through the UNCTAD Liner Code. The Code is often administered by developing countries in such a way that it is more restrictive in fact than on paper. The Code division of freight between country *A* and country *B* is 40:40:20 – 40 per cent in *A* ships, 40 per cent in *B* ships, and 20 per cent reserved for cross-trade. In many trades, however, the *de facto* division is reported to be 50:50:0.

Over and above the liner code, cargo reservation systems, whereby government regulation reserves a certain amount of cargo for national carriers, can also act as a major impediment. USTR (1985) reports that 18 countries operate such schemes. Fifteen are developing countries.

Restrictions affecting establishment

For service industries in general, restrictions on establishment are a much more important impediment to international transactions than restrictions on trade. Some restrictions that affect establishment are general. Limits on the repatriation of profits, for example, are likely to deter investment in any sector, and limits or barriers on the deployment of personnel, or on trans-border data flows will affect the operations of firms in many sectors. Other restrictions, however, apply to specific service industries.

Establishment is directly affected by two broad types of restriction. The first type either places restrictive conditions upon initial establishment or simply bans it (*de jure* or *de facto*). The second type limits the activities of establishments of foreign producers of services: locally-established foreign producers may not be able to enter certain lines of business, for example, or service particular classes of customer, or open new branches. The financial services sector is heavily affected by restrictions on establishment. Some governments completely prohibit their establishment; others will allow only a representative office, which cannot engage in any form of banking business. Restrictions on the opening of branches and on the acquisition of domestic banks through takeover are also common.

Even where establishment is allowed, foreign-owned banks are often treated differently from domestically-owned banks. Foreign-owned banks are often subject to discriminatory reserve requirements; to higher requirements on capital–asset ratios; or face higher taxation than domestic banks. A frequest complaint of foreign-based banks is that they do not have access to the rediscount facilities of the host central bank, or to subsidised lines of credit, such as export guarantees. They are restricted in the range of services that they can offer, and in the assets they can acquire (Walter, 1987, supplies a detailed analysis of the restrictions placed on foreign banks).

A similar picture emerges for insurance. Some governments prohibit access by foreign insurers. Others require local incorporation. Foreign-owned insurers are often subject to discriminatory capital and deposit requirements, and are also restricted in the assets they can acquire (Carter and Dickinson, 1987).

Establishment problems are cited as a major barrier to entry in advertising, accountancy, and professional services in general; indeed, whenever establishment is necessary for the provision of services, barriers are reported.

10.4 POLICY ISSUES FOR DEVELOPING COUNTRIES

Discussion of appropriate policy for developing countries is most easily organised around two simple propositions. The first is that an economy will perform best when the residents of the country are able to receive services at the best available price-quality combination. the second is that this objective will best be achieved by a policy of competition in the provision of services and of free entry of new competitors into industries providing services.

This does not necessarily mean a total absence of government intervention in the provision of services. There is a case for the regulation of service industries (Hindley, 1987b). A government trying to achieve the best available price – quality combination for its residents might therefore intervene as a regulator, or by appointing regulators. It would, however, wish to ensure that regulations were demonstrably in the interests of the receivers of a service and, especially, tht regulations did not unnecessarily block the entry of firms into the provision of services or otherwise impede competition between service providers.

Few governments of developing countries (and, indeed, few governments of developed ones) apply such policies. The question therefore arises as to what their policy objectives are. What is on the other side of the coin? Might governments have valid objectives whose attainment clashes with efficiency in the provision of services? If entry barriers are raised and competition is restricted, what is the case for that policy?

One dividing line is between domestic and international providers of services. Competition and free entry for *domestic* providers of services are one thing, it might be said; free entry of *foreign* providers of services and the outcome of their competition with domestic producers is quite another. To a large extent, the arguments stemming from this division are simply a replay of those deriving from the similar division over the protection of domestic suppliers of goods against competing goods from abroad. In that area, the governments of most developing countries have revealed a preference for a policy of protection. This is despite the negligible intellectual case for that policy, and although all available evidence indicates that policies of protection have had high costs in terms of foregone economic growth (Bhagwati, 1986).

This precedent is not encouraging to proponents of a policy of competition in the service sector of developing countries. Moreover, two features of the service sector which are not present – or not present to the same degree – militate against a policy of openness. The first is the fact, already noted, that international transactions in services often require some form of establishment – that is, inward investment – in the country in which the services are to be provided. In the service sector, developing country sensitivities towards foreign investment combine with those invoked by the import of goods from abroad to produce attitudes that are even more antagonistic to foreign transactions. The second feature is institutional. It is that there has been virtually no control of governmental policies towards international transactions in the service sector, by the GATT or by any other body. The protective policies that have in fact been pursued have thus set up major vested interests.

These are brute political facts. But those who live by brute political facts like to provide themselves with intellectual justification. Those justifications pose the question that is relevant here. Do any of them stand up to analysis? There are in fact two groups of justifications. The first group contains arguments that are economic, the primary ones being first, the infant industry argument and second, the need to balance international payments. members of the second group base themselves upon a need to achieve aims such as the protection of cultural integrity and national security. Assessment of such goals is beyond the scope of economic analysis – the means proposed to achieve them, however, are not. As a defence of protection in the service sector, the two economic arguments have one major strength and one major weakness. The strength is institutional; Article XVIII of the GATT accepts them as valid reasons for protection of industries producing goods in developing countries. The weakness is intellectual; properly analysed, neither of them provides anything other than third or fourth best arguments for protection.

An extensive literature deals with the difficulties of constructing a case for trade protection from the infant industry argument (Bhagwati and Ramaswami, 1963; Johnson, 1965), and also with the fact that protection will in many circumstances be an ineffective response to balance of payments deficits (Johnson, 1961). These general arguments have been applied to services (Hindley, 1982; Hindley and Smith, 1984), and they seem if anything less applicable to services than to goods industries.

The infant industry argument starts from the postulate that a country has an inherent comparative advantage in the production of some good or service. The comparative advantage, however, does not reveal itself in current production because the competition of foreign producers makes impossible the establishment of a local industry. But, the argument continues, if the local industry were protected from that foreign competition, there could be a process of learning by doing and its comparative advantage would be revealed. At some time in the future, the local industry would be viable without protection and would provide an economic gain to the country.

The difficulties of knowing where there is an *inherent* comparative advantage, one that is not manifesting itself in current production, have long been recognised. The costs of protecting infant industries that never grow up may outweigh by far the benefits of finding one that does (of which, in fact, there are no good examples). So have the problems of knowing whether the industry will grow up fast enough to justify the costs of protecting it. Even if full knowledge is granted on these points, however, the argument is still unpersuasive.

The problem occurs in the conjunction of the propositions, both necessary to make the case for infant industry protection, that:

1. encouragement of the activity by protection is *socially* worthwhile, which is to say that the losses to buyers resulting from

212 Economic Development and Services

the protection are outweighed by the gains of producers when both are appropriately discounted, but

2. it is not *privately* worthwhile for potential producers to enter the industry in the absence of protection – that is, the future gains of producers will be insufficient to offset the losses they will experience in establishing the industry.

How can these conditions simultaneously hold? Protection of the industry will transfer income from buyers to producers, but the gains of producers from protection cannot be larger than the losses of buyers (and will usually be smaller, since protection has a real cost). If condition 1 is true, therefore, how can condition 2 also be true?

The apparent contradiction can be resolved in at least three ways. One is that potential producers are making a mistake. The industry will be profitable even without protection, but this is recognised only by politicians and civil servants, who are unable to persuade any potential entrepreneur that it is true. This argument, however, justifies any intervention – if this is the basic issue, there is no reason to invoke the infant industry argument.

The second argument is that the private rate of discount, used by potential producers to assess the present value of entry into the industry, is higher than the social rate of discount, as used to assess the social value of the industry. If that is so, it presumably applies to other investment decisions also. The appropriate action in that case is to formulate a general policy with respect to defects in the capital market, not one that is specific to the putative infant industry.

The third argument is intellectually more satisfactory, but severely limites the applicability of the thesis. It is that potential producers cannot appropriate all of the returns to the investment they must make to enter the industry. A standard example is that a firm entering the industry requires some kind of specialised labour, which is not currently available in the economy. Suppose, however, that the first firm to enter the industry undertakes the expense of the necessary training, hoping to recoup the invest-ment by paying less than the marginal product of the trained workers. If new firms enter the industry, they will be able to bid away the trained workers by offering them their marginal product (or will force the first firm to pay the workers their marginal product in order to retain the labour). The first firm to enter the industry will therefore not be able to earn a return on its investment in training.

In these circumstances, there is a first-mover disadvantage. No firm will wish to be the first to enter the industry. The industry will not be established even though it would be socially worthwhile. If such misappropriability is at the root of the infant industry argument, a government clearly has available better policies than protection against foreign suppliers. In the example above, for instance, it could supply the training itself, or make it possible for potential trainees to finance their own training.

This analysis fundamentally weakens the case for protection of infant industries. It identifies the features that must be present to make the case, but it also indicates that when those features are present, so also must be better policies than protection.

Yet if the argument is difficult to apply to industries producing goods, it is even more difficult to apply to services. In the first place, it is very difficult to see what inappropriability of the returns to private investment could exist in the case of a service industry. Moreover, when provision of a service by a foreign-based firm requires establishment in the local market, some or all of the training function will be carried out by foreign firms.

The infant industry argument carries very little weight as a guide to appropriate policy towards the service sector in developing countries. There is a good case for the government to facilitate the acquisition of the skills involved in supplying a service. That is a quite general case, involving policy towards education. The infancy of service industries in developing countries does not provide good economic grounds for any other intervention by governments.

The connection between the balance of payments and service trade in developing countries derives in part from the belief of governments of many developing countries that their economies have a comparative disadvantage in the provision of many services. These services are regarded entirely as an import good – an item which, were the economy open to the world, would add to the import bill of the developing country without any corresponding increase in its exports. This may be a short-sighted view. In the first place developing countries may have a comparative advantage in the provision of some services. In the second place, the importance of services as an input into other productive processes suggests that a simplistic analysis of the effects of liberalisation on the balance of payments might be seriously misleading. The import of superior foreign services might improve the performance of service-*using* industries and hence increase exports or reduce imports.

The cause and cure of deficits in the balance of payments is a topic in macroeconomic analysis, and a complicated one at that. To simplify matters, a proposition derived from models of floating exchange rates when the nominal wage rate is floating is useful. The proposition is that protection will have no effect on the level of output or employment, but will primarily affect the exchange rate. A reduction in the level of protection will thus cause the exchange rate to depreciate but, to a first approximation, will have no effect on the level of output (Mundell, 1961; Krugman, 1982).

From this proposition about floating exchange rates another, about fixed exchange rates, follows. It applies when an exchange rate is fixed but over-valued, so that the equilibrium value of the exchange rate is lower than the actual exchange rate. In that circumstance, there is likely to be a conflict between full employment and balance of payments equilibrium, and that problem could be resolved by an increase in the level of protection. The increase in protection will increase the equilibrium value of the exchange rate, and could increase it by so much that it becomes equal to the actual exchange rate. In a regime of rigidly fixed exchange rates, this might be an important proposition (though, of course, to say that objective O can be achieved by policy action P *is a very long way from saying either that* P is the *only* way of achieving O, or that P *should* be employed to achieve O). But we live in an era in which the exchange rate of many developing countries floats or is determined by analogous means. Under such systems, in which the exchange rate can adjust or can readily be adjusted to produce payments balance, what is a 'balance of payments problem'? A country with an over-valued fixed exchange rate might be forced to reduce its level of output and employment to obtain payments equilibrium. It might reasonably take that possibility to be a major component of its 'balance of payments problem'. But under a floating exchange rate, protection affects the exchange rate and not output or employment. There is no analogous problem. For a country with a floating exchange rate, there is no good economic case for restrictions on trade for balance of payments purposes, whether the restrictions apply to goods or to services.

The economic arguments for a policy of protection against foreign providers of services are not compelling. Arguments based upon national sovereignty and security, however, cannot be disposed of so easily, at least by economic analysis. Economic analysis may have something to say about appropriate means of achieving policy objectives but it has little that is useful to say about the value of the ultimate objectives themselves.

Moreover, the feelings that lie behind such arguments are again heightened by the fact that international transactions in services often require some form of factor movement and, in the limiting case, permanent establishment in the country where the services are to be provided. The quality of a retailing or local transportation system might be improved as a result of the involvement of foreigners in the supply of the services through foreign investment or franchising, or as a result of the use of foreign consultants. There is little possibility of achieving this through direct trade in the services themselves, at least currently.

From the standpoint of assessing the potential economic costs of protection in the service sector, the distinction between delivery through trade and delivery through local establishment may not be important. The relevant question from that standpoint is whether price can be reduced, or quality improved, through the involvement of foreign providers of services. The exact way in which they are involved is less important. However, the residents of developed countries are not in a strong position to rebut arguments from developing countries based upon concern about local sovereignty or culture. The United States, for example, insists that companies supplying a variety of services in the United States should be owned by United States nationals (for example, in broadcasting, maritime transport and airlines). Developing countries who maintain that their communications, banks or insurance companies, or entertainment industry should be controlled by their nationals therefore have satisfactory precedents to cite.

Even after all of this is conceded, however, there is still scope for economic examination of policies. One ground is cost. A national insurance industry may be thought important to national life. Translation of that judgement into support of such an industry, however, is unlikely to be independent of the true cost of the policy. A second ground, related to the first, is provided by the means employed to achieve the stated ends. To accept that it is a valid national goal to have locally-owned suppliers of insurance is very far from accepting that any policy that impedes foreign suppliers is therefore justified. The point will emerge again in section 10.5.

10.5　APPROPRIATE PUBLIC POLICY

The policies towards the service sector of many developing countries invite economic losses. These losses cannot yet be quantified, but the possibility that they are substantial seems clear. Are different policies available that will achieve the ends of policy, but reduce the costs?

From the standpoint of international trade theory, the issue is the ranking of instruments of protection. A standard proposition of international trade theory is that if the object of policy is to sustain the output of an import-competing industry at a higher level than would otherwise exist, then a subsidy to the output of the industry is superior to tariffs as a means of achieving that end (Corden, 1957).[10]

The assessment of quantitative restrictions is more complex because there are so many ways of administering such restrictions. Two key variables, however, determine their social costs. They are the destination of the rents associated with the quota rights, and the state of competition in the affected industry. At one extreme, in which domestic residents receive quota rents and there is perfect competition in all relevant markets, it can be shown that tariffs and quotas are equivalent in a comparative static sense. If the quota rents go to foreigners (as in the case of voluntary export restraints), however, a quota is from a national point of view a much more expensive means than a tariff of expanding the output of the import-competing industry.

Moreover, the effects of quotas and tariffs can be quite different from one another in the presence of imperfect competiton (Bhagwati, 1969). Measures affecting the price of imports – such as tariffs in the case of goods – do not create problems of monopoly even when there is only one or a few domestic producers. Imports can be substituted for home output at the world price plus tariff, so that the domestic industry faces an infinitely elastic demand curve, albeit at a higher level than before the tariff. Quantity restrictions on imports of goods, however, prevent such substitution. They therefore have the capacity to *create* monopoly power for the domestic industry. When there is a single domestic producer, for example, it is easily shown that a policy that imposes the free trade level of imports as a quota will cause the domestic producer to *reduce* his output.

Quotas on imports can therefore be an extremely expensive means of expanding the output of the import-competing industry, and may actually cause it to contract. From a national standpoint, they are most expensive – and their effects on the output of the protected industry most dubious – when they shelter an industry consisting of one or a few firms, and the quota rents go to foreigners. This kind of analysis yields a ranking in terms of economic cost of policies to expand the output of an import-competing industry that produces a good. Where $X > Y$ denotes that X is less costly than Y the ranking is:

Subsidy to output $>$ tariff $\geqslant$ quota

where, as explained, equality between tariffs and quotas demands quite restrictive conditions, and the costs of a quota may be very much greater than those of a tariff.

The relevant question is whether this kind of analysis can be applied to international transactions in services. It has been shown that the measures by which domestic providers of services are protected are often different from those adopted in goods industries, and the details of the measures by which particular services are protected often differ from one another. Nevertheless, those means can be separated into two broad types. The first type of protective measure imposes a cost disadvantage on foreign producers (or provides a cost advantage to domestic producers). The second type imposes quantitative limits on the sales of foreign producers – a category which includes total bans on sales of any kind of foreign producers.

From an analytical point of view, the provision of a price or cost advantage to local producers can be viewed as equivalent to a subsidy to output in the case of trade in goods, and the imposition of price or cost disadvantages upon foreign producers can be viewed as equivalent to a tariff. The policies differ in that the latter will cause a deterioration in the price–quality of service combination that foreigners are able to offer in the local market, while the provision of a price advantage to domestic producers retains for local buyers the option of purchasing the best price–quality combination available to them on the international market.

The result from the theory of trade in goods – that a subsidy to output is superior to a tariff as a means of expanding the output of the import-competing industry – is based precisely on the fact that the tax on buyers that is implicit in a tariff does nothing to further the objective of the policy, and is therefore deadweight loss. That is true in the present case. From the standpoint of economic efficiency, therefore, a policy of providing a cost advantage to domestic producers is superior to one of placing a cost disadvantage on foreign producers.

The costs associated with quotas on imports when the quota rents go to foreigners, or when the protected industry consists of one or a few firms also survive the transition to services. The enhanced profits of those foreign firms that have access to the quantity-protected market now play the role of quota rents for foreigners. A plausible conjecture about the hesitation of European service industries to support the US initiative on services in the GATT is that some important members of those industries have 'grandfathered' subsidiaries in the heavily-protected markets of their nation's former colonies, and that any thorough-going liberalisation would threaten the profits of these subsidiaries. If that is true, it is not in the economic interests of developing countries to pursue policies that perpetuate the high profits.

Analysis of quota protection of monopolistic industries also finds an application here. Some service industries in developing countries contain few firms. Moreover, the potential for oligopolistic behaviour is reinforced by the presence of regulators with strong powers, which the local producers may have 'captured'. Where such an industry is protected by a quantity restriction placed upon foreign producers, there is every reason to suppose that a consequence will be monopolistic exploitation of domestic buyers by domestic sellers of the service. The behaviour of any foreigners permitted in such a market will, of course, be affected. Since the quantitative restriction will not permit them to increase sales, the price of the service they provide is likely to rise. Where this reflects itself in enhanced profits, an equivalent of the worst outcome yielded by a quota in theoretical analysis of goods trade appears.

When due modification is made for the nature of the policy instruments that can be applied to the service sector, it appears that the ordering of policies for the support of import-competing industries applies to services as well as to goods. As a matter of practical policy, the prevalence of quantitative restrictions in the service sector, and the possibility (and probability) that the harm they cause may be high, suggests a clear first step for reviews of policy towards international transactions in the service sector. This is to ensure that measures limiting the quantity of sales of services by foreigners are necessary for the achievement of policy goals; where such measures can be replaced by others, affecting the relative costs of foreign and domestic producers, there is a very strong presumption that the replacement will lead to economic gains.

This discussion can be summarised by considering the implications of the analysis for various practices pursued in developing countries.

Restrictions on imports

There is no good economic case for restricting imports of services, and this is emphatically true of bans on imports of a service that could in principle be imported. The best way to maintain a larger import-competing industry than would exist under free trade is by subsidizing domestic producers of the service. It follows that many of the practices complained of by US service suppliers, which amount to subsidies to domestic producers of a service, are defensible. To be precise, the arguments in favour of these policies are as strong as the argument for expanding the import-competing industry beyond the size that it would otherwise have. If that goal is accepted, then a policy of subsidisation to achieve the goal should also be accepted. Of course, the ends to which policy is directed are very much open to debate – even though economic theory is not a useful ground upon which to debate them.

Any proposal for subsidies runs into the objection that it calls for disbursement of governmental revenue rather than its collection, which a policy of taxing foreign suppliers would achieve. The objection is regarded as very much more compelling by finance ministries than it is by many economists.[11] It must therefore be supposed that some finance ministries will look with more favour upon a policy of supporting import-competing industries by taxing foreign suppliers than one of directly subsidizing domestic producers. If the judgement of finance ministries is accepted, along with the judgement that it is socially worthwhile to support a domestic industry, then another set of the policies complained of by service suppliers from developed countries – discriminatory taxes on their products – can be justified. The argument from raising revenue, however, now cuts in another direction. There can be very little sense in policies, such as bans on trade or investment, that reduce the competitive ability of foreign suppliers in the local market but do not raise revenue. Such policies will indeed help local providers, but they are the only ones who will gain from them. There is a strong case for using tax on foreign providers rather than bans on trade or investment.

It is difficult to make a case for a ban or quantitative restriction on foreign suppliers either in terms of revenue collection or economic efficiency. Given the availability of alternative and superior policies to assist the domestic industry, a ban on any operations by foreign suppliers requires extremely stong justification. For most service industries, the terms in which such a justification could be formulated are not evident.

Impediments to establishment

Establishment may touch politically sensitive nerves, but from an economic standpoint it is simply an alternative to imports as a means of delivering a service. The comments above on imports of services also apply to services delivered through establishment. If the aim of supporting the import-competing industry is accepted, then the best means of supplying that support is by the payment of subsidies to that industry and the second best means of supporting it is by taxing foreign suppliers, whether they are locally established or provide their services through trade. Impediments to the competitive efficiency of foreign suppliers which do not raise revenue are unlikely to constitute good policy. Bans and quantitative restrictions cannot be defended, either in terms of economic efficiency or of raising revenue.

Regulation

Regulatory powers are often justified on the basis that domestic buyers of a service need protection from lazy or rapacious sellers of the service. Both theory and observation suggest that such powers are sometimes used instead to protect domestic sellers of a service from the impact of competition from abroad – and therefore to exploit domestic buyers of the service. Where this has occurred, governments must decide on whose behalf they want the regulatory powers to be used – the interests of receivers of the service or thos of providers. There is no good economic case to use regulatory powers on behalf of suppliers; support of the domestic industry would be better achieved by the meausres suggested above. The protection of users of services is a legitimate function of regulation; but if the powers granted for the exercise of that function are used on behalf of local providers of the service – and therefore *against* users of the service – it might be better to do away with the regulatory authority and permit users to fend for themselves.

10.6 CONCLUDING COMMENTS

As a practical matter, the resistance of the governments of developing countries to liberalisation in the service sector is in some degree a natural consequence of the prior lack of international rules controlling protection in that sector. Service industries in some economies are very heavily protected. Some members of such industries very understandably prefer the *status quo*, and they are likely to possess very substantial blocking power. It would be foolish to suppose that they will easily be shifted.

Nevertheless, the arguments for protecting the service sector in developing countries are much less solid than the structures of protection that are built upon them. The restrictive policies pursued by some governments are likely to impose substantial costs upon their economies. To have that conclusion backed by more research and by practical experience of liberalising services in developing countries would be valuable. Enough is already known, however, strongly to support the conjecture that for most developing countries, reviews of policy towards the service sector that focus on obtaining the best possible price–quality combination for domestic *users* of a service will yield a number of possibilities of economic gain. For some developing countries, these gains are likely to be large, both in terms of the level of income and of its rate of growth.

11 Structural Adjustment: A General Overview, 1980–9

PAUL MOSLEY

11.1 BACKGROUND

Structural adjustment, for the purposes of this essay, is that part of development policy which is devoted to achieving a boost to the supply side of an economy by the removal of market imperfections; it is therefore to be contrasted with *stabilisation*, which seeks to control the demand side, and also with long-term supply-side policies such as research and sectoral investment policy. In the 1980s the phrase was used by many as a synonym for appropriate development policy and treated, like motherhood, as a good and necessary thing in itself; but even among those using our own strict definitions, there remain multiple differences between those who, like the Latin American structuralists of the 1980s, favour the removal of imperfections through state intervention (for example, in land and credit markets) and those who, like the World Bank of the 1980s, favour their removal by state withdrawal. And within the latter group, disputes persist concerning which markets should be liberalised and in what order, which are further clouded by enormous inter-country differences in what is politically feasible. Figure 11.1 provides a map of the various pathways into which development policy, and the debate about it, ramifies.

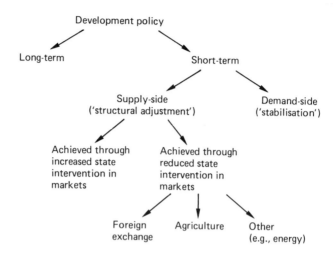

FIGURE 11.1   'Structural adjustment' in relation to other elements of development policy

The focus of this essay is on structural adjustment, in the sense defined above, and on the extent to which it has been able to bring about a lasting improvement in output and living standards in less developed countries (LDCs). The World Bank in the 1980s staked its reputation on the claim that 'outward-looking' economies showed higher levels of production efficiency than 'inward-looking economies' (e.g., World Bank, 1983, Ch. 4; World Bank, 1989a, Table 20) and that governments of all developing countries could increase living standards by making their economies more 'outward-looking' – that is, by implementing a structural adjustment programme of the state intervention-reducing variety. We shall be concerned to test this claim: Section 11.2 deals with the extent of implementation of structural adjustment programmes, section 11.3 with their aggregate effectiveness and section 11.4 attempts to discover why the effectiveness of structural adjustment has varied between countries. The essay arrives at two general conclusions. First, whereas there is indeed a statistically significant payoff to 'structural adjustment' considered as a package, certain elements of the package appear to be vital – notably exchange rate policy and the rationalisation of government investment – and other elements – notably privatisation and foreign trade liberalisation – are irrelevant. Second, that such effectiveness as can be observed is acutely sensitive to a cluster of intermediate variables, of which some relate to the behaviour of the nation's political economy (the extent of real wage compression and political tolerance of it, the nature of the private sector response to liberalisation, the extent of political cohesion amongst exporters) and others to the relationship between the structural adjustment effort and the success of the government's stabilisation and long-term development policies. In general, it will be argued, 'appropriate structural adjustment' means an entirely different thing in a resource poor economy with a shattered infrastructure than in a Newly Industrialising Country (NIC).

11.2 THE IMPLEMENTATION OF 'STRUCTURAL ADJUSTMENT' POLICIES

We begin from the truism that no country can choose *whether* to adjust to external shocks, only *how* to do so; from this point of view, the distinction often made (for example, World Bank, 1988b; World Bank, 1989a) between 'adjusting' and 'non-adjusting' countries is unfortunate. A country which experiences an increase in its balance of payments deficit (i.e., an increase in the net value of claims by nationals of overseas countries on its own domestic economy) must either meet these claims directly, persuade creditors to accept deferred payment, or (if it chooses to repudiate the claim) work out strategies to mitigate the consequences of any retaliatory behaviour by creditors. All of these behaviours have a right to be called an 'adjustment policy'. If we examine the behaviour of LDCs as a group to the shock imposed by the oil crisis and world depression of 1979–83, moreover, what is striking is that *all* LDCs, not only those who have been happy to accept economic support packages from the World Bank and the IMF, have chosen to adopt policies which have sharpened incentives to producers to increase supply. In other words, they have adopted policies of structural adjustment, as well as simple stabilisation. As Table 11.1 demonstrates, even in those LDCs characterised, in the World Bank's view, by 'weak or no reform programmes'. the real effective exchange rate has declined since 1980, and on-farm prices for agricultural exports and real interest rates have

TABLE 11.1   Adjustment indicators for LDCs as a group, 1980–8

	1980 all LDCs	1988 all LDCs	'Strong reform programmes' **	'Weak or no reform programmes' **
Real effective exchange rate (index 1978=100)	104	78	68	82
Public sector deficit as share of GDP	10.2	7.2	6.1	8.0
Real interest rates	−7.9	0.2 *	8.6	−6.5
Agricultural export prices (index 1980–2=100) (*Africa only*)	96	125 *	146	108

Notes: * Data for 1986; ** For the first three indicators a 'strong reform programme' is defined by the existence of a World Bank policy-based lending programme in that country.

Sources: Interest rates, World Bank (1989c) Figure 4.2; exchange rates, World Bank (1989c) Figure 1.7; agricultural prices, World Bank (1989a) Table 19, p. 29; public sector deficit, World Bank (1988b) Figure 3.3, p. 61.

risen. As a broad generalisation, policy adjustment has gone furthest in respect of those policy instruments, such as public expenditure and the exchange rate, which can be manipulated within the central bank or the ministry of finance without any need for legislative sanction or complex institutional planning, and to which political barriers are therefore smallest.

All nations, therefore, have adjusted; but each nation has adjusted in its own way, reflecting its own political imperatives and social priorities as well as the variations in the shocks to which it has been subjected. At this point a major difference between stabilisation and structural adjustment becomes apparent: whereas it is common ground between all parties that aggregate demand needs to be reduced (whether through cutting expenditure or raising taxes) if any economy's balance of payments or inflation problem is to be stabilised, there is no common ground concerning the right way to increase aggregate supply for those wishing to embark on a structural adjustment programme; there is no analogue on the supply side, either in the World Bank or anywhere else, to the IMFs 'Polak Model', which prescribes the amount by which domestic absorption must be reduced if the balance of payments is to be improved by $x. There is a presumption, backed by some empirical analysis in World Bank (1983), that few market distortions are better than many, but there is nothing in economic theory to tell us which distortions should be removed in which order, or even that it will necessarily help if any one distortion is removed.

This territory is still ruled, after thirty years, by the Theory of Second Best (Lipsey and Lancaster, 1956), which warns that in an economy characterised by many market imperfections there is no presumption that the removal of any one such imperfection will necessarily 'make things any better' – i.e., take the economy closer to its production possibility frontier. Any 'structural adjustment programme' – i.e. programme to remove a cluster of such imperfections – is therefore not an application of economic principles but rather an improvisation, a gamble based on the premiss that if past microeconomic policies have yielded unsatisfactory results, an alteration of those policies may help.

Perhaps for this reason, the structural adjustment programmes actually implemented in the Third World have shown extraordinary diversity. The World Bank, which has been responsible for designing a good number of them in conjunction with the economic ministries of LDCs, certainly escapes the censure which has often been levelled at the Fund's stabilisation programmes, of imposing identikit packages on different countries without consideration of differences in economic structure or capacity to adjust. It is, of course, necessary to make a distinction between programmes as *designed* and programmes as *implemented*. In Table 11.2 we set out, in the left-hand column the frequency with which different types of structural adjustment reform were advocated by the Bank and, in the right-hand column the nature of the reforms recommended and implemented in a sample of nine countries studied by a team led by the author (Mosley, Harrigan and Toye, 1991: vol. II, case studies).

TABLE 11.2 Types of policy measures recommended and implemented by World Bank in return for programme finance, 1980–8

Policy measure	% of SALs (1980–7) subject to conditions in this area	Measures recommended and implemented in:									Implementation percentage by type of condition
		Turkey	Philippines	Thailand	Kenya	Malawi	Ghana	Jamaica	Guyana	Ecuador	
Trade policy											
Remove import quotas	57	⊗	⊗		x		x	⊗	x	x	42
Cut tariffs	24	⊗	x	x					x		25
Improve export incentives	76	⊗		⊗	⊗			x	⊗	⊗	67
Resource mobilisation											
Reform budget or taxes	70		⊗	⊗		⊗			⊗		100
Reform interest rate policy	49	⊗					x	x			50
Strengthen external debt management	49				x				⊗		50
Improve financial performance of public enterprise	73	⊗	⊗	⊗	x	⊗	⊗	⊗	x	⊗	77
Efficient use of resources											
Revise priorities of public investment programme	59	⊗	x				⊗	⊗	x	x	50
Raise agricultural prices	73				⊗	x	⊗		⊗		75
Dissolve or reduce powers of state marketing boards	14	x		⊗	x	x	x	x	x	x	13

		90	62	65	45	60	65	35	35	
Reduce or eliminate agricultural input subsidies	27					x				0
Raise energy prices	49	⊗	⊗					x	x	56
Introduce energy conservation measures	35			x						0
Develop indigenous energy sources	24			x						
Revise industry incentive system	68				⊗		⊗		x	66
Institutional reforms										
Strengthen capacity to formulate and implement public investment programme	86	⊗	x		x	⊗	⊗		x	50
Increase efficiency of public enterprise	57				x	x				66
Remove price controls	49		⊗		⊗		⊗		x	50
Implementation percentage by country		90	62	65	45	60	65	35	35	28

Note: X in a cell denotes condition *recommended* in country stated; ⊗ denotes condition *implemented* in country stated.

Sources: Left-hand column, Mosley (1987) Table 2; right-hand column, case studies in Mosley, Harrigan and Toye (1991) vol. 2.

As he looks down the left-hand column of Table 11.2, the alert reader will immediately notice something missing: where is the exchange rate, long cited by the World Bank as the key price which has to be set right in the microeconomy of developing countries? Answer: the IMF is supposed to have sorted it out beforehand. By a division of labour between the two Bretton Woods institutions reconfirmed in 1966 (Feinberg, 1986), the IMF takes primary responsibility for advice on the exchange rate, as a key instrument of stabilisation; the difficulty, as we have moved into the age of structural adjustment, is that it is also a key instrument of resource allocation, which must be at a competitive level if the Bank's other measures are to be expected to work. In principle this difficulty has been sorted out by requiring any developing country to have an IMF standby agreement in position before it is able to negotiate with the World Bank for a structural adjustment loan. Table 11.1 testifies to the Fund's success in bringing this element in the adjustment process into being, but there have been a good number of cases – Jamaica and the Philippines between 1981 and 1985, for example – where for various reasons the Fund, having concluded a standby, allowed the real exchange rate to appreciate in the middle of a Bank structural adjustment programme, thereby provoking the need for a second stabilisation episode which temporarily terminated all adjustment on the supply side.

The second thing to be noted is that not all structural adjustment measures which the Bank asked to be performed have actually been implemented. In its own internal evaluation (World Bank, 1988b, Table 4.1) the Bank estimates the percentage of suggested reforms that have been implemented at 60 per cent, and in our own country case studies, which are intended to be a balanced sample, it ranges from 25 per cent to 90 per cent and averages at less than 50 per cent. This draws attention to two fundamentally important features of structural adjustment. The first is that for a variety of reasons (less precise performance criteria; less power held by the Executive Board; greater pressure to disburse) the World Bank has weaker leverage over the structural adjustment process than the IMF has over the stabilisation process. If an IMF performance criterion is not met, disbursement of the loan is suspended; if a World Bank performance criterion is not met, disbursement of the loan nearly always proceeds. The second is that the political odds are stacked much more heavily against the implementation of structural adjustment than the implementation of stabilisation. Most stabilisation instruments (exchange rate, public investment programme, money supply) can be changed in an afternoon by one official in the central bank or ministry of finance, whereas to 'rationalise the structure of protection' or 'make arrangements to privatise the Maize Marketing Board' (both typical conditions of structural adjustment programmes) takes a lot longer and involves many more people; in addition, the political threat posed by structural adjustment measures is much more direct than that posed by stabilisation measures, since the costs of the latter are scattered across the entire population whereas the costs of the former are borne by specific holders of privileges ('rent-holders' in the World Bank jargon, e.g. local industrialists who lose from the abolition of import quotas, rich maize farmers who lose from the abolition of maize movement restrictions) often have considerable political power. If these two considerations are set side by side, policy-makers in developing countries have a strong temptation to take advantage of the World Bank's bargaining weakness in order to avoid arousing political opposition at home, which they can do by negotiating a structural adjustment loan and then complying only with selected, 'harmless' conditions. The financing of structural adjustment, then, is a game in which the recipient has considerable bargaining power, and in the circumstances what is remarkable is not how much slippage there has been, but how much policy adjustment there has been (Table 11.1) in spite of the formidable obstacles to it.

What is clear after ten years of experience, however, is that there has been massive variation in implementation experience both between countries and between types of policy. As considerations of bargaining theory might lead one to expect, implementation levels tend to be higher in those countries where economic crisis was most acute, the recipient's financial dependence on the donor was greatest and the donor's aid programme was relatively small – in short, where the recipient's bargaining power was weakest (Mosley, Harrigan and Toye, 1991, Ch. 5). But considerations of domestic politics were also vital: in particular, the successful carrying through of any structural adjustment programme required the technocracy in the central bank and the ministry of finance to build an alliance in support of the programme first of all with their own line agencies (ministries of agriculture, commerce and industry, for example), who were most vulnerable to lobbying by aggrieved rent-holders, and beyond that with the industrialists and farmers' representatives directly affected. So powerful are the political barriers to this process, as previously described, that the number of countries where one can truly speak of a 'coalition in support of structural adjustment' can be counted on the fingers of one hand: Turkey, Mauritius, and the Philippines under Aquino for a couple of years. Elsewhere the technocrats, assuming they were unable to impose their will by force (as in Chile) had to fight a somewhat lonely battle, adjusting those instruments which they could (classically the exchange rate and interest rates) but often being forced to accept defeat even in respect of those instruments which lay under their direct control: import quotas, privatisation, composition of the public investment programme (this 'politically biased' pattern of structural adjustment shows up clearly in the final column of Table 11.2). For reasons which we shall develop in section 11.4, this mattered less than it might have been expected to do.

11.3   EFFECTIVENESS

In assessing the effectiveness of structural adjustment programmes we confine ourselves to those sixty or so countries which have conducted those programmes with the World Bank, ignoring that significant number (e.g., India) which have implemented major supply-related reform programmes without involving the Bank. In evaluating structural adjustment efforts, we are in essence comparing what actually happened in a given country with our best guess of what would have happened in the absence of structural adjustment policies. Since the latter is hypothetical, there is always room for honest disagreement regarding what such policies achieved. In principle, there are three possible ways of comparing the 'with-policy' and 'without-policy' situation: comparisons of 'structural adjustment lending' countries with a control group of countries which are similar in all respects to the first group except for the specific supply-side policies which they implemented; cross-section regressions in which the structural adjustment effort features as one among several independent variables influencing growth; and

simulation exercised on econometric models of individual countries. For reasons of space our discussion of the third approach
here will be minimal. (For a report on results from the modelling
approach see Mosley, Harrigan and Toye, 1991, Ch. 8). We shall
also confine our discussion to those performance indicators
stressed by the World Bank – growth and trade performance –
and ignore the important distributional effects of structural adjustment.

Table 11.3 compares the levels of GNP growth, export growth,
balance of payments, investment, consumption and foreign private
capital inflow – five of the main targets of World Bank structural

TABLE 11.3   Comparison of economic performance in adjustment lending and non-adjustment lending, LDCs,
1982–6

Performance criteria	Average value in 20 'adjustment lending' countries, 1982–6	Average value in 20 'non-adjustment lending' countries, 1982–6
Real GNP growth (% p.a.)	1.7	2.0
	[2.95]	[2.12]
Consumption (% of GNP)	86.7	81.4
	[5.0]	[11.4]
Investment (% of GNP)	17.0	20.5
	[4.0]	[7.9]
Balance of payments deficit on current account (% of GNP)	4.0	6.8
	[4.6]	[5.6]
Real export growth (% p.a.)	−0.4	−1.3
	[6.2]	[7.5]

Source: Mosley, Harrigan and Toye (1991) Ch.6. Figures in
brackets are standard deviations.

adjustment lending programmes – as between twenty countries which received World Bank structural adjustment programmes and a 'control group' of developing countries which did not receive adjustment loans but which in other respects (income level, prior growth rate, trend in terms of trade) were selected to be as similar as possible to the adjustment lending group. We observe (without comment at this stage) that the balance of payments performance of adjustment lending countries is substantially better than the performance of the control group, the performance of GNP and export growth trivially better (average export growth being negative in both groups), but the performance of investment a good deal worse.

We now move to the regression approach. Table 11.4 shows the results of an OLS regression estimated on a sample of nineteen countries receiving World Bank Structural Adjustment Loans (SALs) for the seven years 1980–6 (133 observations) in which the dependent variables are the targets which the Bank has declared to be the objectives of structural adjustment (GDP growth, export growth, investment and the inflow of private foreign finance), and the independent variables are the finance provided by, and the implementation of the policy conditions attached to, World Bank adjustment loans, plus a cluster of additional independent variables which may also be expected to exert an influence on growth (weather, terms of trade, IMF finance). Once again we discover that the influence of structural adjustment on exports and GNP growth appears to be mildly positive, and on investment negative. But from this exercise we also discover that the influence of SAL *money* on its own appears to be negative, whereas the implementation of SAL *conditions* has a positive (but lagged) effect. The influence of structural adjustment programmes on inflows of private foreign investment, which it was intended to stimulate, is statistically insignificant.

Finally let us bring together the results of these two exercises with some results from our modelling work on Malawi and from the World Bank's own internal review of adjustment lending (World Bank, 1988b). The results show a remarkable consistency, as displayed in Table 11.5.

We would draw attention in particular to two implications of the above results. First, the immediate negative effect of World Bank loan finance, coupled with the positive effects of implementation

TABLE 11.4 Results of regression analysis, all SAL countries

Dependent variable (R^2 in brackets)	Regression coefficients on independent variables (Student's t-statistic in brackets beneath coefficient)												
	Constant	IMF(t)	SAL(t)	SAL(t-1)	SAL(t-2)	CI(t)	CI(t-1)	CI(t-2)	W(t)	TOT(t)	EPI(t)	INV(t)	gEX(t)
GDP growth (0.40)	-24.68** (-5.65)	-0.11 (-0.46)	0.09 (0.05)	-1.05* (-2.54)	0.90 (1.30)	0.29 (0.50)	1.35** (2.87)	0.20 (0.52)	0.12** (4.54)	0.16** (4.07)	N/A	0.01 (0.16)	0.04 (2.57)
Export growth (0.17)	-0.51 (-0.02)	2.64 (1.83)	-10.08** (-3.08)	3.72 (0.84)	1.09 (0.41)	9.68** (3.96)	-6.04* (-2.15)	1.72 (0.64)	-0.15 (-0.97)	N/A	0.20 (0.94)	-0.25 (-0.71)	N/A
Import growth (0.13)	24.84 (0.93)	2.91* (1.99)	-6.13 (-1.86)	-2.07 (0.46)	3.57 (0.77)	6.69** (2.71)	-4.50 (-1.61)	0.94 (0.13)	-0.18 (-1.13)	-0.15 (-0.63)	N/A	0.12 (0.34)	N/A
Investment as % of GDP (0.25)	-16.37* (-2.43)	0.00 (0.00)	-0.70 (-0.83)	0.53 (0.46)	-0.72 (-0.60)	-0.38 (-0.60)	0.49 (0.67)	-0.20 (-0.28)	0.10* (2.39)	0.32** (6.03)	N/A	N/A	N/A
Private foreign finance (0.10)	-1269.71* (-1.97)	-61.81 (-1.76)	-30.62 (-0.39)	-16.16 (-0.159)	-100.64 (-0.97)	-25.46 (-0.43)	-2.04 (-0.03)	62.43 (0.96)	0.17* (2.15)	6.67 (1.17)	N/A	16.99* (2.01)	N/A

Note: ** denotes significance of a coefficient at the 1% level; * denotes significance of a coefficient at the 5% level.

Notation: IMF = drawing of IMF finance as % of GDP

SAL = SAL and SECAL finance as % of GDP

CI = % implementation of policy conditions set by world bank of SALs and SECAL

W = weather index (rainfall in capital city for years stated as % of 25 years index 1961–6)

TOT = Terms of trade index (1980=100)

EPI = Export price index (1980=100)

INV = investment as a share of GDP

gEX = growth rate of exports.

Source: Mosley, Harrigan and Toye (1991) Ch. 7, Table 10

TABLE 11.5   Effectiveness of structural adjustment: summary of results

Methods	Real GDP growth	Real export growth	Invest-ment	Balance of payments	Foreign finance
1 Tabular com-parisons with 'control group':					
(a) Mosley, Harrigan and Toye (1991)	Neutral/ weak +ve	−ve	+ve	N/A	
(b) World Bank (1988)	Neutral	−ve	+ve	N/A	
2 Multiple regressions	weak +ve	−ve	+ve	Neutral	
3 Single country simulations (Malawi, Morocco)	weak +ve (Morocco only)	Neutral (Morocco only)	-ve	N/A	

Sources: World Bank (1988b); Mosley, Harrigan and Toye (1991)

of loan conditions, suggest that such finance, far from acting as a leverage mechanism to encourage structural adjustment reforms, may in a larger number of countries have simply reduced the immediate pressure to adjust by delaying the moment when radical measures had to be undertaken (see also Mosley, Hudson and Horrell, 1987); but when they were undertaken they seem on balance to have helped. Second, however, there is the worrying evidence, at a time when attention is being switched from concerns of 'adjustment' to those of 'sustainable growth', that structural adjustment programmes have acted to reduce investment, and hence long-term growth prospects. Hypotheses concerning the causal mechanisms at work are various: adjustment lending is not project-tied, and hence can more freely be diverted to consumption; adjustment lending is limited to stabilisation programmes of which the part most faithfully carried out has been cuts in public investment; private investment, as revealed by Table 11.4, has failed to respond to the intended stimulus of SALs, possibly because the private sector sees the implementation of adjustment programmes itself as a sign of weakness, and expects that any changes implemented under a structural adjustment programme will be soon reversed. Whatever the reasons for it, the fact of declining investment levels is worrying, more particularly because, as we shall proceed to argue, in the poorest countries a boost to public investment is the key element in a correctly designed structural adjustment programme.

11.4 INTER-COUNTRY VARIATIONS IN EXPERIENCE

The findings reported in section 11.3 have been aggregative; the high standard deviations of Table 11.3 provide a warning of how much adjustment experiences varied between countries. Just as Lance Taylor's study (1988) for the World Institute for Development Economics Research (WIDER) has reminded us that there are 'varieties of stabilisation experience', so even the most casual review of what happened in different developing countries during the 1980s makes one aware that the stimuli listed in Table 11.2 produced enormously diverse responses. Again we confront the fact that structural adjustment is not a standard and reliable cure for a clearly identified disease, but an improvisation, a collection of measures thrown together in the hope of inducing greater supply-side efficiency in a wide variety of economies. In this section we speculate in summary manner (drawing on the case studies in Mosley, Harrigan and Toye, *vol. II* 1991) on some of the factors, over and above the political variables discussed in section 11.2, which may have differentiated the effective from the ineffective programmes.

Three such factors which stand out as potential influences on the effectiveness of structural adjustment are:

- The response of domestic and overseas investment to the structural adjustment programme

- The behaviour of real wages, and as a consequence the size of the competitive advantage conveyed by devaluation
- whether or not the structural adjustment exercise was interrupted mid-term by a stabilisation episode.

Figure 11.2 graphs these potential explanatory variables onto the relationship between the implementation of structural adjustment measures and growth examined in section 11.4. In simple two-variable form this becomes:

$$\text{GDP growth} = -1.8 + 0.032 \text{ (level of implementation of structural adjustment conditions)}, r^2 = 0.41$$

Let us now see whether the variables mentioned above explain any tendency for countries to perform better or worse than this regression line might predict. Malawi, Ghana and Jamaica, of our case-study countries, lie very close to the regression line, and so can be disregarded for this purpose. The status of the others in relation to our chosen indicators is as set out in Table 11.6.

The indicators set out in Table 11.6 should not be mistaken for econometric evidence (which cannot be provided with a sample of only nine countries); nonetheless, it does appear at least as though the less-than-expected performance of foreign investment inflows and the unexpected stabilisation episodes may have something to do with the lower-than-predicted growth rates observed in Guyana and the Philippines. But Kenya's structural adjustment process was interrupted by a stabilisation episode, which it managed to shrug off; nor did a rise in real wages in Thailand manage to prevent it becoming one of the most successful of all developing economies, with double-digit growth rates of both GDP and exports, during the second half of the 1980s. At the very least, therefore, falling real wages do not constitute a necessary condition for the success of a structural adjustment programme.

We would additionally draw attention to the case of Guyana, by some measure the poorest performer within our sample. Jane Harrigan's case study of this country (Mosley, Harrigan and Toye, 1991; Ch. 18) makes it clear that this fiasco is by no means solely due to its failure to implement the policy advice of the World Bank, nor even to the collapse of public expenditure and foreign

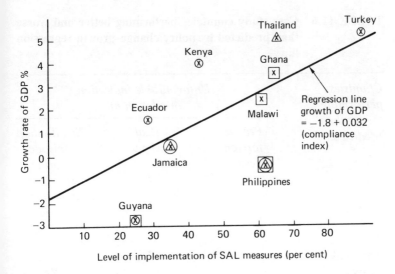

FIGURE 11.2 Relation between slippage and growth of GDP, with possible explanation of 'outliers'

investment which occurred during the stabilisation episode. Rather, in a country where infrastructure and the export sectors' capital stock had decayed, 'structural adjustment' should have taken the form of rehabilitation of the productive structure, rather than privatisation and liberalisation. As one of the World Bank's most percipient senior economists has acknowledged,

> Conventional text-book economics is not written for economies in decline, but for static or growing economies. One can structurally adjust an economy which is growing but growing inefficiently, or one that is static. But an economy in cumulative decline forces one to confront a systemic problem. Such an economy requires transformation of a Keynesian type, in which the emphasis is on the quantity and quality of investment, particularly the stimulative role of public sector investment. The Bank's structural adjustment programmes however are rooted in the marginality theories of neo-classical text-book economics with their emphasis placed on price incentives, exchange rate adjustments, and trade liberalisation (cited in Mosley, Harrigan and Toye, 1990, Ch. 18).

TABLE 11.6   Case-study countries performing better and worse than predicted by policy change–growth regression line

Countries performing 'better than predicted'	Unfavourable indication in relation to:		
	Private foreign investment	Real wages	Stabilisation episode during structural adjustment period
Turkey			
Thailand		Yes	
Kenya			Yes
Countries performing 'worse than predicted'			
Guyana	Yes		Yes
Philippines	Yes		Yes

Note: A rise in real wages during the adjustment period is treated as an 'unfavourable indication'.

Source: Harrigan and Mosley (1991); World Bank (1989c).

The importance of this observation is that it is not, of course, the economy of Guyana alone which is in 'cumulative decline', but that of many of the world's poorest countries, including much of sub-Saharan Africa. Mozambique, Sudan, Ethiopia, Somalia, Sierra Leone, Guinea, Zaire, even Nigeria: all of these, as much as Guyana, require 'transformation of a Keynesian type', plus state intervention to make land and smallholder credit available to those who need them, rather than stimuli for a 'private capitalist sector' which in many of the poorest countries scarcely exists. Our reading of the structural adjustment experience of the poorer developing countries, then, leads us to take inspiration from the Latin American structuralists of the 1950s, who advocated that the state itself should promote development by removing bottlenecks in the economy – the left-hand branch of the two structural adjustment options in Figure 11.1 – rather than from the 'new structuralist' experiments of the 1980s.

11.5 SYNTHESIS AND HISTORICAL CONTEXT

The cluster of reforms known as 'structural adjustment', then, has been implemented intitially across the entire less developed world during the 1980s, but in a patchy manner which reflects the fact that exchange rate and public expenditure reforms, being administratively simpler and politically less visible, are easier to implement than liberalisation and privatisation. Where implemented they appear to have raised income and exports, but to an extent which varied across countries according to the response of private foreign investment and the incidence of emergency stabilisation measures. The liberalising brand of structural adjustment fashionable in the 1980s appears to have more relevance to richer than to poorer LDCs and least of all to those which are in absolute decline.

It remains to ask how this episode fits into its historical context. Gerschenkron (1965) comparing the industrialisation patterns followed by successive countries before 1914, observed that each such process appeared to be more heavy industry-oriented, more monopolistic and more heavily state-protected than the last; but as has frequently been noted (for example Hirschman, 1968; Ranis, 1990) this trend towards progressively increasing state intervention has been bucked by the 'late late industrialisers' of the twentieth century, many of whom (classically Hong Kong and Singapore) have been remarkably sparing in their use of industrial protection. In an attempt to make sense of the complex reality of post-colonial industrialisation, Fei and Ranis (1988, pp.15–23) have argued that the general pattern is for an initial inward-looking (import substitution) phase (artificially prolonged in Latin America) to be succeeded by a trend towards progressively increasing liberalisation and export orientation, as the economy becomes more complex and less manipulable by a few powerful rent-holders. This long-term trend will be interrupted by exogenous shocks provoked by the world business cycle, primary product prices, etc. Where does the structural adjustment episode of the 1980s fit into this long-term pattern?

What immediately becomes clear is that the appropriateness of packages such as those set out in Table 11.2 depends entirely on the stage of development which the recipient country has reached. In countries such as Turkey and the Philippines the World Bank was able to achieve spectacular success by catching the point of transition from the inward-oriented to the export-oriented phase, at a point when an internal political change had made it unnecessary, and indeed undesirable, for the state to propitiate most of the rent-holders from the previous *ancien régime*. In countries such as Kenya and Malawi it tilted at windmills by asking for liberalisation at a point when the country was *still, and rightly, in its inward-oriented phase*, and needed protection for its infant activities both industrial and agricultural before a switch to export-led growth could make any policy sense. In countries such as Guyana and Ghana in the early 1980s, caught in a process of systemic decline, 'structural adjustment' in the liberalising sense can be described only as a historical irrelevance, but many elements of the Bank's approach to Ghana in 1984–6 showed that the Bank had learned to appreciate the need for a phase of capital stock rehabilitation in advance of any changes in the structure of industrial protection or ownership. In the early 1980s one of the architects of structural adjustment policy at the World Bank described the structural adjustment process as a necessary item of consumption for all LDCs, designed to confront 'the central problem of development at present' (Stern, 1983, p.107). The experience of the 1980s has taught us to see structural adjustment in the Bank's sense, rather, as a somewhat specialised, and on balance a middle-income, item of consumption.

Notes and References

CHAPTER 3

1. Technological innovation in agriculture can also be viewed as a response to growing population pressure, particularly in pre-industrial societies (Boserup, 1965). Boserup argues that the response of food supplies to population growth is elastic, even in poor countries, *due to the adoption by farmers of new technology which increases the productivity of land*. But the theory says nothing about the origins of technical innovations. The existence of a stock of unused innovations is assumed. Boserup's hypothesis has been tested empirically, with some success, in SSA (Pingali, Bigot and Binswanger, 1987).
2. See Ghatak and Ingersent (1984, Ch. 6, pp. 155–8) for a fuller treatment of the theory of factor-biased technical change, including its effects on total output and employment.
3. See Ghatak and Ingersent (1984, Ch. 6, pp. 158–60 and 166–9) for a further treatment of the concepts of LATC and LDTC and the issue of selective mechanisation.
4. The existence of inter-industry linkage effects is quite independent of the existence of a formal input–output matrix which some LDCs lack the capacity to prepare.
5. A succinct general review of the impact of technical change on agricultural output and income in LDCs, including both conceptual and empirical aspects, and emphasising the effects of farm mechanisation, is given by McInerney *et al.* (1984).
6. This subsection draws on Dalrymple (1985) and World Bank (1986b).

7. Conceptually, the HYV technology represents a discrete shift in the production function (yield–fertiliser relationship) (see, for example, Herdt and Capule, 1983).

8. The initiation of a system of IARCs in the 1960s and 1970s was facilitated by the success of an agricultural science programme set up in Mexico in 1943 by the Rockefeller Foundation. This programme (headed by Norman Borlaug) developed semi–dwarf wheat varieties incorporating stem rust resistance which successfully expanded wheat production in Mexico. In 1963 the Rockefeller Foundation Institute was reorganised with Ford Foundation help as the International Centre for the Improvement of Maize and Wheat. The two Foundations also initiated a rice research programme via the setting up of the International Rice Research Institute (IRRI) in the Philippines in 1962. The international research system was formalised in 1971 with the formation of the Consultative Group on International Agricultural Research (CGIAR) with sponsorship from the World Bank, The Food and Agricultural Organisation, the United Nations Development Programme, nine national governments and three foundations. The international research system expanded rapidly and the number of institutions now includes ten IARCs and three research related programmes.

9. Mexican varieties of wheat bred at the International Centre for the Improvement of Maize and Wheat were initially transferred to regions with similar agroecology (latitude and climate), particularly India and Pakistan. Likewise initial transfers of rice from IRRI went to regions with similar agroecology. The impact of the GR came from the development of varieties modelled on IARC strains.

10. Burma, Bangladesh, China, India, Indonesia, the Philippines, Sri Lanka, Thailand.

11. The complementarity between factors makes it difficult to isolate the contribution of the separate factors, but the broad picture is clear.

12. Alauddin and Tisdell (1986) argue that the real contribution of the GR in Bangladesh lies in increased land productivity via multiple cropping rather than extension of the area cultivated or increased yields from single cropping.

13. For example, Prahladachar (1983), Herdt and Capule (1983), Hayami and Ruttan (1985). The evidence relates to Asia.

14. Pinstrup-Anderson (1982) pp. 102–4 reports internal rates of return generally approaching 50 per cent from 50 studies relating the growth of agricultural output to research expenditure in LDCs excluding SSA.

15. For details see, for example, Nolan (1983), Nolan and Paine (1986) and Perkins (1988).

16. McMillan *et al.* (1989) actually measure Total Factor Productivity (TFP) as the residual from an 'institutional' production function relating output to (a) aggregate non-labour inputs and (b) the stock of labour measured by number of workers. The intercept of the function is a mixture of (invariant) technological and taste parameters and labour incentive and price variables. The residual is then related to movements in the incentive and price variables. They then find that about 75 per cent of the TFP increase in 1978–84 resulted from incentive effects and the remainder from price changes. See also Lin (1988) for theoretical models and empirical results of an analysis of the incentive systems under the collective and the household responsibility system.

17. This section draws on Buttel and Barker (1985) and Buttel, Kenney and Kloppenburg (1985).

18. A broad definition of biotechnology is 'the manipulation of living organisms in order to alter their characteristics in some fashion, to encourage them to produce some desired product, or to use them as a component of a broader production process' (Buttel *et al.* p. 13). Biotechnology includes the techniques of recombinant DNA (the insertion of genetic material from one organism into the genetic code of another – or 'genetic engineering') and plant cell and tissue culture.

19. Hybrids confer natural proprietary protection for seed producers since farmers must repeatedly purchase hybrid seed. However, with open pollinated crops, farmers can multiply the seed themselves and farmers are the dominant competitor to seed firms.

20. There is a tendency for corporate-sponsored research in universities to replace public funding. Increasing stress in research orientation is being placed on the direct 'economic' returns from research.

21. UNIDO has sponsored the establishment of the International Centre for Genetic Engineering and Biotechnology

with a mandate to research into applications in a Third World context, but its budget is small compared to those of leading genetic engineering firms.

CHAPTER 5

1. This paper has benefited from comments by Stephen Coate, Michael Lipton and Martin Ravallion. The usual disclaimer applies.
2. See the contributions in Garfinkel (1982).
3. Kanbur (1987a) reviews the issues in the light of recent US and UK policy.
4. On these issues see Atkinson (1987), Kanbur (1987b).
5. It requires the state to have perfect information about individuals' tastes and characteristics so that individuals are prevented from 'pretending' to have incomes below the poverty line in order to claim a transfer.
6. For developed countries there has been some collation of evidence. Kesselman (1982) classified several programmes into 'universal' or 'tested'. Of the seven UK programmes considered two were universal and five tested. Administrative costs as a percentage of benefits were 3.8 per cent and 3.5 per cent for the universal programmes, while they ranged from 5.2 per cent to 15.4 per cent for the tested programmes. In the US, the old age, survivors, disability and health insurance programme (a universal programme) had administrative costs of 2.5 per cent of benefits, while for public assistance and unemployment insurance (tested programmes) the figures were 12.1 per cent and 11.8 per cent. The veteran's welfare programme, a tested programme, had an incredible administrative costs to benefits ratio of 95.2 per cent. What seems to be needed is systematic compilation and analysis of such data for developing countries.
7. The latter has been much discussed in the developed country literature (see, for example, Moffitt, 1983) but very little, if anything, has been written on it in the developing country context.
8. This is the motivation for the analyses of optimal income tax

problems, first analysed by Mirrlees (1971).

9. Besley (1988) provides simulations which suggest that means testing is still very often widely preferable to a universalistic programme, in spite of these effects.

10. Much work has been done in the developed country context. In a recent exercise based on US data, Sadka, Garfinkel and Moreland (1982) conclude that:

> the results presented in this paper are sufficient to call into question the consensus among economic experts that transfer programmes which provide benefits only to those with low incomes are more efficient than those which provide benefits to all regardless of income.

11. A theoretical analysis of the impact of political economy constraints on the analysis of price reform is provided in Braverman and Kanbur (1987).

12. Such as those being conducted, with World Bank support in Côte d'Ivoire, Peru, Ghana and Mauretania.

13. Those interested in the details should consult Kanbur (1986; 1987b).

14. I.e., the aggregate of individual shortfalls of income from the poverty line for poor people.

15. For an overview of how the available published evidence for Latin America might be used, see Kanbur (1987d).

16. Besley and Kanbur (1988) also presents generalisation of this rule.

17. For further discussion, see Besley and Coate (1988).

CHAPTER 6

1. We would like to thank Mike Gavin and Ricardo Hausmann for helpful comments.

2. See Bevan, Bigsten, Collier and Gunning (1988).

3. See Bevan, Collier and Gunning (1989a).

4. See Corden (1984) for a survey.

5. On Indonesia see Warr (1986), on Egypt see Martin and van Wijnbergen (1986) and on Nigeria see Collier (1983, 1987, 1988).

6. See Bevan, Collier and Gunning (1990).
7. We are here assuming, for simplicity, that stochastic outcomes are independently distributed between periods. Otherwise, particular outcomes may lead to revised forecasts even when they are consistent with past expectations.
8. See Bevan, Collier and Gunning (1989b).
9. As can be seen the two unrevised cases are very similar. The distinction between them becomes important in the context of taxation; see section 6.8 below.
10. This is not necessarily the case when depreciation is taken into account for then there is an incentive to increase (net) investment in one sector while reducing (gross) investment in the other sector and the net effect on total investment is ambiguous. We will assume that the net effect is positive but, clearly, this is not necessarily so.
11. There may be an additional effect if the two sectors differ in the composition of the investment they require. Suppose that the tradable sector uses only tradable capital goods whereas the non-tradable sector uses both tradable and non-tradable capital goods. Now when the tradable sector is the favoured sector the cost of capital does not fall in terms of its output, whereas when the non-tradable sector is the favoured sector the average cost of a unit of capital (a composite) does fall in terms of its output. Hence, in this case, *ceteris paribus*, the investment stimulus would be more pronounced with a positive shock.
12. There is no more reason for tradable and non-tradable capital goods to be perfect substitutes than for tradable and non-tradable consumer goods to be so, and the Theory of Dutch Disease is predicated upon the reasonable idea that tradables and non-tradables in general are not perfect substitutes.
13. See, for example, Bruno and Sachs (1982), Brock (1988) and Gavin (forthcoming).
14. There may be a phase at the onset of the boom during which there is domestic investment but no foreign asset acquisition. Similarly the repatriation of foreign financial assets could precede the end of the windfall. Figure 6.3b abstracts from these possibilities.

15. The generalisation of the effect depicted here as a special case is that the opportunity cost of funds for domestic investment falls as the country's net foreign assets are increased (or its net liabilities are reduced).

16. Whether or not the price of capital goods (in units of tradables) ends up above or below its pre-boom level depends upon intersectoral differences in factor proportions. Figure 6.3e depicts the case in which the price reverts to its initial level.

17. The unaccommodated extra demand for money will tend to lower the price level, giving rise to a wealth effect which may reduce the propensity to save.

CHAPTER 9

1. The figures measure *gross* external debt, or the disbursed and outstanding contractual liabilities of countries' residents to pay interest and/or principal to non-residents (Joint Report, 1988, p. 19). They are gross values in that they neglect the foreign assets (e.g. reserves), of the countries involved. They also exclude foreign held equity investments in local enterprises, since no contractual obligation exists in this case other than a claim to residual streams of income. A final significant definitional aspect of the figures is the distinction between 'public and publicly guaranteed' debt and 'private non-guaranteed' claims. The guarantee arises where the government of the debtor country has accepted ultimate responsibility for the debt service commitment on foreign loans to local (often parastatal) entities. These loans therefore have the same 'security' as loans to the government itself.

2. 'Low Income Africa' is a sub-group of thirty SSA countries which receive World Bank finance only on concessional terms through its International Development Association affiliate.

3. Capital flight in a certain period is calculated indirectly as follows: net direct investment inflows (FDI) + increases in gros external debt – the sum of recorded current account deficits over the period – increases in foreign assets (includ-

ing foreign exchange reserves) of the country's banking sector. Capital flight thus represents the difference between reported foreign exchange receipts and payments (for uses). For a discussion of the limitations of this measure see Morgan (1986, p. 13).

4. The 'Paris Club' is an intergovernmental forum which meets to renegotiate debts to official creditors, (donor governments and their agencies), with OECD countries being the principal members. Traditionally, Paris Club negotiations have permitted the rescheduling of interest as well as principal. Rescheduling means the postponement of repayments of principal on a loan. It does not imply a reduction in the burden of payments unless the new loans are to be financed at lower interest rates than the old ones. Otherwise, rescheduling allows only a 'bunching' of maturing debt to be spread out over a longer time period.

5. Sometimes the Commercial Bank Advisory Committees are referred to as the 'London Club'. A basic difference with the Paris Club, at least until 1987, was that rescheduling of interest payments was not permitted.

6. A difficulty with debt–equity swaps is that the local currency created may add to domestic inflation. 'Round tripping' can also arise when foreign assets of local residents are used to buy the debt as a means of obtaining national currency at the favourable rate. The proceeds may then be used to purchase dollars for re-export on the local black market. The associated tendency for the black market price of dollars to rise may heighten the inflationary expectation of an official devaluation.

7. Corden (1988a) adopts a wider, more controversial, definition of debt relief which *includes* debt rescheduling and concerted lending on the grounds that these arrangements involve the provision of finance at interest rates well below what the country would need to offer 'new' external lenders.

8. It has proved difficult in the international context to create loans with varying degrees of seniority: an 'old' claim is as likely to be repaid as a 'new' one. '*Pari passu*' and 'negative pledge' clauses in bank loan agreements, for instance, seek to ensure that prior right of security cannot be given to one creditor in preference to another.

CHAPTER 10

1. UNCTAD Secretariat (1985, Ch. III) discusses definitions and their effects on statistics such as those cited above.
2. A report in the *Financial Times* (15 November 1988) illustrates the point. The headline is 'Zambian maize left to rot by the roadside'. The report goes on to say, in part, that 'road haulage is the most serious problem of all. About 1000 trucks are needed and all long-haul contract trucks in Zambia have been forbidden by law to leave the country in an attempt to marshall the maximum number. But truckers have resisted taking their vehicles onto remote and badly maintained roads where breakdowns are common and spare parts non-existent . . . As a cooperative farmer from Central Province ruefully puts it "We just do not understand why we should be encouraged to grow more food when nobody comes to collect it or even cover it to protect it from the rains" '.
3. Bauer and Yamey (1951, p. 753), discussing (and disputing) the proposition that services grow in importance with development, observe that: 'Over a considerable period of development many activities, especially trading, porterage and domestic service, would not be regarded as separate occupations either by official enumerators or by the subjects themselves. As specializations become more definite and pronounced and as these activities are carried out by specialists, the performers and their performance are more easily identified and recognised and their quantitative extent looms larger, possibly much larger in occupational statistics, even though in total the volume of these activities may be unchanged or even reduced'.
4. The actions a government can take with regard to international trade in goods is to some extent limited by the General Agreement on Tariffs and Trade (GATT). There is no such legal restraint on the actions that a government can take with respect to international transactions in services.
5. Of course, direct regulation of inputs also occurs in goods trade – as when a government, on health grounds, insists that it must inspect a food-processing or pharmaceuticals plant before the output of that plant can be sold in its territory. An example is British behaviour towards UHT milk imports, in

which inspection was required by local authorities but no funds were available for the inspectors to travel abroad. The effect was of a total prohibition on imports of UHT milk.

6. US policy towards maritime transport policy provides an interesting example of a service affecting exports of a good. US cabotage law requires lumber shipped from Seattle to use US bottoms. Lumber shipped from Vancouver can be shipped at international rates. The difference apparently gives Canadian lumber a competitive advantage in the South-Eastern states of the US.

7. The results reported by by Cecchini are only for the countries shown in Table 10.1. Research by the Bureau of European Consumer Organisations (Beuc), however, apparently suggests that the differences are even larger in some of the remaining member states. According to Beuc, a 10-year term insurance policy will cost a 30-year old male non-smoker ten times the UK price in Portugal and four times the UK price in Greece (reported in the *Financial Times*, 9 March 1988).

8. A fact that might be noted by those looking for topics for Ph.D. research! De Soto (1989) provides an illuminating discussion of conditions in Peru.

9. UNCTAD Secretariat (1985) presents a similar though more detailed classification and discussion.

10. The same theorem states that the most efficient means is not independent of objective – in particular, if the objective is to restrict imports, then a tariff is superior to a subsidy. In some service industries, the goal might indeed be to restrict imports – for example, where foreign films or television programmes are seen as a threat to local culture – and the ranking would then be reversed. Moreover, to rank a subsidy to output as superior to a tariff assumes the country is unable to affect the terms of trade – or at least with a level of tariff protection that is less than the optimal tariff. For most developing countries, and perhaps for all, this appears to be a plausible assumption with respect to services.

11. It does not seem relevant to economists because, first, an industry can be 'subsidized' by placing a tax on other industries. 'Subsidies' therefore do not require disbursement of government revenue. To tax other industries clearly may not make good *political* sense. However, taxes on foreign

suppliers will allow domestic producers to raise their prices also – or, in other words, to collect a 'tax' direct from purchasers of their product. The mere fact that the 'tax' does not go through the finance ministry does not seem very relevant to a judgement on overall social welfare.

Bibliography

Akerlof, G. (1978) 'The Economics of 'Tagging' as Applied to the Optimal Income Tax, Welfare Programs and Manpower Planning', *American Economic Review*, 68(1) (March): 8–19.

Alamgir, M. (1980) *Famine in South Asia – Political Economy of Mass Starvation in Bangladesh* (Cambridge, Mass: Oelgeschlager, Gunn & Hain).

Alauddin, M. and Tisdell, C. (1986) 'Decomposition Methods, Agricultural Productivity Growth and Technological Change: A Critique Supported by Bangladeshi Data', *Oxford Bulletin of Economics and Statistics*, 48: 353–72.

Alderman, H. (1987) 'Allocation of Goods Through Non-price Mechanisms: Evidence on Distribution by Willingness to Wait', *Journal of Development Economics*, 25: 105–24.

Alexandratos, N. (ed) (1988) *World Agriculture: Towards 2000* (Belhaven, by arrangement with FAO).

Amsden, A. (1989) *Asia's New Giant: South Korea and Late Industrialisation* (New York: Oxford University Press).

Anand, S. and Kanbur, S.M.R. (1987) 'Public Policy and Basic Needs Provision in Sri Lanka', in J. Drèze and A. K. Sen (eds), *Hunger: Economics and Policy* (Oxford: Oxford University Press).

Arroyo, G. M. (1984) *The Services Sector in the Philippines*, working paper, 2 (Kuala Lumpur and Canberra: ASEAN–Australia Joint Research Project).

Atkinson, A. B. (1987) 'On the Measurement of Poverty', *Econometrica*, 55(4) (July): 49–64.

Baer, W. (1987) 'The Resurgence of inflation in Brazil 1974–86', *World Development*, 15: 1007–34.

Balassa, B. (1979), 'Intra Industry Trade and the Integration of the Developing Countries in the World Economy', in H. Giersch (ed.), *On the Economics of Intra Industry Trade* (Tübigen: J.C.B. Mohr).

Balassa, B. (1989) 'Outward Orientation', in H. B. Chenery and T. N. Srinivasan (eds), *Handbook of Development Economics*, vol. 2 (Amsterdam: North-Holland).

Balassa, B. *et al.* (1982) *Development Strategies in Semi-Industrial Economies* (Baltimore: Johns Hopkins University Press).

Balassa, B. and Bauwens, C. (1988) *Changing Trade Patterns in Manufactured Goods* (Amsterdam: North-Holland).

Baldwin, R. E. (1969) 'A Critique of Infant Industry Protection', *Journal of Political Economy*, 17: 295–305.

Baldwin, R. and Flam, H. (1989) 'Strategic Trade Policies in the Market for 30–40 Seater Commuter Aircraft', seminar paper, 431 (Stockholm: Institute for Internal Economic Studies).

Bardhan, P. (1988) 'Alternative Approaches to Development Economics', in H. Chenery and T. N. Srinivasan (eds), *Handbook of Development Economics*, vol. 1 (Amsterdam: North Holland).

Bardhan, P. (1989) 'The new Institutional Economics and Development Theory: A Brief Critical Assessment', *World Development*, 17, 9 (September).

Basu, D. (1986) 'Sen's Analysis of Famine: A Critique', *Journal of Development Studies,* 22: 598–603.

Bates, R. H. (1981) *Markets and States in Tropical Africa: The Political Basis of Agricultural Policies* (Berkely: University of California Press).

Bates, R. H. (1983) *Essays on the Political Economy of Rural Africa* (Cambridge: Cambridge University Press).

Bauer, P. and Yamey, B. S. (1951) 'Economic Progress and Occupational Distribution', *Economic Journal*, 61(244) (December): 741–55.

Bell, M., Ross-Larson, B. and Westphal, L.E. (1984) 'Assessing the Performance of Infant Industries', *Journal of Development Economics*, 16: 101–28.

Berg, A. and Sachs, J. (1988) *The Debt Crisis: Structural Explanations of Country Performance*, NBER working paper, 2607 (June).

Berry, D.A. and Cline, W.R. (1979) *Agrarian Structure and Productivity in Developing Countries* (Baltimore: Johns Hopkins University Press).

Besley, T.J. (1988) 'Means Testing Versus Universal Provision in Poverty Alleviation Programs', *Economica*, 10.

Besley, T.J. and Coate, S. (1988) 'Workfare vs. Welfare: Incentive Arguments for Work Requirements in Poverty Alleviation Programs', Woodrow Wilson School discussion papers in Economics, Research Program in Development Studies, 142.

Besley, T.J. and Coate, S. (1989) 'Universal Public Provision of Private Goods and the Redistribution of Income', Woodrow Wilson School, Princeton University (mimeo).

Besley, T.J. and Kanbur, S.M.R. (1988) 'Food Subsidies and Poverty Alleviation', *Economic Journal*, 98 (March–June): 701–19.

Bevan, D.L., (1989) *Peasants and Governments: An Economic Analysis* (Oxford: Oxford University Press).

Bevan, D.L., (1990) *Controlled Open Economies: A Neoclassical Approach to Structuralism* (Oxford: Oxford University Press).

Bevan, D.L., Bigsten, A., Collier, P. and Gunning J.W. (1988) 'Incomes in the United Republic of Tanzania during the 'Nyerere Experiment'', in W. van Ginneken (ed.), *Trends in Employment and Labour Incomes* (Geneva: ILO) : 62–83.

Bevan, D.L., Collier, P. and Gunning, J.W. (1989) 'Fiscal Response to a Temporary Trade Shock: the Aftermath of the Kenyan Coffee Boom', *World Bank Economic Review*, 3:359–78.

Bhagwati, J. N. (1958) 'Immiserising Growth: A Geometrical Note', *Review of Economic Studies* (June).

Bhagwati, J. N. (1969) 'On the Equivalence of Tariffs and Quotas', in J. N. Bhagwati (ed.), *Trade, Tariffs and Growth* (London: Weidenfeld and Nicolson).

Bhagwati, J.N. (1978) *Anatomy and Consequences of Exchange Controls Regimes* (New York: National Bureau of Economic Research).

Bhagwati, J. N. (1987a) 'International Trade in Services and its Relevance for Economic Development', in O. Gravini (ed.), *The Emerging Service Economy*, Services World Economy series, 1 (New York: Pergamon Press).

Bhagwati, J. N. (1987b) 'Trade in Services and the Multilateral Trade negotiations', *World Bank Economic Review*, 10.

Bhagwati, J.N. (1988) 'Export-Promoting Trade Strategy: Issues and Evidence', *World Bank Research Observer*, 3, 1: 27–58.

Bhagwati, J. N. and Ramaswami, V.K. (1963) 'Domestic Distortions, Tariffs and the Theory of Optimum Subsidy', *Journal of Political Economy*, 71: 44–50.

Bhalla, S.S. and Roy, P. (1988) 'Misspecification in Farm Productivity Analysis: The Role of Land Quality', *Oxford Economic Papers*, 40: 55–73.

Bienen, H.S. and Gersovitz, M. (1985) 'Economic Stabilization, Conditionality and Political Stability', *International Organization*, 10.

Biggs, T. and Levy, B. (1990) 'Strategic Interventions and the Political Economy of Industrial Policy in Developing Countries', forthcoming in D. Perkins and M. Roemer (eds), *Economic Systems in Developing Countries* (Cambridge Mass.: Harvard University Press).

Binkley, J.K. and Harrer, B. (1981) 'Major Determinants of Ocean Freight Rates for Grains: An Econometric Analysis', *Journal of Agricultural Economics*, 10: 44–57.

Binswanger, H. and Pingali, P. (1988) 'Technological Priorities for Farming in Sub-Saharan Africa', *World Bank Research Observer*, 3: 81–98.

Boserup, E. (1965) *The Conditions of Agricultural Growth* (London: Allen & Unwin).

Brander, J. and Spencer, B. (1982) 'Tariff Protection and Imperfect Competition', in H. Kierskowski (ed.), *Monopolistic Competition and International Trade* (Oxford: Oxford University Press).

Brander, J. and Spencer, B. (1984) 'Trade Warfare: Tariffs and Cartels', *Journal of International Economics*, 16: 227–42.

Braverman, A. and Kanbur, S.M.R. (1987) 'Urban Bias and the Political Economy of Agricultural Price Reform', *World Development*, 10.

Brecher, R. and Diaz-Alexandro, C. (1977) 'Tariffs, Foreign Capital and Immiserising Growth', *Journal of International Economics*, 7: 317–22.

Brock, P.L. (1988) 'Investment, the Current Account, and the Relative Price of Non-traded goods in a Small Open Economy', *Journal of International Economics*, 24: 235–53.

Bruno, M. and Sachs, J. (1982) 'Energy and Resource Allocation:

a Dynamic Model of the 'Dutch Disease'', *Review of Economic Studies*, 49: 849–50.

Bulow, J. and Rogoff, K. (1988) 'The buyback boondoggle', *Brookings Papers on Economic Activity*, 2: 675–98.

Buttel, F.H. and Barker, R. (1985) 'Emerging Agricultural Technologies, Public Policy and Implications for Third World Agriculture: The Case of Biotechnology', *American Journal of Agricultural Economics*, 67: 1170–5.

Buttel, F.H., Kenney, M. and Kloppenburg, J. (1985) 'From Green Revolution to Biorevolution: Some Observations of the Changing Technological Bases of Economic Transformation in the Third World', *Economic Development and Cultural Change*, 33: 31–55.

CAA, (1983) *A Comparison Between European and United States Fares*, CAA paper, 83006 (London: Civil Aviation Authority).

Calvo, G.A. (1987) 'On the Cost of a Temporary Policy', *Journal of Development Economics*, 27: 245–61.

Calvo, G.A. (1988) 'Costly Trade Liberalizations', *International Monetary Fund Staff Papers*, 35, 3: 461–73.

Cantwell, J. (1989) *Technological Innovation and Multinational Corporations* (Oxford: Basil Blackwell).

Carter, R. and Dickinson, G. (1987) *Problems of International Transactions in the Insurance Industry*, Thames Essay (London: Trade Policy Research Centre).

Cecchini, P. (1988) *1992: The European Challenge* (London: Gower).

Chenery, H.B., Robinson, S. and Syrquin, M. (1986) *Industrialization and Growth: A Comparative Study* (New York: Oxford University Press).

Clayton, E.S. (1972) 'Mechanisation and employment in East African agriculture', *International Labour Review*, 105,4.

Cohen, W.M. and Levinthal, D.A. (1989) 'Innovation and Learning: The Two Faces of R & D', *Economic Journal*, 99: 569–96.

Collier, P. (1983) 'Oil and Inequality in Rural Nigeria', in D. Ghai and S. Radwan (eds), *Agrarian Policies and Rural Poverty in Africa* (Geneva: ILO).

Collier, P. (1987) 'Oil and Poverty in Nigeria', *IDS Bulletin*, 18(1).

Collier, P. (1988) 'Oil and Food Security in Nigeria', *International Labour Review*,

Commission of the European Communities (CEC) (1988) *Food Security Policy: Examination of Recent Experiences in Sub-*

Saharan Africa (28 July 1988, SEC (88) 76). (mimeo).

Congressional Research Service (1983) *Cargo Preference Programs* (Washington DC).

Corden W.M. (1957) 'Tariffs, Subsidies and the Terms of Trade', *Economica*, reprinted with additional notes as Ch. 2 in W.M. Corden (ed.) (1985) *Protection, Growth and Trade* (Oxford: Basil Blackwell).

Corden, W. M. (1967) 'Monopoly, Tariffs and Subsidies', *Economica*, 34: 50–8.

Corden, W.M. (1984) 'Booming Sector and Dutch Disease Economics: Survey and Consolidation', *Oxford Economic Papers*, 36,3: 359–80.

Corden, W.M. (1988a) *Is debt relief in the interests of creditors?*, IMF working paper (unpublished) (8 August)

Corden, W.M. (1988b) 'Debt relief and adjustment incentives', *IMF Staff Papers*, 35: 628–43.

Corden, W.M. and Neary, J.P. (1982) 'Booming Sector and De-Industrialisation in a Small Open Economy', *Economic Journal*, 92: 825–48.

Cox, D. and Harris, R. (1985) 'Trade Liberalization and Industrial Organisation: Some Estimates for Canada', *Journal of Political Economy*, 3: 115–45.

Dahlman, C., Ross-Larson, B. and Westphal, L.E. (1989) 'Managing Technological Development: Lessons from Newly Industrializing Countries', *World Development*, 15,6: 759–75.

Dalrymple, D.G. (1985) 'The Development and Adoption of HYVs of Wheat and Rice in Developing Countries', *American Journal of Agricultural Economics*, 67: 1067–73.

Dean, E. (ed.) (1984) *Education and Economic Productivity* (Cambridge Mass.: Ballinger).

Deaton, A.S. and Stern, N.H. (1986) 'Taste Differences, Lump-Sum Grants and Uniform Taxation', *Economics Letters*, 20.

Dertouzos, M.L., Lester, R.K. and Solow, R.M. (1989) *Made In America: Regaining the Productive Edge* (Cambridge Mass.: MIT Press).

De Soto, Hernando, (1989) *The Other Path* (New York: Harper & Row).

Dias, D. Carneiro (1988) 'Brazil and the IMF: the story of a stalemate', in S. Griffith-Jones (ed), *Managing World Debt* (Brighton: Wheatsheaf).

Dixit, A.K. and Stiglitz, J. (1977) 'Monopolistic Competition and

Optimum Product Diversity', *American Economic Review*, 67: 297–308.

Donaldson, G.F. and McInerney, J.P. (1973) 'Changing machinery, technology and agricultural adjustment', *American Journal of Agricultural Economics*, 55,5.

Dooley, M.P. (1988a) 'Capital flight: a response to differences in financial risks', *IMF Staff Papers*, 35: 422–36.

Dooley, M.P. (1988b). 'Buybacks and market valuation of external debt', *IMF Staff Papers*, 35: 215–30.

Dooley, M.P. (1988c) 'Self financed buybacks and asset exchanges', *IMF Staff Papers*, 35: 714–22.

Dooley, M.P. (1989a) 'Assessing buyback benefits: Reply to Snowden', *IMF Staff Papers*, 36: 736–7.

Dooley, M.P. (1989b) 'Debt relief and leveraged buy-outs', *International Economic Review*, 30: 71–5.

Dornbusch, R. (1985a) 'External debt, budget deficits, and disequilibrium exchange rates', in G.W. Smith and J.T. Cuddington (eds), *International Debt and the Developing Countries* (Washington, D.C.: World Bank).

Dornbusch, R. (1985b) 'Policy and performance links between LDC debtors and industrial nations', *Brookings Papers on Economic Activity*, 2, 303–56.

Dornbusch, R. and Park, Y.C. (1987) 'Korean growth policy', *Brookings Papers on Economic Activity*, 2: 389–444.

Downs, A. (1982) 'Comment on Tullock', in I. Garfinkel (ed.), *Income-Tested Transfer Programs: The Case For and Against* (New York: Academic Press).

Drèze, J. (1986) 'Famine Prevention in India', in J. Drèze and A.K. Sen (eds), *Hunger: Economics and Policy* (Oxford: Oxford University Press).

Enos, J. (forthcoming) *Learning How: The Creation of Technological Capability in Developing Countries* (Geneva: International Labour Office).

Erlich, P.R. and Erlich, A.H. (1972) *Population, Resources, Environment: Issues in Human Ecology* (San Francisco: Freeman).

Fagerberg, J. (1988) 'Why Growth Rates Differ', in G. Dosi *et al.* (eds), *Technical Change and Economic Theory* (London: Frances Pinter).

FAO (1973) *The State of Food and Agriculture* (Rome: Food and

Agriculture Organisation of the United Nations).

FAO (1987) *Agriculture Toward 2000* (ROME: Food and Agriculture Organisation of the United Nations).

Farrell, M. J. (1957) 'The Measurement of Productive efficiency,' *Journal of Royal Statistical Society,* Series A, 120: 254–6.

Fei, J.C.H. and Ranis, G. (1988) *The political economy of development change: a comparative study of Thailand and the Philippines,* Economic Growth Center, Yale University (unpublished paper).

Feinberg, R. (1986) *The changing relationship between the World Bank and IMF* (Washington, D.C.: Overseas Development Council) (unpublished paper).

Fransman, M. (1986) *Technology and Economic Development* (Brighton: Wheatsheaf Books).

Froot, K.A. (1989) 'Buybacks, exit bonds and the optimality of debt and liquidity relief', *International Economic Review,* 30: 49–70 (February).

Garfinkel, I. (ed.) (1982) *Income-Tested Transfer Programs: The Case For and Against* (New York: Academic Press).

Gavin, M. (forthcoming) 'Structural Adjustment to a Terms of Trade Disturbance: the Real Exchange Rate, Stock Prices and the Current Account', *Journal of International Economics.*

Gelb, A., Knight, J.B. and Sabot, R.H. (1988) 'Lewis Through a Looking Glass: Public Sector Employment, Rent-Seeking and Economic Growth', World Bank, Country Economics Department, working paper series, 133 (Washington, D.C.).

Gerschenkron, A. (1965) *Economic Backwardness in Historical Perspective* (Cambridge Mass.: Harvard University Press).

Ghatak, S. and Ingersent, K.A. (1984) *Agriculture and Economic Development* (Brighton: Wheatsheaf Books).

Gray, H.P. (1973) 'Two Way International Trade in Manufactures: A Theoretical Underpriming', *Weltwirtschaftliches Archiv,* 109: 19–39.

Green, R.S. (1988) 'Unmanageable-toward Sub-Saharan African debt bargaining', in S. Griffith-Jones (ed.) *Managing World Debt* (Brighton: Wheatsheaf).

Greenaway, D. (1987) 'The New Theories of Intra Industry Trade', *Bulletin of Economic Research,* 37: 95–130.

Greenaway, D. and Milner, C.R. (1986) *The Economics of Intra Industry Trade* (Oxford: Basil Blackwell).

Greenaway, D. and Nam, C.H. (1988) 'Industrialization and macroeconomic Performance in Developing Countries Under Alternative Trade Strategies', *Kyklos*, 41: 419–35.

Griffin, K. and Knight, J. (1989) 'Human Development: The Case for Renewed Emphasis', *Journal of Development Planning*, 19: 9–40.

Gurria, A.T. (1988) 'Debt restructuring: Mexico as a case study', in S. Griffith-Jones (ed.), *Managing World Debt* (Brighton: Wheatsheaf).

Harbison, F.H. and Myers, C.S. (1964) *Education, Manpower and Economic Growth* (New York: McGraw-Hill).

Harrigan, J. and Mosley, P. (1991)   'Impact of World Bank Structural Adjustment Lending: 1980–87', *Journal of Development Studies*, (April).

Havrylyshyn, O. and Civan, E. (1985) 'Intra Industry Trade Among Developing Countries', *Journal of Development Economics*, 18: 253–72.

Hayami, Y. and Ruttan, V.W. (1971) *Agricultural Development: An International Perspective* (Baltimore: Johns Hopkins University Press).

Hayami, Y. and Ruttan, V.W. (1985) *Agricultural Development: An International Perspective* (Baltimore: Johns Hopkins University Press) revised edn.

Herdt, R.W. and Capule, C. (1983) *Adoption, Spread and Production Impact of Modern Rice Varieties in Asia* (Manila: International Rice Institute).

Hill, T.P. (1977) 'On Goods and Services', *Review of Income and Wealth,* 23: 315–38.

Hindley, B. (1982) *Economic Analysis and Insurance Policy in the Third World*, Thames Essay, 32 (London: Trade Policy Research Centre).

Hindley, B. (1987a) 'A Comment on Jagdish Bhagwati's Geneva Association Lecture', in O. Giarini (ed.), *The Emerging Service Economy*, services world economy series, 1 (New York: Pergamon Press).

Hindley, B. (1987b) 'Trade in Services within the European Community', in H. Giersch (ed.), *Free Trade in the World Economy* (Tübigen: J.C.B. Mohr).

Hindley, B. (1988) 'Integrated World Markets in Services: Problems and Prospects', in H. Giersch (ed.) *Services in the World*

Economy (Tübigen: J.C.B. Mohr).

Hindley, B. and Smith, A. (1984) 'Comparative Advantage and Services', *The World Economy*, 7.

Hirschman, A. (1968) 'The political economy of import-substituting industrialisation in Latin America', *Quarterly Journal of Economics*, 82: 1–32.

Hopper, W.D. (1965) 'Allocation efficiency in a traditional Indian Agriculture', *Journal of Farm Economics*, 47,3.

Horton, D. (1986) 'Assessing the Impact of International Agricultural Research and Development Programs', *World Development*, 14: 453–68.

International Civil Aviation Organization (ICAO) (1983) *Regional Differences in Fares, Rates and Costs for International Air Transport 1981*, Circular 180-AT/69 (Montreal:ICAO).

Jarrett, F.G. (1985) 'Sources and Models of Agricultural Innovation in Developed and Developing Countries', *Agriculture Administration*, 18.

Johnson, D.G. (1988) 'Economic Reforms in the People's Republic of China', *Economic Development and Cultural Change*, 35: S225–45.

Johnson, H.G. (1961) 'Towards a General Theory of the Balance of Payments', in H.G. Johnson (ed.), *International Trade and Economic Growth* (Cambridge, Mass.: Harvard University Press):153–68.

Johnson, H.G. (1965) 'Optimal Trade Intervention in the Case of Domestic Distortions', in Robert E. Baldwin *et al.* (eds), *Trade Growth and the Balance of Payments* (Chicago: Rand McNally).

Johnson, H.G. (1968) 'A New View of Infant Industry Protection', in R.H. Snape and D. MacDougall (eds), *Issues in World Trade*, 16.

Joint Report (1988) *External Debt; Definition, Statistical Coverage and Methodology,* (Paris: joint report of IBRD, IMF, BIS, OECD).

Judd, M.A. Boyce, J.K. and Evenson, R.E. (1986) 'Investing in Agricultural Supply: The Determinants of Agricultural Research and Extension Investment', *Economic Development and Cultural Change*, 34: 77–113.

Kanbur, S.M.R. (1986) 'Budgetary Rules for Poverty Alleviation', Institute for International Economic Studies, University of Stockholm, seminar paper, 363.

Kanbur, S.M.R. (1987a) 'Targeting, Transfers and Poverty', *Economic Policy*.

Kanbur, S.M.R. (1987b) 'Measurement and Alleviation of Poverty: With an Application to the Impact of Macroeconomic Adjustment', *IMF Staff papers*, 34: 60–85.

Kanbur, S.M.R. (1987c) 'Structural Adjustment, Macroeconomic Adjustment and Poverty: A Methodology for Analysis', *World Development*, 15.

Kanbur, S.M.R. (1987d) 'Malnutrition and Poverty in Latin America', in J. Drèze and A.K. Sen (eds) *Hunger: Economics and Policy* (Oxford: Oxford University Press).

Kanbur, S.M.R. (1988) 'Poverty Alleviation Under Structural Adjustment in Côte d'Ivoire', SDA Unit, World Bank.

Kanbur, S.M.R. and Keen, M.J. (1987) 'Optimum Income Taxation for Poverty Alleviation', University of Warwick (mimeo).

Kay, J.A. and King, M.A. (1978) *The British Tax System* (London: Macmillan).

Katz, J. (ed.) (1987) *Technology Generation in Latin American manufacturing* (London: Macmillan).

Kesselman, J.R. (1982) 'Taxpayer Behaviour and the Design of a Credit Income Tax', in I. Garfinkel (ed.) *Income-Tested Transfer Programs: The Case For and Against* (New York: Academic Press).

Keynes, J.M. (1926) *The End of Laissez Faire* (London: Hogarth Press).

Knight, J.B. and Sabot, R.H. (1990) *Education, Productivity and Inequality. The East African Natural Experiment* (New York: Oxford University Press).

Krishna, R. (1975) 'Measurement of the direct and indirect employment effects of agricultural growth with technical change', in L.G. Reynolds (ed.), *Agriculture in Development Theory* (New Haven: Yale University Press).

Krueger, A.O. (1983) *Trade and Employment in Developing Countries*, vol. 3 (Chicago: University of Chicago Press).

Krueger, A.O., Schiff, M. and Valdes, A. (1988) 'Agricultural incentives in Developing Countries: Measuring the Effect of Sectoral and Economywide Policies', *World Bank Economic Review*, 2,3.

Krugman, P. (1982) 'The Macroeconomics of Protection with a Floating Exchange Rate', *Carnegie–Rochester Conference Series on Public Policy*, 16 (North Holland: Amsterdam).

Krugman, P.R. (1984) 'Import Protection as Export Promotion', in H. Kierzkowski (ed.), *Monopolistic Competition and International Trade* (Oxford: Oxford University Press).

Krugman, P. (1988) 'Financing vs. forgiving a debt overhang', *Journal of Development Economics*, 29: 253–68.

Kula, Erhun (1988) 'The Inadequacy of the Entitlement Approach to Explain and Remedy Famines', *Journal of Development Studies* (October).

Lal, D (1983) *The Poverty of Development Economics*, Hobart Paperback 16 (London: Institute of Economic Affairs).

Lall, S. (1985) *Multinationals, Technology and Exports* (London: Macmillan).

Lall, S. (1987) *Learning to Industrialize: The Acquisition of Technological Capability by India* (London: Macmillan).

Lall, S. (1989) 'Human Resource Development and Industrialization. With Special Reference to Sub-Saharan Africa', *Journal of Development Planning*, 19: 129–48.

Lall, S. (1990) *Building Industrial Competitiveness in Developing Countries* (Paris: OECD Development Centre).

Lancaster, K. (1979) *Variety, Equity and Efficiency* (Oxford: Basil Blackwell).

Leamer, E.E. (1981) *Sources of International Comparative Advantage* (Cambridge, Mass.: MIT Press).

Lewis, W.A. (1984) 'The State of Development Theory', *American Economic Review*, 74,1 (March): 1–10.

Lin, J.Y. (1988) 'The Household Responsibility System in China's Agricultural Reform: A Theoretical and Empirical Study', *Economic Development and Cultural Change*, 36: S199–224.

Lipsey, R.G. and Lancaster, K. (1956) 'The general theory of second best', *Review of Economic Studies*, 24: 11–32.

Lipton, M. (1968) 'The theory of the optimising peasant', *Journal of Development Studies*, 4,3.

Lipton, M. (1987) 'Limits of price policy for agriculture: which way for the World Bank?', *Development Policy Review*, 5: 197–215.

Lipton, M. (1988) 'The Place of Agricultural Research in the Development of Sub-Saharan Africa', *World Development*, 16: 1231–57.

Little, I.M.D. (1982) *Economic Development: Theory, Policy and*

International Relations (New York: Basic Books).

Little, I.M.D., Scitovsky, T. and Scott, M.F. (1970) *Industry and Trade in Some Developing Countries* (Oxford: Oxford University Press).

Lundberg, C. (1982) 'Intra Industry Trade: The Case of Sweden', *Weltwirtschaftliches Archiv*, 118: 303–16.

MacBean, A.I. and Nguyen, D.T. (1989) *Commodity Policies: Problems and Prospects* (London: Croom Helm).

Macedo, R. (1987) 'The Mistargeting of Social Programs in Brazil: the federal Health and Nutrition Programs', University of São Paulo (mimeo).

Martin, R. and Selowsky, M. (1988) 'External Shocks and Demand for Adjustment Finance', *World Bank Economic Review*, 2: 105–21.

Martin, R. and van Wijnbergen, S. (1986) 'Shadow Prices and the Intertemporal Aspects of Remittances and Oil Revenues in Egypt', in J.P. Neary and van Wihnbergen (eds), *Natural Resources and the Macroeconomy* (Oxford: Basil Blackwell): 142–68.

Matthews, R.C.O. (1986) 'The Economics of Institutions and the Sources of Growth', *Economic Journal*, 96: 903–18.

McInerney, J., Lingard, J., Thornton, D.S. and Ingersent, K.A. (1984) 'Symposium on the Impact of Technical Change on Output and Income Distribution in LDC Agriculture', *Journal of Agricultural Economics*, 35, 3.

McKinnon, R.I. (1981) 'The Exchange Rate and Macroeconomic Policy: Changing Postwar Perceptions', *Journal of Economic Literature*, 19, 2: 531–57.

McMillan, J. Whalley, J. and Zhu, L. (1989) 'The Impact of China's Economic Reforms on Agricultural Productivity Growth', *Journal of Political Economy*, 97: 781–807.

Meadows, D.H., Meadows, D.L., Randers, J. and Behrend III, W.W. (1972) *The Limits of Growth* (Washington, D.C.: Potomac Associates).

Mirrlees, J.A. (1971) 'An Exploration in the Theory of the Optimum Income Tax', *Review of Economic Studies*, 35: 175–208.

Mody, A. (1989) 'Institutions and Dynamic Comparative Advantage: The Electronics Industry in South Korea and Tiawan', World Bank, Industry and Energy Department working paper, Industry series, 9.

Moffitt, R. (1983) 'An Economic Model of Welfare Stigma', *American Economic Review*, 73: 1023–35.

Morgan, I.P. (1980) *The Impact of the Jones Act on Selected United States Industries,* Harvard University: DBA dissertation.

Morgan, P. (1986) *World Financial Markets* (New York: J.P Morgan Inc.) (March)

Morgan, P. (1988) *World Financial Markets* (New York: J.P. Morgan inc.) (December).

Mosley, P. (1987) 'Conditionality as bargaining process: structural adjustment lending 1980–86', *Princeton Essays in International Finance*, 168 (Princeton, N.J.).

Mosley, P., Harrigan, J. and Toye, J. (1991) *Aid and Power: The World Bank and Policy-Based lending in the 1980s* (London: Routledge).

Mosley, P., Hudson, J. and Horrell, S. (1987) 'Aid, the public sector and the market in less developed countries', *Economic Journal*, 97: 616–42.

Mundell, R.A. (1961) 'Flexible Exchange Rates and Employment Policy', *Canadian Journal of Economics and Political Science*, 27.

Murray, C. (1984) *Losing Ground: American Social Policy, 1950–1980* (New York: Basic Books).

Neary, J.P. and van Wijnbergen, S. (eds) (1986) *Natural Resources and the Macroeconomy* (Oxford: Basil Blackwell).

Nelson, R.R. (1981) 'Research on Productivity Growth and Productivity Differences: Dead Ends and New Departures', *Journal of Economic Literature*, 19: 1029–64.

Nelson, R.R. and Winter, S.J. (1982) *An Evolutionary Theory of Economic Change* (Cambridge Mass.: Harvard University Press).

Newbery, D.M.G. (1988) 'The Theory of Food Price Stabilisation', University of Cambridge, Economic Theory discussion paper, 133.

Newbery, D.M.G. and Stiglitz, J. (1981) *The Theory of Commodity Price Stabilisation* (Oxford: Clarendon).

Nicholls, A.L. and Zeckhauser, R. (1982) 'Targeting Transfers via Restrictions on Recipients' *American Economic Review, Papers and Proceedings*, 72: 372–7.

Nolan, P. (1984) 'De-Collectivisation of Agriculture in China 1979–82: a Long Term Perspective', *Cambridge Journal of Economics*. 7: 381–403.

Nolan, P. and Paine, S. (1986) 'Towards an Appraisal of the Impact of Rural Reform in China, 1978–85', *Cambridge Journal of Economics*, 10: 83–99.

ODM (1976) *British Aid Tractors in India: An Ex-Post Evaluation* (London: Ministry of Overseas Development).

OECD (1987) *Structural Adjustment and Economic Performance* (Paris: OECD).

OECD (1988) *Development Cooperation 1988 Review* (Paris: OECD).

Pack, H. (1988) 'Industrialization and Trade', in H.B. Chenery and T.N. Srinivasan (eds). *Handbook of Development Economics*, vol. 1 (Amsterdam: North-Holland).

Pack, H. and Westphal, L.E. (1986) 'Industrial Strategy and Technological Change: Theory versus Reality', *Journal of Development Economics*, 21: 87–128.

Peltzman, S. (1976) 'Towards a more General Theory of Regulation', *Journal of Law and Economics*, 19: 211–40.

Perkins, D.H. (1988) 'Reforming China's Economic System', *Journal of Economic Literature*, XXVI: 601–45.

Pingali, P., Bigot, Y. and Binswanger, H.P. (1987) *Agricultural Mechanisation and the Evolution of Farming Systems in Sub-Saharan Africa* (Baltimore: Johns Hopkins University Press).

Pinstrup-Anderson, Per (1982) *Agricultural Research and Technology in Economic Development* (London: Longman).

Prahladachar, M. (1983) 'Income Distribution Effects of the Green Revolution Varieties: A Review of the Empirical Evidence', *World Development*, 11: 927–44.

Pryke, R. (1987) *Competition Among International Airlines*, Thames Essay, 46 (London: Trade Policy Research Centre).

Ranis, G. (1990) 'Asian and Latin American experience: lessons for Africa', *Journal of International Development*, 2 (April).

Ranis, G. and Fei, J.C.H. (1988) 'Development Economics: What Next?', in G. Ranis and T.P. Schultz (eds), *The State of Development Economics: Progress and Perspectives* (Oxford: Basil Blackwell).

Rao, J.M. (1989) 'Getting Prices Right', *Food Policy*, 14,1.

Ravallion, M. (1987) 'Land-Contingent Policies for Rural Poverty Alleviation', *World Development*, 15.

Ravallion, M. and Chao, K. (1987) 'Targeted Budgetary Allocations of Poverty Alleviation: Algorithms and Examples', *Journal of Policy Modeling*.

Rawski, T.G. (1982) 'Agricultural Employment and Technology', Ch. 8 in R. Barker and R. Sinha (eds), *The Chinese Agricultural Economy* (London: Croom Helm).

Riskin, C. (1986) *Feeding China: The Experience Since 1949*, (Helsinki: WIDER).

Roberts, K.W.S. (1983) 'The Theoretical Limits to Redistribution', *Review of Economic Studies*.

Rottenburg, S. (ed.) (1980) *Occupational Licensure and Regulation* (American Enterprise Institute for Public Policy Research).

Roumasset, J. (1976) *Price and Risk* (Amsterdam: North-Holland).

Roush, C.T., Jr (1984) *The Benefits of Eliminating an Alaskan Crude Oil Export Ban: an Economic Analysis*, Bureau of Economics Staff Report to the Federal Trade Commission (Washington, D.C.).

Roy, S. and Blase, M.G. (1978) 'Farm tractorisation, productivity and labour employment: a case study of India, Punjab', *Journal of Development Studies*, 14, 2.

Ruttan, V.W. (1974) 'Induced technical and institutional change and the future of agriculture', in K.E. Hunt (ed.), *The Future of Agriculture* (Oxford: Institute of Agricultural Economics).

Ruttan, V.W. (1982) *Agricultural Research Policy*, (Minneapolis: University of Minnesota Press).

Ruttan, V. and Thirtle, C. (1987) *The Economics of Technical Innovation*, (Second World Basque Congress, Bilbao, Spain) (September).

Ruttan, V.W. and Thirtle, C. (1989) 'Induced Technical and Institutional Change in African Agriculture', *Journal of International Development*, 1, 1.

Sachs, J. (1985) 'External debt and macroeconomic performance in Latin America and East Asia', *Brookings Papers on Economic Activity*, 2: 523–64.

Sachs, J. (1986) 'Managing the LDC debt crisis', *Brookings Papers on Economic Activity*, 2: 397–431.

Sachs, J. (1988) 'Comprehensive debt retirement: the Bolivian example', *Brookings Papers on Economic Activity*, 2: 705–13.

Sadka, E., Garfinkel, I. and Moreland, K. (1982) 'Income Testing and Social Welfare: An Optimal Tax-Transfer Model', in I. Garfinkel (ed.) *Income-Tested Transfer Programs: The Case For and Against*, (New York: Academic Press).

Sampson, G.P. and Snape, R.H. (1985) 'Identifying the Issues in

Trade in Services', *The World Economy*, 8: 171–82.

Schluter, M. and Mount, T. (1974) *Management Objectives of the Peasant Farmers: An Analysis of Risk Aversion in the Choice of Cropping Patterns, Surat District India*, Cornell University, Department of Agricultural Economics, occasional paper, 78.

Schultz, T.W. (1964) *Transforming Traditional Agriculture* (New Haven: Yale University Press).

Sen, Amartya (1981) 'Public Action and the Quality of Life in Developing Countries', *Oxford Bulletin of Economics and Statistics*, 43, 4 (November) 287–320.

Sen, Amartya (1982) *Poverty and Famines: An Essay on Entitlement and Deprivation* (Oxford: Clarendon Press).

Sen, Amartya, (1983) 'Development: Which Way Now?', *Economic Journal*, 93: 745–62.

Sen, Amartya, (1984) *Resources, Values and Development* (Oxford: Basil Blackwell).

Sen, Amartya (1989) 'Development as Capability Expansion', *Journal of Development Planning*, 19: 41–58.

Sieh, LML (1984) *The Services Sector in Malaysia*, working paper 18 (Kuala Lumpur and Canberra: ASEAN–Australia Joint Research Project).

Simonsen, M.H. (1985) 'The developing country debt problem', in G.W. Smith, and J.T. Cuddington (eds) *International Debt and the Developing Countries* (Washington, D.C.: World Bank).

Smith, L.D. (1989) 'Structural Adjustment, Price Reform and Agricultural Performance in Sub-Saharan Africa', *Journal of Agricultural Economics*, 40, 1.

Snowden, P.N. (1989) 'The interpretation of market discounts in assessing buy-back benefits: Comment on Dooley', *IMF Staff Papers*, 36: 733–5.

Srinivasan, T.N. (1985) 'Neo-classical Political Economy, the State and Economic Development', *Asian Development Review*, 3, 2: 38–58.

Stanyer, P.W. and Whitley, J.A. (1981) 'Financing world payments balances', *Bank of England Quarterly Bulletin*, 21: 187–97.

Stern, E. (1983) 'World Bank financing of structural adjustment', in J. Williamson (ed.), *IMF Conditionality* (Cambridge, Mass.: Institute for International Economics–MIT Press).

Stern, N.H. (1987) 'The Effects of Taxation, Price Control and

Government Contracts in Oligopoly and Monopolistic Competion', *Journal of Public Economics*, 32: 133–58.

Stern, N. (1989) 'The Economics of Development: A Survey', *Economic Journal*, 99: 597–685.

Stigler, G.J. (1971) 'The Theory of Economic Regulation', *Bell Journal of Economics*, 3.

Stiglitz, J.E. (1986) 'The New Development Economics', *World Development*, 14, 2: 257–65.

Stiglitz, J.E. (1989) 'Markets, Market Failures and Development', *American Economic Review, Papers and Proceedings*, 79, 2: 197–202.

Tang, A.M. (1980) 'Food and Agriculture in China: Trends and Projections 1952–77 and 2000', in A.M. Tang and B.F. Johnston, *Food Production in the People's Republic of China*, research report, 15 (Washington, D.C.: IFFRI).

Taylor, L. (1988) *Varieties of Stabilisation Experience: towards sensible macroeconomics in the Third World* (Oxford: Oxford University Press).

Teitel, S. (1982) 'The Skill and Information Requirements of Industrial Technologies: On the Use of Engineers as a Proxy', in M. Syrquin and S. Teitel (eds), *Trade, Stability, Technology and Equity in Latin America* (New York: Academic Press): 333–48.

Teitel, S. (1984) 'Technology Creation in Semi-Industrial Economies', *Journal of Development Economics*, 16: 39–61.

Tharakan, P.K.M. (1984) 'Intra Industry Trade Between the Industrial Countries and the Developing World', *European Economic Review*, 26: 213–27.

Thirtle, C.G. and Ruttan, V.W. (1987) *The Role of Demand and Supply in the Generation and Diffusion of Technical Change* (London: Harwood Academic Publishers).

Timmer, C.P. (1986) *Getting Prices Right* (Ithaca: Cornell University Press).

Timmer, C.P. (1989) 'Food Price Policy, the Rationale for Government Intervention', *Food Policy*, 14, 1.

Timmer, C.P., Falcon, W.P. and Pearson, Scott R. (1983) *Food Policy Analysis* (Baltimore: Johns Hopkins University Press).

Toye, J. (1985) 'Dirigisme and Development Economics', *Cambridge Journal of Economics*, 9, (March): 1–14.

Tullock, G. (1982) 'Income Testing and Politics: A Theoretical Model', in I. Garfinkel (ed.) *Income-Tested Transfer Programs:*

The Case For and Against (New York: Academic Press).

UNCTAD Secretariat (1985) *Production and Trade in Services: policies and their underlying factors bearing upon international service transactions*, TD/B/941 (New York: United Nations).

US General Accounting Office (GAO) (1982) *Cargo Preferences Add to Costs of Title II Food Peace Programs* (Washington, DC).

US General Accounting Office (GAO) (1984) *Economic Effects of Cargo Preference Laws* (Washington, D.C.).

USTR (1985) *Selected Programs Encountered by US Service Industries in Trade in Services* (Washington D.C.: Office of the United States Trade Representative) (mimeo).

Villarreal, R. (1988) 'External debt and adjustment policies: the case of Mexico 1982–6', in S. Griffith-Jones (ed.) *Managing World Debt* (Brighton: Wheatsheaf).

Wade, R. (1982) 'The System of Administration of Political Corruption: Land Irrigation in South India', *Journal of Development Studies*, 19: 283–328.

Wade, R. (1988) 'The Role of Government in Overcoming Market Failure. Taiwan, Republic of Korea and Japan', in H. Hughes (ed.), *Achieving Industrialization in East Asia* (Cambridge: Cambridge University Press).

Walter, Ingo (1987) *Global Competition in Financial Services* (Washington, D.C.: American Enterprise Institute).

Warr, P.G. (1986) 'Indonesia's Other Dutch Disease: Economic Effects of the Petroleum Boom', in J.P. Neary and S. van Wijnbergen (eds), *Natural Resources and the Macroeconomy* (Oxford: Basil Blackwell): 288–320.

Weiss, J. (1988) *Industry in developing Countries* (London: Croom Helm).

Westphal, L.E. (1982) 'Fostering Technological Mastery by Means of Selective Infant-Industry Protection', in M. Syrquin and S. Teitel (eds), *Trade Stability, Technology and Equity in Latin America* (New York: Academic Press).

White, L.J. (1986) *International Trade in Ocean Shipping Services: the United States and the World* (Cambridge, Mass.: Ballinger).

Wiens, T.B. (1982) 'Technological Change', Ch.7 in R. Banner and R. Sinha (eds), *Agricultural Economy* (London: Croom Helm).

Willmore, L.N. (1974) 'The Pattern of Trade and Specialization in the Central American Common Market', *Journal of Economic Studies*, 2: 113–34.

Wolgin, J.M. (1975) 'Resource allocation and risk: a case study of smallholder agriculture in Kenya', *American Journal of Agricultural Economics* 54, 1.

Wong, L. (1983) *Agricultural Productivity in China and India: A Comparative Analysis*, University of Minnesota, Economic Development Center, Bulletin 87–3.

World Bank (1978) *World Development Report 1978* (Washington, D.C.: World Bank).

World Bank (1981) *Accelerated Development in Sub-Saharan Africa* (Washington, D.C.: World Bank).

World Bank (1983) *World Development Report 1983* (Washington, D.C.: World Bank).

World Bank (1985) *World Development Report 1985* (Washington, D.C.: World Bank).

World Bank (1986a) *Poverty and Hunger: Issues and Options for Food Security in Developing Countries* (Washington, D.C.: World Bank).

World Bank (1986b) *World Development Report 1986* (Washington, D.C.: World Bank).

World Bank (1987) *World Development Report 1987* (Washington, D.C.: World Bank).

World Bank (1988a) *Report of the Task Force on Food Security in Africa* (30 June 1988) (Washington, D.C.) (mimeo).

World Bank (1988b) *Report on adjustment lending*, Report R88–199. Country Economics Department (Washington, D.C.).

World Bank (1988c) *World Debt Tables: 1988–9*, vol. 1 (Washington, D.C.: World Bank).

World Bank (1988d) *World Development Report 1988* (Washington, D.C.: World Bank).

World Bank (1989a) *Africa's adjustment and growth in the 1980s*, World Bank joint report with UNDP (Washington, D.C.).

World Bank (1989b) *Quarterly Review of Commodity Markets* (March) (Washington, D.C.).

World Bank (1989c) *World Development Report 1989* (Washington, D.C.: World Bank).

World Bank (1989d) *The Role of Foreign Direct Investment in Financing Developing Countries* (Washington, D.C.: World Bank).

Yotopoulos, P.A. and Nugent, J.B. (1976) *Economics of Development* (New York: Harper & Row).

Yudelman, N., Butler, G. and Banerji, R. (1971) *Technological Change in Agriculture and Employment in Developing Countries* (Paris: OECD).

Author Index

275

Subject Index

279